For Reference

Not to be taken from this room

The American Congress

Recent Titles in the
CONTEMPORARY WORLD ISSUES
Series

Books in the **Contemporary World Issues** series address vital issues in today's society such as genetic engineering, pollution, and biodiversity. Written by professional writers, scholars, and nonacademic experts, these books are authoritative, clearly written, up-to-date, and objective. They provide a good starting point for research by high school and college students, scholars, and general readers as well as by legislators, businesspeople, activists, and others.

Each book, carefully organized and easy to use, contains an overview of the subject, a detailed chronology, biographical sketches, facts and data and/or documents and other primary source material, a forum of authoritative perspective essays, annotated lists of print and nonprint resources, and an index.

Readers of books in the Contemporary World Issues series will find the information they need in order to have a better understanding of the social, political, environmental, and economic issues facing the world today.

The American Congress

A REFERENCE HANDBOOK

Sara L. Hagedorn and Michael C. LeMay

 ABC-CLIO™

An Imprint of ABC-CLIO, LLC
Santa Barbara, California • Denver, Colorado

Copyright © 2019 by ABC-CLIO, LLC

Library of Congress Cataloging in Publication Control Number: 2019941121

ISBN: 978-1-4408-6580-0 (print)
     978-1-4408-6581-7 (ebook)

23 22 21 20 19   1 2 3 4 5

This book is also available as an eBook.

ABC-CLIO
An Imprint of ABC-CLIO, LLC

ABC-CLIO, LLC
147 Castilian Drive
Santa Barbara, California 93117
www.abc-clio.com

This book is printed on acid-free paper ∞

Manufactured in the United States of America

5   DATA AND DOCUMENTS, 221

The United States of America is the oldest democratic form of government operating under the authority of a single document—a constitution. *The American Congress: A Reference Handbook* discusses the first branch of the American government—the American Congress. The founding fathers of the United States created a new republican form of government that was intended to establish a more powerful and effective government than the one that had been established under the Articles of Confederation. But the founders also distrusted the idea of a central government that could become too powerful or too prone to abuse that power. As this institutional analysis demonstrates, their solution was an elaborate system of governmental powers that entailed two fundamental principles with respect to governmental power and authority that were ingeniously designed to achieve those two goals: the separation of power into three branches of government and a system of checks and balances incorporated into the separate branches of government intended to limit government by so structuring power that each branch had some constitutionally prescribed powers to offset or check and balance the powers of the other two branches.

Article I of the U.S. Constitution, adopted in 1789, details the authority, concept, powers, and bicameral structure of the legislative branch of the new republican form of the U.S. government. From the founding of the constitutional government until World War I, the American Congress was the more powerful of the three branches, and Article I is the longest and most elaborately detailed of the Articles, each of which establishes a separate branch of the national government as part of a federal union designed to delegate some power to the national level but to reserve power not otherwise specified to the state governments. As this book makes clear, the Constitution purposively allowed for the evolution of the national government to adapt to a changing world. The document, and the government it established, has served the nation admirably for more than two hundred years.

The basic form of government and the structuring of political power and authority depend not only on the constitutional base but also on those who occupy the offices of the branches of government as, over time, they give life and meaning to the words enshrined in the founding document. How the Congress evolved over two hundred years is one of the more fascinating aspects of American political history. Congress had to confront innumerable problems over those two hundred years. How those problems were faced raised issues, both legal and political, as solutions were sought. Prior to World War I, Congress had the upper hand because all laws to govern the nation had to be passed in identical language by both chambers of Congress. It had the power of the purse. It had oversight power over the executive branch. It had design authority over the federal judiciary and approved nominees to the federal courts. In the eighteenth and nineteenth centuries, the United States was not yet a major world power, and the president, as commander in chief, was not the dominant role-player. Most occupants of the office viewed the role of the president as simply seeing that the laws passed by Congress were faithfully executed. Presidents did not control or set the legislative agenda. Congress had the sole power to declare war, and presidents generally deferred to Congress in decisions to engage the military in foreign entanglements. So too, the power of judicial review had to be asserted and established in *Marbury v. Madison* (5 U.S. 1, 1803).

The American Congress shows how Congress, as an institution, evolved over time: in its own powers, in its relationships with the other two branches, in its internal practices and procedures, and in its influence over American politics and society. The book, aimed at the general reader and undergraduate college and university students, follows the format of all volumes in the Contemporary World Issues series.

Chapter 1 discusses the history and background of congressional politics. It covers who became the major stakeholders in congressional politics. It examines the internal structure and procedures of the U.S. House of Representatives and of the U.S. Senate and how they changed over time. The historical background chapter is designed to provide the context through which the reader can better understand current events and problems and issues that Congress faces. It presents that discussion in a comprehensive and unbiased manner, allowing readers to form their own judgment on the issues.

Chapter 2 covers in detail the major problems related to congressional policy making. It addresses the efforts taken to cope with the problems and how congressional politics frame the issues and discusses some proposed solutions to the problems that are now on the agenda of national level of government, especially as Congress attempts to achieve some consensus on the issues.

Chapter 3 is comprised of eight original essays by scholars and stakeholders involved in congressional politics and policy making. The chapter brings together voices from diverse disciplinary perspectives to examine many sides of the issues and to enrich the perspective that the primary authors are able to provide.

Chapter 4 describes the key organizations and people who are involved in congressional politics. In brief profiles, it presents the many organizations, both governmental and nongovernmental, that advocate for or against various policy proposals to cope with the problems highlighted in Chapter 2. It covers the various actors who, as individuals, are major participants involved in crafting solutions to the problems and acting politically to enact, oppose, or implement those solutions.

Chapter 5 presents some key data and documents gathered from a variety of government sources. They are presented in graphic form (line, bar, and pie charts), in a series of tables of important data, and in excerpts and summaries of primary source documents.

Chapter 6 is a resource chapter. It is comprised of a list of annotated books on the subject and on an annotated list of the major scholarly journals devoted to discourse on the subject. The chapter briefly presents some important films and videos as nonprint sources that hopefully give "life" and a "face" to the discourse. Together these resources provide the reader with a comprehensive review of the discourse on congressional politics. Hopefully, the chapter will direct the reader to further research on the topic.

A chronology of key moments in the history of Congress and congressional politics is then provided in Chapter 7. Finally, a glossary offers easy access to definitions of the key terms used in the debate concerning congressional politics. These terms define the key concepts and explain any jargon associated with congressional politics, some of which may be unfamiliar to many readers. The volume closes with a comprehensive index.

The American Congress

Introduction

The United States is notable as a constitutional democracy—the longest operating such democracy in the world governed by a written constitution. The Constitution has lasted, remarkably, as the basis for the government since 1789. The genius of the Constitution is its dynamic nature. It has served as the fundamental document governing American politics despite the profound changes in American society that have occurred over the past 230 years. The United States has evolved from thirteen states huddled along its eastern coast to fifty states that span the continent and beyond to the noncontiguous states of Alaska and Hawaii. Demographically speaking, the United States has changed since 1790 from a highly homogeneous population of about 3.5 million to the nation with the world's most diverse population of more than 325 million as of 2016. It has evolved from an overwhelmingly rural population of small farmers to the world's leading industrial society in which more than 80 percent of the population resides in 389 metropolitan statistical areas, based on the 2010 census. In 1790, the United States was a decidedly minor power, economically, militarily, and diplomatically. Today, it is the world's sole superpower, with the largest economy, the most powerful military, and, diplomatically, the leading nation of the free world (LeMay 2013).

Powerful Speaker of the House Joseph Gurney Cannon (R-IL) was instrumental in supporting a U.S. defense buildup, including the "Fifty Million Dollar Bill" that helped prepare the nation for the Spanish-American War. (Library of Congress)

The Constitution-Based Functions and Powers of the American Congress and How They Have Changed over Time

The framers of the Constitution were attempting to craft a government that struck a balance between two conflicting aims. On the one hand, they wanted a strong national government that overcame the inefficiencies of the Continental Congress under the Articles of Confederation (1777–1789), while, on the other hand, they sought to limit the national government from behaving in an arbitrary or antidemocratic way—what they perceived was the autocratic ways of the British monarchy against which they had fought in the Revolutionary War.

The framers of the Constitution gave the national government large grants of well-defined authority, such as the power to tax and to spend. They placed in the American Congress the largest share of the national power. However, to reduce the possibility of systematic abuse of power by willful congressional majorities, they included three fundamental elements: (1) representation by a multiplicity of interests within an extended republic, (2) the separation of powers at the national level into three branches of government, and (3) the creation of a bicameral (two-chamber) legislative body (Davidson and Oleszek 1998; Loomis and Schiller 2016: 21–22; Madison 1981).

Only can a dynamic constitution account for its extraordinary ability to govern a nation that evolved so profoundly since its inception. As mentioned, among the Constitution's defining characteristics are the dual principles of the separation of powers and a system of checks and balances. These two fundamental concepts are structured into the constitutional basis for the American government, designed to limit the power of the central government. The national government is divided into three coequal branches: legislative, executive, and judicial. The Constitution enumerates the powers granted to and prohibited from each branch and the powers specified or implied for each branch that enables one branch to check and balance any excessive use of power by any other branch (Howell and Peve-house 2007; Loomis and Schiller 2016: 22–23).

This book describes the legislative branch—the American Congress. It discusses the basic functions and powers of Congress and how those have changed so profoundly over the nation's history. It examines congressional norms and customs; its internal structures, politics, size, and scope; and the way its members are elected. It discusses the lawmaking function of the American Congress. The Constitution's language in Article I, Section 7 is expansive: "To make all laws which shall be necessary and proper for carrying into Execution the foregoing Powers vested by this Constitution in the Government of the United States, or in any Department or Officer thereof." This chapter describes how that function evolved from primacy in lawmaking in 1789 to playing second fiddle to the executive office and outside lobbying groups, which collectively now play a prominent if not dominant role in crafting legislative proposals.

The chapter also discusses the changing role in the representation function of the Congress. Article I grants Congress the "powers of the purse" to craft the federal budget. Over the years, however, Congress increasingly only authorizes or revises (usually only slightly so) a budget now crafted by the presidential administration. In recent years, Congress has often relied on continuing budget resolutions rather than authorizing a fiscal year budget or even a temporary omnibus budget (Farrier 2004; Fenno 1966; Keith and Schick 2003; LeLoup 2005; Pfiffner 1979; Rubin 2003; Schick 2000; Wildavsky 1964).

There has also been a profound change in congressional war-making powers. Until World War II, only the American Congress could declare war. Since the end of World War II, however, the nation has been committed to war mostly by actions of the U.S. president exercising the commander in chief powers granted to the office (Fisher 2000; Howell and Pevehouse 2007; Stevenson 2007).

The U.S. Constitution charges the Congress with an oversight function to check the implementation by executive-branch departments and agencies of the laws it has enacted. That role, too, has changed dramatically in size and scope as the nation evolved into a superpower. Article II of the Constitution grants to the U.S. president the power and function to negotiate treaties with other nations but with the approval, known as the "advice and consent," of the U.S. Senate. So too, the president appoints persons to the major departments and agencies of the federal government, as well as justices to the U.S. Supreme Court and many federal courts, but again with the advice and consent of the Senate. Those functions and roles have shifted considerably during the nation's long history of governing under the Constitution.

The Changing Role of the Lawmaking Function of the American Congress

Article I, Section 1 of the U.S. Constitution specifies that all legislative powers are vested in the Congress, which is divided into two chambers, a U.S. Senate and a U.S. House of Representatives. Section 7 of Article I lays out the lawmaking function of the Congress. Among Section 7's provisions, it details those of a bill, a law, a resolution, the veto, pocket veto, veto override, and the use of the roll call vote and such votes being recorded in the Journal (i.e., the Congressional Record of its actions). Section 7 reads as follows:

> All Bills for raising Revenue shall originate in the House of Representatives; but the Senate may propose or concur with Amendments as on other Bills.
>
> Every Bill which shall have passed the House of Representatives and the Senate, shall, before it become a Law, be presented to the President of the United States: If he approve he shall sign it, but if not he shall return it, with his Objections to that House in which it shall have

originated, who shall enter the Objections at large on their Journal, and proceed to reconsider it. If after such Reconsideration two thirds of that House shall agree to pass the Bill, it shall be sent, together with the Objections, to the other House, by which it shall likewise be reconsidered, and if approved by two thirds of that House, it shall become a Law. But in all such Cases the Votes of both Houses shall be determined by yeas and Nays, and the Names of the Persons voting for and against the Bill shall be entered on the Journal of each House respectively. If any Bill shall not be returned by the President within ten Days (Sundays excepted) after it shall have been presented to him, the Same shall be a Law, in the Manner as if he had signed it, unless the Congress, by their Adjournment prevent its Return, in which Case it shall not be a Law.

Every Order, Resolution, or Vote to which the Concurrence of the Senate and the House of Representatives may be necessary (except on a question of Adjournment) shall be presented to the President of the United States, and before the Same shall take Effect, shall be approved by him, or being disapproved by him, shall be repassed by two thirds of the Senate and House of Representatives, according to the Rules and Limitations prescribed in the Case of a Bill.

Lawmaking during the Early Years of Congress: 1789–1830

The Constitution gives the largest amount of functions and powers to Congress. In 1789, the entire nation was small and the federal government, at best, was rudimentary. In 1790, the U.S. House of Representatives had only sixty-five members and twenty-six senators. There were no congressional offices for individual members. Members of Congress often met in their hotels; the term "lobbyist" derives from the days of the British Parliament when constituents and persons advocating on behalf of then small interest groups hung around hotel lobbies in hopes of advocating for their interests. In the days before the American Congress had an office building, lobbyists met its members going to or returning from the Capitol Building (Loomis and Schiller 2016: 49–52; Smith, Roberts, and Vander Wielen 2011: 351).

Congress operated through ad hoc committees prior to 1825, when standing committees that spanned sessions of Congress were first established (Loomis and Schiller 2016: 25). Individual members of the House and the Senate wrote the bills they sponsored. There were no formal (or really even informal) party organizations in Congress. The famous "factions" that James Madison discussed in the Federalist Papers were informal caucus meetings of like-minded legislators (Madison 1981). The term "King Caucus" came to signify a principal difference between the organization of the first protoparties and the organization of those that emerged with the mass party system of the Jacksonian era. The caucus was "king" in the sense that it implied an undemocratic, nonrepublican system in which elites (the members of the Congress) in their party caucuses selected national party nominees (Aldrich 2012; LeMay 2017: 6).

The first "protoparties," which came to be known as the Federalists and the Anti-Federalists, were factions in the legislature until 1800. That began to change with the election of Thomas Jefferson, who had formed the Jeffersonian Republican Party (the first true national party organization and the ancestor of the modern Democratic Party) to help him win the presidential election of 1800 and to pursue his policy agenda for the national government (Chambers and Burnham 1967; Gerring 2001; LeMay 2017: 4; Schlesinger 1973; Witcover 2003: 8).

By 1813, when the nation had expanded from thirteen to eighteen states, Congress was comprised of 181 members in the House and thirty-six senators. The Twenty-First Congress, which convened in 1830 after the election of President Andrew Jackson, had 213 members in the House, plus three nonvoting delegates, and forty-eight senators from the then twenty-four states. Martin Van Buren, who led his Albany Regency party organization in New York, organized the development of the first true mass party organization, the Jacksonian Democratic Party, which led to General Andrew Jackson's election to the presidency in 1828 (Aldrich 2012; LeMay 2017; Van Buren 1867). The development of national political parties, particularly the mass party, provided a counterbalance (a centripetal force toward party-based centralization) to the institution's centrifugal forces pushing Congress toward greater decentralization and the influence of the individual member (Davidson and Oleszek 1998; Loomis and Schiller 2016: 7–9).

The Decentralized Congress: 1830–1860

During the pre–Civil War period, centrifugal forces dominated lawmaking. Those forces are exemplified by the congressional careers of such luminaries as Senator John C. Calhoun (Democratic-Republican, South Carolina), Daniel Webster (Whig, New Hampshire), Henry Clay (Whig, Kentucky), and Thomas Benton (Democrat, Missouri). In an effort to stave off a civil war, Senator Clay proposed the famous Compromise of 1850. Prompted by the coming statehood of California, the Compromise of 1850 echoed the Missouri Compromise of 1820. The Senate debate by Senators Calhoun and Webster over Clay's Compromise of 1850 proposal was one of the most famous debates in U.S. Senate history. A brief synopsis of their notable careers in the American Congress illustrates their centrifugal impact on both chambers of Congress.

Senator Henry Clay (1777–1852) was born in Virginia. He became a frontier lawyer in Kentucky, where he served as a Kentucky senator and then a member of the U.S. House of Representatives. He served as U.S. secretary of state under President John Quincy Adams. Senator Clay was known as the "Great Compromiser." He strongly opposed the Alien and Sedition Act of 1798. As an attorney, he represented Aaron Burr in Burr's 1806 treason case. He was appointed to fill an unexpired term in the U.S. Senate in 1806. In 1811, Clay was elected to the U.S. House of Representatives, serving multiple terms (1811–1814, 1815–1821, 1823–1825). In the House he rose to the office of Speaker of the House. Clay was elected to and served in the U.S. Senate several times (1806–1807, 1810–1811, 1831–1842, 1849 until his death in 1852). In the House, Clay was instrumental in pushing the United States going to war against England in the War of 1812. He advocated for a national bank and successfully negotiated the settlement between the slave-owning states and the rest of the country over the nation's western policy by means of his bill that became the Missouri Compromise of 1820. Senator Clay crafted the Compromise Tariff of 1833, which helped prevent South Carolina from secession that year. As stated, Clay negotiated the Compromise of 1850 to stave off bloodshed by crafting a bill that allowed California to enter the union as a free state without a counterbalancing slave state entrance by covering a settlement of the Texas boundary line.

Senator Daniel Webster (1782–1852) was born in New Hampshire where he studied law and was admitted to the bar in 1801. As a Federalist, Webster was elected to the U.S. House of Representatives from New Hampshire, serving from 1816 to 1817. He moved to Massachusetts where he achieved notoriety by representing Dartmouth College before the U.S. Supreme Court in 1816–1819. He served as a delegate to the Massachusetts constitutional convention in 1820 and served in the Massachusetts delegation to the U.S. House of Representatives from 1823 to 1827. Notably for his growing influence on lawmaking, he chaired the Judiciary Committee in 1827. He was elected to the U.S. Senate as an anti-Jackson partisan in 1827 and was reelected as a Whig, serving from 1833 to 1839. Webster was the unsuccessful Whig candidate for the U.S. presidency in 1836. He served as secretary of state to President William Henry Harrison (1841) and, upon Harrison's death, to President John Tyler (1841–1843). He was again elected to the U.S. Senate, as a Whig, in 1845, serving until 1850, when he left the Senate to serve as secretary of state to President

Millard Fillmore, in which office he served until his death in October 1852.

Senator John C. Calhoun (1782–1850) was a prominent U.S. diplomat and defender of the slave-plantation system that dominated the antebellum South. As a member of the U.S. House of Representatives from South Carolina, Calhoun helped push the U.S. entrance into the War of 1812. He strongly advocated for the creation of the Second Bank of the United States in 1812. In the executive branch, Calhoun served as U.S. secretary of war, vice president, and secretary of state. He opposed the Mexican-American War and the admission of California into the union as a free state. He ran for president in 1824 but dropped out of the race to serve as vice president. When Andrew Jackson was sworn in as president in 1829, Calhoun was isolated from national affairs. He supported the Tariff of 1828 until it unfairly assessed the agrarian South to benefit the industrializing North. In an essay opposing the tariff policy, he famously advocated for a state veto or "nullification" of any national law held to impinge on minority interests (i.e., states' rights). He resigned from the vice presidency to be elected to the U.S. Senate from South Carolina. After serving as President Tyler's secretary of state, he was reelected to the U.S. Senate in 1845. He opposed the Compromise of 1850, and in the Senate during great debates over the bill, Calhoun articulated the position of the slave states. Senators Benton, Calhoun, Webster, and Clay and President Andrew Jackson dominated American political life from 1815 to 1850. A gifted debater, Senator Calhoun was nicknamed the "Cast-Iron Man."

Senator Thomas Hart Benton (1782–1858) was born in North Carolina, attended Chapel Hill College (now the University of North Carolina), and was admitted to the bar in Nashville, Tennessee, in 1806. He served in the Tennessee state senate from 1809 to 1811. During the War of 1812, he was an aide-de-camp to General Andrew Jackson and a colonel of a regiment of the Tennessee volunteers. He went on to serve as a colonel of the U.S. Infantry from 1813 to 1815. He moved to

Missouri where he edited a newspaper, the *Missouri Inquirer*. In 1820, when Missouri entered the union, Benton was elected to the U.S. Senate as a Democratic-Republican and later as a Jacksonian-Democrat. Benton was reelected in 1827, 1833, and 1839. In the Senate he served on three major committees: Indian Affairs, Military Affairs, and Foreign Relations. He authored the resolution to expunge from the Senate Journal the resolution of censure of Andrew Jackson. Ironically, he failed to win reelection to the Senate in 1850 when censure proceedings were initiated against him. He was elected as a Democrat to the Thirty-Third Congress (1853–1855) and failed in a reelection bid in 1854 and in a bid to be the governor of Missouri in 1856. A notable orator and debater, after leaving the Congress, he pursued a literary career in Washington, D.C., until his death there in 1859 (Loomis and Schiller 2016: 24–27).

The Rise of the Two-Party System and Evolution of the Modern Congress, 1860–1920

After the Civil War, the modern two-party system of national political parties arose and evolved, resulting in significant centripetal forces within the American Congress (Aldrich 2012; Gould 2003; Haas 1994; Kleppner 1979; LeMay 2017: 21–29; Loomis and Schiller 2016: 27–32; Witcover 2003).

As political scientists Burdett Loomis and Wendy Schiller note so succinctly:

> Over the 1860–1920 period, the Congress experimented with strong party leadership in both chambers, created and then limited a separate committee for appropriations, first dominated a series of weak presidents and later looked to the president for coherent leadership initiatives, and eventually moved toward a mixture of standing committee decentralization and oligarchy that would characterize the institution until the mid-1960s. (2016: 27)

Obviously, the lawmaking function was affected as the number of bills and resolutions introduced during each two-year congressional session rose from the hundreds to the thousands and eventually to the tens of thousands. This expansive trend in lawmaking followed naturally as the country expanded after the Civil War, the number of states grew, and the total population expanded by natural birth and by the massive waves of immigration that occurred after 1865. In 1860, the United States was still 80 percent rural and its economy still overwhelmingly agricultural (LeMay 2013). By the 1920 census, however, the urban population of the nation topped 50 percent for the first time ever. Between 1860, when there were thirty-six states, and 1912, when there were forty-eight, the size of the Senate correspondingly grew from seventy-two to ninety-six and the U.S. House of Representatives grew from 241 members in 1863 to 435 members in 1913. In accordance with the constitutional provision of one House member representing thirty thousand persons (Article I, Section 2), the 1910 census set the number of representatives at 435. The Congress could not agree after the 1920 census on how to apportion the seats, however, and essentially the number of members has remained fixed at 435 ever since 1910. The size of the House was then legally set by the Permanent Apportionment Act of 1929. In 1941, Congress adopted the current formula for reapportioning those 435 House seats (Thirty-Thousand.org 2006).

As the size of the Congress grew, the number of bills introduced by lawmakers rose dramatically during this period. In the 1867–1868 session of Congress, a total of 3,003 bills were introduced. By 1891–1893, members had introduced 14,518 bills. By 1907–1909, the number of bills introduced had increased twelvefold in forty years to 38,000 bills (Davidson and Oleszek 1998: 30; Loomis and Schiller 2016: 31). Obviously, the way Congress conducted its lawmaking function had to adjust to that trend of ever-expanding bills and resolutions (Smith, Roberts, and Vander Wielen 2011: 29–54).

The sheer size of the Congress acted as a centrifugal (decentralizing) force. Individual members, pursuing their respective careers, introduced bills and resolutions to please constituents, address problems experienced in their states and districts as the nation industrialized, and respond to lobbying efforts by an ever-growing number of interest groups seeking to influence public policy lawmaking on behalf of their group members.

As Loomis and Schiller note, "Since World War II, Congressional resources have grown steadily and profoundly. Personal office and committee staff members have risen sharply, as have the number of special interest caucuses, the budgets of legislative support agencies (e.g. Government Accountability Office, Congressional Research Service, and Congressional Budget Office), and campaign expenditures" (2016: 189; for the growth of standing committees, see Smith, Roberts, and Vander Wielen 2011: 171–216).

To counterbalance that trend and to make lawmaking more manageable and expeditious, several centripetal forces developed as well: the growing impact of national mass parties, an increasingly elaborate committee system, and the growing power and influence of a congressional leadership structure. As the two major party system became entrenched, party leadership in the Congress became formalized. Party leaders, known as floor leaders, were elected by their respective parties in closed-door caucuses by secret ballot. The most important such leadership positions became the majority leader and majority whip and the minority leader and minority whip (Davidson, Hammond, and Smock 1998; Dodd and Oppenheimer 2005; Ripley 1967; Sinclair 1995; Volden and Wiseman 2014).

In terms of a centralizing effect on lawmaking (as well as on other functions and procedures of Congress), the most important during the 1865–1920 period was the emergence of strong positions of Speaker of the House and majority leader of the Senate, as well as chairs of several notably powerful committees, particularly Appropriations, Ways and Means, and Rules.

In Article I, Section 2, the Constitution specifies the office of Speaker of the House. It reads, "The House of Representatives shall chuse their Speaker and other Officers; and shall have the sole Power of Impeachment." The Constitution is notably silent, however, on the manner by which they shall "chuse"— that is, select—the Speaker. Nor does it specify the powers and authority of the office in conducting the day-to-day business of the House. It says nothing about appointive powers to committees or to the chairs of committees or the ability to send what bills to what committees. Those aspects of the lawmaking conduct of Congress evolved with the role of the political parties in Congress, about which the Constitution is again notably silent, as norms and customs by which Congress conducted its business.

During this period, four notably important Speakers ruled Congress and are described next to illustrate their centralizing impact on Congress: Tom Reed, Charles Crisp, Joe Cannon, and Oscar Underwood.

Thomas Brackett Reed (1839–1902, R-Maine) was elected to the House in 1877. He became chair of the House Judiciary Committee in 1881 and member and soon chair of the Rules Committee where he became a master of parliamentary rules. He served as Speaker from 1889 to 1891, when Republicans controlled the House, and again from 1895 to 1899, when they regained control. Tom Reed was admitted to the bar in 1865, served in Maine's House of Representatives (1868–1869), served as attorney general of Maine (1870–1872), and was elected to Congress in 1877. He used so well his command of the rules that he was nicknamed "Czar Reed" and controlled matters in the House by "Reed's Rules." He resigned in 1899 and died in 1902.

Charles Crisp (1845–1896, D-GA) was less influential than Reed but nonetheless was an important Speaker by employing the rules developed by Speaker Reed. Crisp served as Speaker between Reed's two terms in the office, when his party took control of the House. Crisp, a Democrat from Georgia, was

Speaker from 1891 to 1895. He ran for the U.S. Senate in 1896, but declining health resulted in his death in October 1896, about a month before the general election.

Arguably the most powerful Speaker of the House was Joseph Gurney "Uncle Joe" Cannon (1836–1926, R-IL). Cannon was born in North Carolina but later moved to Illinois. He was admitted to the bar in 1858. He was elected to the House as a member from Illinois and served as Speaker of the House from 1902 to 1911. He served in the American Congress for nearly five decades. He chaired three of the most influential committees of the time: Appropriations, Expenditures in the Post Office Department, and Rules. Cannon was simultaneous chair of the Rules Committee and Speaker of the House. His autocratic style and power earned him the moniker "Czar Cannon," who ruled with "an iron fist." As Speaker, Cannon was leader of the Republican Party. Uncle Joe Cannon was the second-longest continuously serving Republican Speaker (the longest was Dennis Hastert, who served as Speaker from 1999 to 2007) and the longest serving Republican member of Congress from Illinois. He often clashed with Republican president Theodore Roosevelt.

In 1910, a group of Republican members, led by George Norris (R-NE), along with Democrats, revolted against Cannon's imperial style. They stripped him of the power to serve on the Rules Committee while he was Speaker and of the power to assign members to committees by establishing a Committee on Committees. By a vote of 191–156, the insurgents created a new system of seniority by which members could move ahead even against party leadership's wishes. Norris is a good example of centrifugal forces in the Senate that enable individual senators to play a prominent role in lawmaking, often putting their "stamp" on particular policy matters. Norris served in the House from 1903 to 1913 and in the Senate from 1913 to 1943. He was the leader of progressive and liberal causes in Congress and was noted for his insurgency against party leaders, isolationist foreign policy views, support for labor unions, and creating the Tennessee Valley Authority, which earned him the nickname "Father of the TVA." Many scholars rank him as one of the five best senators in U.S. history. Norris died in 1944.

Preceding Speaker Cannon was Oscar Underwood (1862–1929, D-AL). Underwood served as Speaker from 1899 to 1901. Oscar Underwood exemplifies congressional influence arising through seniority and the committee chairpersonship that comes through it. He served in the Congress for three decades, from 1895 to 1927. He earned his law degree from the University of Virginia and was admitted to the bar in 1884. He was elected to the House in 1895 and served there until 1915. He was chair of the powerful House Ways and Means Committee and drafted the Underwood Tariff Act of 1913. He went on to serve two terms in the U.S. Senate (1915–1927). Underwood was the first officially designated Democratic minority floor leader. He ran for but lost his party's nomination for the presidency to Woodrow Wilson in 1912. Demonstrating party loyalty, he supported Wilson's programs, notably the Federal Reserve Act of 1913 and the U.S. participation in the League of Nations. Underwood served as a member of the U.S. delegation to the Washington Conference on arms limitations (1921–1922). He sought the presidential nomination again in 1924, but he denounced the Ku Klux Klan and opposed prohibition, and those stands cost him the support of the southern wing of the party and he lost the nomination (see Ripley 1967).

In the Senate, from 1865 until about 1880, when the size of the chamber grew from seventy-two members to seventy-six members, centrifugal forces remained strong. Individual senators could conduct their lawmaking business pretty much as they had before the Civil War. That pattern began to change in the 1880s and 1890s. By 1900, the Senate had grown to ninety members. Increasingly, party caucuses and the party leaders determined who sat on which committees. The leaders determined the calendar of senate business. As a result, senators sought to curry the favor of party leadership in order to have influence on policy and pass bills they sponsored. In the Senate, party leadership, through the party caucuses, and chairs of the major standing committees joined forces to impose a high degree of roll call discipline on members (Loomis and Schiller 2016: 29; Rothman 1969: 4, 58–59).

Examples of the centralizing force in the Senate are two of the most influential senators of the time: William B. Allison and Nelson Aldrich. They chaired the Republican Conference (as the party caucus is called) and the Senate Steering Committee. William Boyd Allison (1829–1908, R-IA) represented Iowa in the U.S. House of Representatives from 1863 to 1871 and in the U.S. Senate from 1872 to 1909. He was the longest serving senator from Iowa and the longest serving chair of a standing committee, as chair of the Senate Committee on Appropriations (1881–1893, 1896–1908). Nelson Aldrich (1841–1915, R-RI) served as senator from Rhode Island from 1881 to 1911 and as a member of the U.S. House of Representatives from 1879 to 1881. Before being elected to the U.S. House of Representatives, Aldrich served as Speaker of the Rhode Island House of Representatives. The grandfather of Nelson Rockefeller and great-grandfather of John D. Rockefeller, he was first appointed to the U.S. Senate in 1881 and reelected in 1886, 1892, 1898, and 1904. He chaired the powerful Rules Committee and the Committee on Finance. He died in 1915.

Processing tens of thousands of bills required, as it still does, a mechanism to handle the flow. The complex committee system was the organizational response. By 1918, the House had sixty standing committees and the Senate had seventy-four (Loomis and Schiller 2016: 31). The reliance on committees to move proposals through the chambers of Congress in a predictable and timely manner led to occasional reform of their respective committee systems, such as in 1919 and 1946. Committee service and position advanced on the basis of seniority or tenure on a given committee. The Legislative Reorganization

Act of 1946 decreased the number of standing committees in both chambers but thereby increased the value of the remaining standing committees. Today there are twenty standing committees in the House and sixteen in the Senate (Davidson, Hammond, and Smock 1998; Dodd and Oppenheimer 2005; Frisch and Kelly 2006; Loomis and Schiller 2016: 322; Ripley 1967; Sinclair 1995).

The Textbook Congress: 1920–1970

The Congress of the 1920s–1970s has been characterized as "the Textbook Congress" in that it responded to three competing imperatives—geographical, jurisdictional, and partisan. Lawmaking operated in an arena involving members who were influenced by pressures from their constituencies, by committees, and by a party-based coalition (Chubb and Peterson 1989; Loomis and Schiller 2016: 32–33; Shepsle 1989: 238–66). In the 1950s and 1960s, the congressional lawmaking function was especially influenced by two leaders who individually and in particular played a centralizing role: Speaker of the House Sam Rayburn and Senate Majority Leader Lyndon B. Johnson.

Speaker Sam T. Rayburn (1882–1961, D-TX) was the longest-serving Speaker in the history of the House and was debatably its most revered. He served seventeen years as Speaker during the period 1940–1961, when the Democrats held the majority in the House (1940–1947, 1949–1953, and 1955–1961). Unlike Reed and Cannon, Sam Rayburn influenced the House through skillful persuasion and humor rather than an imperial rule. Rayburn was especially skillful in brokering legislative initiatives among a group of strong and often conflicting committee chairs to whom much of the power in the House had devolved (Loomis and Schiller 2016: 32–33). He expanded membership of the powerful House Rules Committee, which influenced major civil rights and other legislation in the mid- to late 1960s (i.e., the Great Society program of President Lyndon Johnson). Sam Rayburn was the longest-serving member in the House's history and died, much admired, in November 1961.

Lyndon Baines Johnson (1908–1973, D-TX) was the thirty-sixth president of the United States who pushed through Congress his Great Society program, arguably the most major legislation that had been passed during any presidential term since Franklin Roosevelt's New Deal. His background as majority leader made him one of the best "nose-counters" in presidential history, and his 1964 landslide electoral victory gave him so many noses to count. The Democratic ticket of Johnson-Humphrey won 61.05 percent of the popular vote to the Goldwater-Miller popular vote of 38.47 percent. The landslide was even more lopsided in the Electoral College vote: Johnson-Humphrey beat Goldwater-Miller 486 votes (90.3%) to 52 votes (9.7%) (Leip, n.d.). The American Congress reflected the presidential coattails: in the U.S. House of Representatives, Democrats had 295 members to the Republicans' 140 seats; and in the U.S. Senate, there were 68 Democrats to 32 Republican seats—a comfortable, filibuster-proof majority (Association of Centers for the Study of Congress, n.d.).

Lyndon Johnson was born in Texas in 1908, taught school there, and served as Texas's director of the National Youth Administration of Roosevelt in 1935. In 1937, Johnson won a special election by a hair-thin margin to fill a vacancy from Texas in the U.S. House of Representatives. He left Congress to serve in the U.S. Navy in the Pacific and was awarded the Silver Star. After the war Johnson was reelected five times, serving in the House until 1949. He was elected to the U.S. Senate in 1949, became the Democratic whip in 1951, and the floor leader in 1953, serving as majority leader from 1953 to 1960. He ran for the presidential nomination of the Democratic Party in 1960 but lost to John F. Kennedy, for whom he served as vice president. As Senate majority leader, he authored what became known as the Johnson Amendment, which changed the Internal Revenue Service's tax code to prohibit tax-exempt religious organizations from endorsing or opposing candidates for political office (LeMay 2018: 186–87).

As political scientists Loomis and Schiller note so well:

The textbook Congress was both decentralized and oligarchic: decentralized in that committee chairs dominated their own policy domains; oligarchic in that top party leaders, committee chairs, and chairs of the thirteen Appropriations Committee subcommittees in each chamber all benefited from their joint control of the domestic policy agenda. (2016: 32)

The equilibrium in Congress began to change in the 1960s, in part because of Johnson's landslide victory over Senator Barry Goldwater (R-AZ) in 1964. In the House, a Democrat reform group, the Democratic Study Group, formed in 1958 and began pushing a reform agenda that began to strip away the power of committee chairs that led to reforms in Congress enacted in the 1970s. Subcommittees gained some independent authority, more roll call votes were taken that opened congressional voting to greater public scrutiny, and the Democratic caucus enhanced the power of the Speaker and the top party leaders (Frisch and Kelly 2006; Loomis and Schiller 2016: 33–34; Oleszek 2007; Shepsle 1989: 256; Sinclair 2006; Volden and Wiseman 2014).

The Reform Congress: 1980–2000

A key leader of the "reform" Congress in the 1980s was the popular Speaker Thomas Philip "Tip" O'Neill (1912–1994, D-MA). Tip O'Neill was a member of the House from 1953 to 1987, elected to the Massachusetts district vacated by John F. Kennedy when Kennedy was elected to the U.S. Senate. Tip O'Neill had served in the Massachusetts House of Representatives, including as its Speaker. He became the Democratic majority whip in 1971, its floor leader in 1973, and Speaker of the House, serving from 1977 to 1987. He was a very popular

Speaker. He worked well across the aisle and personally with President Ronald Reagan. He famously coined the phrase "All politics is local." In 1987, he authored (with William Novak) his memoir book, *Man of the House*. He died in January 1994 (Loomis and Schiller 2016: 34–35).

In the 1980s–1990s Senate, the majority leaders were Robert Byrd (1977–1981 and 1987–1989, D-WV) and George Mitchell (1989–1995, D-ME), and the minority leader was Senator Bob Dole (1987–1995, R-KS; 1995–1996, majority leader). Given the Senate's smaller size and a long-standing tradition allowing for individual senators to influence policy areas, several senators notably played a somewhat maverick role and used the filibuster and other parliamentary tactics to assert their rights and often stalemate progress on legislation they opposed. These included Republican Jesse Helms (1973–2003, R-NC; chair of Foreign Relations in 2001) and Howard Metzenbaum (1974, 1976–1995, D-OH) (Loomis and Schiller 2016: 33–34).

The Republicans gained control of the Congress in 1994 and were the majority from then to 2006, and Newt Gingrich (R-GA) became Speaker of the House (1995–1999) after having served as the minority whip (1989–1995). Senator Bill Frist (1995–2007, R-TN) was majority leader from 2003 to 2007. Democratic senator Harry Reid (D-NV) was the minority leader (2015–2017) and majority whip (2001–2003). He was U.S. senator from Nevada for the 1987–2017 period. He warned against Republicans changing the filibuster rules to limit their use to delay or obstruct the agenda and judicial nominations of President George Bush. In 2006, the Senate changed to Democratic majority and Reid became majority leader. He then backed restrictions on filibustering when the Republican minority used it to block President Barack Obama's nominations. By 2014, the Congress was polarized along party lines. The Senate switched once again in 2014, and Senator Mitch McConnell (R-KY) became the majority leader and Senator Reid the minority leader. McConnell, too, moved to limit the filibuster but retained it in the case of Supreme Court nominees (Loomis and Schiller 2016: 37–39). Arguably, since President Obama's election in 2008, partisanship in Congress has become so intense that its lawmaking function has verged on becoming dysfunctional (Sinclair 2000). The problems arising for lawmaking, and most other functions for that matter, by congressional tribalism will be explored in Chapter 2.

The Changing Role of Congressional Budget Powers Post–World War II

The Constitution gives Congress the "powers of the purse," as stated in Section 7 of Article I:

All Bills for raising Revenue shall originate in the House of Representatives; but the Senate may propose or concur with Amendments as on other Bills.

Section 8 states:

The Congress shall have Power To lay and collect Taxes, Duties, Imposts and Excises to pay the Debts and provide for the Common Defence and general Welfare of the United States: but all Duties, Imposts and Excises shall be uniform throughout the United States; To borrow Money on the credit of the United States; No money shall be drawn from the Treasury, but in Consequence of Appropriations made by Law, and a regular Statement and Account of the Receipts and Expenditures of all public Money shall be published from time to time.

But those general statements on the power to raise revenues and to appropriate the expenditure of funds do not describe a budget process as understood today (Fenno 1966; Wildavsky 1964).

The changes in the budgetary function of Congress since adoption of the Constitution have been among its most profound.

Indeed, as three scholars of Congress note so well, "The budget reflects fundamental choices about the role of government in American life. Action on the annual budget tends to generate the most partisan fights in Washington. The twists and turns of budget politics have strongly influenced winners and losers in elections, shaped the political careers of the most prominent politicians, reshaped congressional decision-making processes, and altered the distribution of power within Congress" (Smith, Roberts, and Vander Wielen 2011: 379).

Throughout the nineteenth century, and essentially prior to World War I, the Congress lacked a cohesive, planned budgetary process. It authorized programs that required appropriations, often in a fragmented manner, by its various committees, each of which received funding requests from the various departments and agencies that they oversaw without a prior sense of what the total spending would be as a result. As long as the country was a relatively minor world power, and when the national government was relatively small, this approach to budgeting worked sufficiently well. Indeed, the national government often had a surplus. World War I, and especially World War II, changed all that. Budget deficits began to grow and become routine, and paying for the interest on the national debt has increased to an ever-larger percentage of the annual budget. In 1921, Congress enacted a budget process that established a framework by which Congress and the president formulated a federal budget by passing the Budget and Accounting Act of 1921 (68 Pub. L. No. 67–13, 42 Stat. 20) and signed into law by President Warren Harding on July 10, 1921. For the first time, it required that the president submit an annual budget to Congress and created the Bureau of the Budget (which subsequently became the Office of Management and Budget [OMB]) to assist in the formulation of the budget. The bureau was housed in the Department of the Treasury from 1921 until it was moved by President Franklin Roosevelt to the Executive Office of the President in 1939 (Budget Counsel Reference, n.d.).

The budget process was amended and elaborated upon by the Congressional Budget and Impoundment Control Act of 1974 (Pub. L. No. 93–344, 88 Stat. 297), signed into law on July 12, 1974, by President Richard Nixon. The 1974 act was prompted by President Nixon's refusal to spend funds allocated by Congress. Republican president Nixon and the Democrat-controlled Congress differed ideologically on policy priorities embodied in the budget. By the 1974 act, Congress created the Congressional Budget Office (CBO), which gained more control of the budget, limiting the power of the president's OMB. In large measure, the 1974 act was passed easily because the administration was embroiled in the Watergate scandal and President Nixon was unwilling to provoke Congress. The Budget Act of 1974 addressed the fragmentation of the budget process. Even after the 1921 act, although the president proposed a unified budget, the House broke the spending proposals up into thirteen parts, each considered by a subcommittee of the House Appropriations Committee. Only after passage of the thirteen separate bills would the Congress and the administration know how much had actually been appropriated. By the early 1970s, political pressures in Congress mounted to establish a more coherent congressional approach to its entire budget making process (Fenno 1966; Keith and Schick 2003; Loomis and Schiller 2016: 58–59; Pfiffner 1979; Smith, Roberts, and Vander Wielen 2011: 383).

As Loomis and Schiller note, "Over the 1980s, a centralizing change, implicit in the new budget arrangements, modified the nature of congressional actions: the *fiscalization* of the policy process" (2016: 59). The current Congress is driven by this fiscal focus. Controlling spending levels and funding for continuing programs have become central to the contemporary Congress, forcing future programs to give way to yesterday's decisions (Schick 1980, 2000). The U.S. deficit grows steadily, sometimes even exponentially, driven by the mandatory portions of the budget. Discretionary spending becomes ever more contentious as debates over policies hinge more heavily on fiscal considerations. This trend enhances the power of members of the budget and appropriations committees and the party leadership whose members have the most leverage in determining policy outcomes. "The very nature of redistributive, or zero-sum, decision making is to empower those whose reach facilitates negotiations and whose power can enforce agreements, as long as they can convince even a bare majority of members to agree" (Loomis and Schiller 2016: 59–60). Increasingly since 2010, when the Republicans controlled Congress, and especially the House where raising the debt level originates, votes over those limits have become contentious. The battles over raising the debt level, and the more frequent use of continuing resolutions instead of a regular-order fiscal budget, have badly tarnished the reputation and support for the institution of the Congress. The percentage of the public viewing the Congress in favorable terms has remained a minority since the mid-1960s, plummeting to new lows since 2014 (Loomis and Schiller 2016: 60–63). The public has increasingly viewed the Congress as dysfunctional, especially with the prominence of filibusters and delay in the Senate and by hyperpartisan and interparty division in the House (Mann and Ornstein 2013).

The formal budget process involves the president submitting to Congress a unified budget formulated over months with the OMB, which works with the various cabinet departments and independent agencies that submit to the OMB their requests. Past budget data, economic projections, and the administration's policy proposals and initiatives and its intended revenue and spending plans for the following fiscal year all shape the fiscal budget. The president submits the unified budget to Congress where it is referred to the House and Senate Budget Committees and to the CBO. Other committees with budgetary responsibilities weigh in during this time. In March, the CBO reports its analysis of the budget requests and projects a baseline, and the budget committees consider the budget resolution (a concurrent resolution). It is not a law and therefore does not require the president's signature (Smith, Roberts, and

Vander Wielen 2011: 382–85). After both chambers pass budget resolutions, a select group of representatives and senators negotiates a conference report to reconcile any differences. In order to be binding, the conference report must be approved by both the House and the Senate. It becomes a blueprint for the actual appropriations and the authorization on new discretionary spending. In recent years, Congress has failed to pass all the appropriations bills before the start of the fiscal year (October 1). In that case, Congress has passed continuing resolutions that provide for the temporary funding of government operations based on the prior year's funding levels of discretionary spending, which, since 2012, are broken down into a dozen appropriations bills. Sometimes multiple bills are combined into one piece of legislation, an omnibus appropriations act. Mandatory spending refers to spending enacted into law but not set by an annual appropriations bill, such as a host of transfer payments like welfare benefits, Social Security benefits, Medicare, and Medicaid (these are also known as "entitlement programs"). The CBO estimates the cost of mandatory spending each year.

The Changing Role of the Representation Function

The Constitution stipulates the representation function in Article I, Section 2 where it specifies how the membership of the House of Representatives and the Senate shall be elected. It specifies only a geographic representation function. Each state, regardless of size or population, elects two U.S. senators, who each represent the whole state. Members in the U.S. House of Representatives, known as "the people's house," are chosen by congressional districts, and each state must have at least one such representative. Members of the U.S. House of Representatives represent people residing in a geographic district within their state.

Chief Justice Earl Warren stated the rationale for the "one person, one vote" rule that requires each district in a single-member district election system contain an equal number of people. The geographic size of the district does not matter; instead, it is the population size that is important:

> Legislators represent people, not trees or acres. Legislators are elected by voters, not farms or cities or economic interests. As long as ours is a representative form of government, and our legislatures are those instruments of government elected directly by and directly representative of the people, the right to elect legislators in a free and unimpaired fashion is a bedrock of our political system. (*Reynolds v. Sims*, 377 U.S. 533, 1964)

What changed over time, and as a result of Supreme Court decisions and constitutional amendments, is who was counted as people. Originally, a person or citizen with the right to vote (and therefore to be represented) was limited to free, white males, over twenty-one years of age, who owned property, who were native-born or naturalized citizens. Native American Indians were not considered native-born or naturalized citizens and therefore could not vote. Blacks were slaves and counted only as three-fifths of a person in determining the population of a state, so they were not allowed to vote. Women were not allowed to vote and were therefore not represented. In the words of Article I, Section 2, "Representatives shall be apportioned among the several States which may be included within this Union, according to their respective numbers, which shall be determined by adding the whole Number of free Persons, including those bound to Service for a Term of Years, and excluding Indians not taxed, three fifths of all other Persons."

The first expansion of citizenship and thereby the right to vote came with the ratification of the Thirteenth, Fourteenth, and Fifteenth Amendments—known collectively as the Civil War Amendments.

- The Thirteenth Amendment ended slavery and was ratified on December 6, 1865.

- The Fourteenth Amendment applied the aforementioned provision to the states by stating that "all persons born or naturalized, including former slaves, are citizens" and forbade states to deny any person life, liberty, or property without due process of law and the equal protection of law. It was ratified on July 9, 1868.

- The Fifteenth Amendment, ratified on March 30, 1870, insured African American men the right to vote, stating, "the right of citizens of the United States to vote shall not be denied or abridged by the United States or by any State on account of race, color, or previous condition of servitude."

Women were not allowed to vote until adoption of the Nineteenth Amendment in 1920 and were therefore not represented. Women began to agitate for suffrage in a few states as early as the 1820s, but the national suffrage movement began in 1848 at the Seneca Falls Convention in New York, led by Elizabeth Cady Stanton, Lucretia Mott, and Susan B. Anthony.

The members of the U.S. Senate represent the states, and until 1913, senators were elected by state legislatures. The Seventeenth Amendment, ratified on April 8, 1913, finally mandated the popular (i.e., direct) election of senators by the state's population rather than its legislature (Smith, Roberts, and Vander Wielen 2011: 43).

The citizens residing in the District of Columbia had been denied the right to elect representatives. That issue was finally addressed and resolved in 1961 with adoption of the Twenty-Third Amendment, which allowed for suffrage in the District, enacted by Congress on March 23, 1961, by Public Law 87–389.

Another change in representation was brought about by the U.S. Supreme Court. Although the Constitution calls for reapportionment after the census years, for many years many states did not do so. In the 1960s, the U.S. Supreme Court finally intervened in the matter. In 1962, in a Tennessee case that came to the court when some of its citizens challenged the state legislature for failing to reapportion its congressional districts, the court first ruled that it could, indeed, enter the political thicket and weigh in on the apportionment issue. By a 6–2 vote, the Supreme Court decided to assert its power of judicial review principle in the case of *Baker v. Carr* (369 U.S. 186, 1962). It followed up that decision with two other decisions in 1964. One was a ruling on a Georgia case, *Wesberry v. Sanders* (376 U.S. 1, 1964), in which the court ruled 6–3 that congressional districts must be apportioned in districts that are equal in population. And in the aforementioned ruling in *Reynolds v. Sims* (377 U.S. 533, 1964), in an Alabama apportionment case, the court ruled 8–1 that the state must reapportion its districts on the basis of "one man, one vote," apportioning the districts as near as practicable equal on the basis of population. In subsequent rulings it held that to ensure the equal population principle, districts could not vary in size greater than 16 percent from one district to another.

Finally, reacting to the Vietnam War, young men eighteen years old and older agitated to change the Constitution to allow eighteen-year-olds to vote, arguing persuasively that if they were old enough to be drafted and possibly die for their country in that war, they should be old enough to vote. The Twenty-Sixth Amendment, passed in 1971, gave suffrage to eighteen-year-olds.

These cases illustrate the fact that representation can involve considerations other than geographic ones, even beyond the equality of population in geographic districts. Women's suffrage, black suffrage, and age of suffrage all concern demographic aspects of representation. If representatives are supposed to be "like" the constituents they represent, then Congress is still decidedly "unrepresentative." Despite having the right to vote, women, blacks, Hispanics, Asians, ethno-religious groups like Muslims, and so on are still underrepresented in the Congress when compared to their percent of the population. Catholics, from the Civil War until after World War II, were similarly underrepresented, although since the 1980s, they have become slightly overrepresented (LeMay 2018: 18–19, 204, 209).

Another factor that could be considered as part of representation is party identification. Because of gerrymandering (manipulating district boundaries to maintain majorities), Democrats and Republicans are often underrepresented in Congress. All minor or third parties are clearly underrepresented; indeed, in Congress they are totally absent. One could also assess representation in terms of political ideology—whether citizens consider themselves conservatives, liberals, or progressives. The geographic means to determine representation does not take ideological perspectives into consideration.

The Changing Role in Congressional War-Making Powers

The war powers functions of Congress are stipulated in Article I, Section 8 by the following enumerated powers:

> To declare War, grant Letters of Marque and Reprisal, and make Rules concerning Captures on Land and Water; To raise and support Armies, but no Appropriation of Money to that Use shall be for a longer term than two Years; To provide and maintain a Navy; To make Rules for the Government and Regulation of the land and naval Forces; To provide for calling forth the Militia to exercise the Laws of the Union, suppress Insurrection and repel Invasions; To provide for organizing, arming, and disciplining, the Militia, and for governing such Part of them as may be employed in the Service of the United States, reserving to the States respectively, the Appointment of the Officers, and the Authority of training the Militia according to the discipline prescribed by Congress.

For the first 150 years of its history, Congress held sway in its war powers functions. From the adoption of the Constitution until the end of World War II, all wars in which the United States engaged were at the declaration of hostilities or war by the American Congress. From 1801 to 1945, Congress declared war and the various presidents, as commander in chief, carried out the war. These included the Tripolitan (or Barbary) War (1801–1805), the War of 1812 (1812–1814), the Mexican-American War (1846–1848), the Spanish-American War (1898), World War I (1914–1919), and World War II (1941–1945) (Smith, Roberts, and Vander Wielen 2011: 297–98).

Since the end of World War II and the development of the United States as the world's superpower, however, Congress essentially ceded many of its war powers functions to the president. Since the Korean War, every major conflict in which the United States has engaged was conducted without a declaration of war by the American Congress. Those include the Korean War (1950–1953), the Vietnam War (1964–1973), the U.S. invasion of Panama (1989), the Persian Gulf War (1990–1991), the Afghanistan War (2001 to present), and the Iraq War, also known as the Second Persian Gulf War (2003–2011) (Smith, Roberts, and Vander Wielen 2011: 297–98).

Beyond the power to declare war, however, congressional war powers functions extend to the establishment, and funding, of the executive branch agencies for executing military actions.

The U.S. Department of Navy began with its inception in 1775 as the Continental Navy, which was disbanded after the Revolutionary War. After adoption of the Constitution, which authorized the creation of a navy, Congress expanded the force by the Naval Act of 1794, which created and equipped six naval frigate vessels, first used against the Tripoli pirates in 1801. On October 10, 1845, Congress moved the Naval School to Annapolis, and it became the U.S. Naval Academy in 1850. Congress authorized the academy to begin conferring BS degrees in 1933. Congress authorized the admission of women to the Naval Academy in 1976 (U.S. Naval Academy, n.d.).

The U.S. Department of War was formed on August 7, 1789, headed by the U.S. secretary of war. Congress established the Army Military Academy at West Point in upstate New York in 1802. The War Department expanded greatly during the Civil War. In 1916, Congress passed the National Defense Act, reducing the War Department's size and support, until the United States entered World War I on April 6, 1917. The War Department was headed by General George Marshall in 1939, when he assumed the office of army chief of staff. He expanded the authority of the chiefs of staff until World War II. The Pentagon was completed in 1943. General Marshall reorganized the army under the War Powers Act of 1941. It was dissolved on September 18, 1947, when Congress established the Department of the Army and Department of the Air Force to join the Department of the Navy as part of the new joint National Military Establishment (NME) created by Executive Order 9877. The executive order assigned primary military functions. The NME was renamed the U.S. Department of Defense, headed by the U.S. secretary of defense, in 1949, when Congress merged the U.S. military forces. As a vestige of its pre–World War II traditions, however, military officers are still trained at the Army War College, the Naval War College, and the Air War College (Fisher 2000; Stevenson 2007).

The president and Congress can sometimes conflict in war policy making. The power of the purse can limit a president's ability to make war as part of his commander in chief role, but presidents have found ways to manipulate the Congress in war policy making (Fisher 2000; Howell and Pevehouse 2007; Stevenson 2007). A good example is President Theodore Roosevelt's use of the newly expanded navy in 1907. He did so partly as his desire to "flex the U.S. muscles" in response to Japan's surprising victory in the Russo-Japanese War in 1905. President Roosevelt wanted to send the fleet of sixteen new battleships (dubbed the Great White Fleet) from the U.S. Atlantic Fleet to make a voyage around the world to the Pacific. Many in Congress balked at doing so, given its expense. In July 1907, Roosevelt commissioned the fleet to depart, and in July 1908, it left San Francisco for eastern Asia, with stops in Hawaii, New Zealand, Australia, the Philippines, Japan, and China. The navy and War Department ran out of authorized funds when the fleet was in Japan. Roosevelt informed the Congress that if it wanted to bring the fleet home, it would have to appropriate additional funds (a supplemental budget) to do so. He cleverly had forced its hands to do so, and on February 22, 1909, the fleet completed its voyage and arrived home in Hampton Roads, Virginia (Library of Congress, n.d.).

In conducting the Vietnam War, Republican president Richard Nixon clashed with the Democratic Party–controlled Congress. "In 1973, Congress enacted, over President Richard Nixon's veto, the War Powers Resolution. This law requires the president to notify Congress of any commitment of military forces within 48 hours and to terminate the commitment within 60 days unless Congress approves an extension or is unable to meet" (Smith, Roberts, and Vander Wielen 2011: 297–98). Obviously, as illustrated by the Afghanistan War now having lasted more than sixteen years, Congress simply neglected to invoke and enforce the provisions of the War Powers Resolution. Many checks and balances work only if the branch having a power to check another branch actively does so.

Presidents have been equally adroit at manipulating the "authorization to use force" that Congress has passed rather than a formal declaration of war (Fisher 2000; Stevenson 2007). President Johnson used the Gulf of Tonkin Resolution to legally justify the escalation of forces in the Vietnam War and to expand the conflict into Cambodia and Laos. To illustrate with two recent examples: "President Obama used two congressional authorizations for the use of military force—provided to President Bush in 2001 and 2002 after the 9/11 attacks to wage war on Afghanistan and Iraq—to do two things. First, he used them to oversee conflicts in those countries when he first came to office, and later to wind down the U.S. military combat roles there. Second, he has used them to launch attacks on terrorist groups such as Al Qaeda and ISIL in Iraq, Yemen, Syria, and Pakistan" (Loomis and Schiller 2016: 105).

In addition to its powers to create military departments in the executive branch, Congress influences U.S. war and military affairs through oversight by a number of its committees (Howell and Pevehouse 2007). Chief among those, of course, are such standing committees of the U.S. House of Representatives and the U.S. Senate as Appropriations, Budget, and Armed Services Committees and the key subcommittees of the Armed Services Committees. The U.S. Senate's Armed Services Committee has seven subcommittees: Airland, Cybersecurity, Emerging Threats and Capabilities, Personnel, Readiness and Management Support, Seapower, and Strategic Forces.

There are seven similar subcommittees of the U.S. House Armed Services Committee: Tactical Air and Land Forces, Military Personnel, Oversight and Investigations, Readiness, Seapower and Projection Forces, Strategic Forces, and Emerging Threats and Capabilities. The jurisdiction of the Armed Services Committees (Senate and House) includes defense policy generally, ongoing military operations, organization and reform of the Department of Defense and Department of Energy, counterdrug programs, acquisitions and industrial base policy, technology transfer and export controls, joint interoperability, cooperative threat reduction programs, Department of Energy nonproliferation programs, and detainee affairs and policy.

Because funding for defense-related programs tends to be well supported by the public, and especially for programs located in congressional home districts of members serving on those key defense-related committees, Congress often funds military and defense projects even beyond what is requested by the executive branch's Department of Defense. This is especially the case if there is a military installation in a congressional district or if the congressional district is home to a major arms manufacturing company or corporation.

The Changing Role in Congressional Oversight of the Other Branches

Oversight refers to the role of Congress to determine that the laws and regulations it passes are faithfully executed by the executive branch. Oversight is a role that has expanded considerably in congressional time and attention as the executive branch and its numerous agencies and programs have grown exponentially in size and scope since the end of World War II. Three political scientists specializing in studying Congress have noted the following:

> A member of Congress dissatisfied with agency performance or with presidential directives to an agency can choose from several oversight strategies to try to bring the bureaucracy into line. Oversight strategies centered on formal hearings include Committee or subcommittee hearings, which regularly bring agency heads in front of legislators, special hearings designed to draw attention to a disputed policy or agency action, and more dramatic investigations . . . usually conducted by special committees. (Smith, Roberts, and Vander Wielen 2011: 309)

As these scholars note, the Legislative Reorganization Act of 1946 charges the various standing committees with the duty to maintain continuous watchfulness over executive branch activities (by the respective departments and their agencies) within their jurisdiction. The 1946 act also established two committees with government-wide oversight responsibilities: now called the House Committee on Oversight and Government Reform and the Senate Committee on Homeland Security and Government Affairs. In particular, they use the special hearings and investigations approach across a wide range of government activities (Smith, Roberts, and Vander Wielen 2011: 188). In 1970, Congress enacted a law with the strongest oversight directives, the Legislative Reorganization Act of 1970. It required committees to write biannual reports on their oversight activities. The House created many oversight subcommittees and authorized the hiring of staff devoted to oversight and enabling committees and subcommittees to organize more hearings and more extensive investigations.

Oversight became an increasingly important part of committee work. In 1961, less than 10 percent of committee hearings and meetings were devoted to oversight matters. By 1983, that had risen to 25 percent. By 1997, 34 percent of their activities concerned oversight matters. In 2009, House rules required each standing committee to hold at least one oversight hearing during each 120-day period to be concerned with waste, fraud, abuse, or mismanagement in the programs and agencies under the committee's jurisdiction (Smith, Roberts, and Vander Wielen 2011: 188).

In addition to the House Committee on Oversight and Government Reform, the Appropriations and Budget Committees have government-wide jurisdiction. Cabinet-level executive branch departments and agencies each have a corresponding House committee that oversees their activity: the Department of Agriculture is overseen by the House and Senate Agriculture Committees; the Department of Commerce is overseen by the House Energy and Commerce Committee and the Senate's Commerce, Science, and Transportation Committee; the House and Senate Armed Services Committees have oversight of the Department of Defense; the Department of Education is under jurisdiction and oversight by the House Education and Workforce Committee and the Senate's Health Education, Labor, and Pensions Committee; the House Foreign Affairs and the Senate Foreign Relations provide oversight of the Department of State; the House Natural Resources and the Senate's Energy and Natural Resources oversee the Department of Energy and the Department of the Interior; the Department of Justice is overseen by the House and the Senate Judiciary Committees; and so on.

Recent examples of the special hearings and investigative type of legislative oversight are the Benghazi investigation and hearings that lasted several years and where a Republican-controlled committee grilled then Secretary of State Hillary Clinton for many hours over several days; the hearings on the backlog of services to veterans by the Department of Veteran Affairs; and the special hearings conducted by the U.S. House and the U.S. Senate Intelligence Committees on Russian cyberattacks and related influence on the 2016 elections.

Congressional members, their staffs, and the assorted committee and subcommittee staffs often employ less formal oversight methods, such as written and telephonic communications with agency heads, discussions with agency heads and interested (i.e., often lobbying) parties during informal office visits, public relations campaigns, and threats of more and harsher regulatory legislation (Smith, Roberts, and Vander Wielen 2011: 309–10). They may push agencies to conduct internal investigations, and congressional staff sometimes pressure agencies and departments not to act when such agencies or programs adversely affect their constituents.

Political scientists have used a helpful distinction in discussing oversight: the "police-patrol" versus the "fire-alarm" approaches. The police-patrol approach to oversight involves Congress using routine, systematic surveillance of executive branch agencies at its own initiative. The fire-alarm approach is more decentralized. It relies on others—agency whistleblowers, interest groups, citizens, and the media—to pull the alarm bringing to congressional attention the failures or problematic rules and procedures of an agency. Congress, or often simply an individual member, can then bring pressure on the agency, motivating the bureaucracy to act. Sometimes by simply putting the bureaucracy under the glare of adverse publicity, a member of Congress, and certainly a committee or subcommittee, can change agency behavior. Congressional members and certainly committee leaders can use the pressure of an on-site visit to accomplish the same goal (Aberbach 1990; Bond and Fleisher 2000; Smith, Roberts, and Vander Wielen 2011: 311–12).

Congressional oversight, particularly using the police-patrol approach, has become more common since the 1970s, when Congress expanded its staff and such support agencies as the Government Accountability Office (GAO), the CBO, and

Congressional Research Service (Aberbach 1990; Bond and Fleisher 2000; Loomis and Schiller 2016; Smith, Roberts, and Vander Wielen 2011). Congress can use the "threat" implicit in the police-patrol approach to oversight to motivate the bureaucracy to change its ways, procedures, and sometimes its rules and regulations. Congress can threaten to use its appropriations powers to reprogram an agency, threaten new legislation to write new rules and procedures, and threaten to require the agency to submit reports to Congress on some problem and how it is addressing the issue. Indeed, often simply the threat of adverse public exposure, and the threat of the inconvenience of an investigation, can produce desired results.

The legislative veto is another congressional oversight strategy, although one that is disputed as to its constitutionality. A *legislative veto* is a provision written into legislation that delegates authority for certain actions to the president or to a department or agency (e.g., an independent regulatory agency), subject to the approval or disapproval of one or both chambers of Congress, certain committees of the Congress, or even designated committee leaders (Smith, Roberts, and Vander Wielen 2011: 313). It gives Congress the means to check executive branch actions without having to pass new laws requiring presidential approval. Use of the legislative veto enables Congress to avoid the often contentious and onerous task of writing detailed legislation. It delegates rulemaking authority to the executive branch while retaining the final say over such executive decisions (Aberbach 1990; Fisher 2000; Smith, Roberts, and Vander Wielen 2011: 313–14).

The legislative veto practice goes back to 1932, when Congress and then President Herbert Hoover reached a reorganization agreement on the executive branch that included a legislative veto provision. The Supreme Court declared legislative vetoes as unconstitutional in the case of *Immigration and Naturalization Service (INS) v. Chadha* (462 U.S. 919, June 23, 1983) (summarized in LeMay and Barkan 1999: 279–80). The Supreme Court noted that some legislative vetoes circumvent the constitutional prescription that all measures be passed by both chambers and violate the constitutional provision that all measures subject to a legislative vote must be submitted to the president for his or her signature or veto (Smith, Roberts, and Vander Wielen 2011: 314). Since the *Chadha* ruling, Congress has tried to get around the decision. It has used more detailed legislation or committee reports to add procedural requirement for agencies. At other times, Congress has used informal agency-committee spending agreements, which require agency notification to certain committees before the agency acts. Such advance notification requirements have been upheld by the courts. An implicit threat of funding reprisal is sometimes sufficient to induce an agency not to proceed with their original plans for fear that the authorizing or appropriations committee will retaliate when the legislation is next before the Congress.

Despite *Chadha* decision, Congress has continued to add legislative vetoes to new laws, adding fifty-three such legislative vetoes by 1985 and, by 1998, had enacted more than four hundred new legislative vetoes. These efforts indicate the desire, by the Congress, presidents, and agencies, to find mutually acceptable ways to balance the delegation of power with checks on the use of that power, largely because the *Chadha* decision seems to have had little practical effect on interbranch relations. Scholarly studies indicate the *Chadha* decision did eliminate a means of resolving conflict. When the executive branch and the Congress are in serious disagreement, the executive branch seems unwilling to accept even symbolic legislative veto provisions, and Congress seems unwilling to delegate power that the executive branch agency seeks, thus undercutting efforts to arrive at cooperative strategies (Smith, Roberts, and Vander Wielen 2011: 314–15).

Another device that is an implicit oversight method is the use of a *sunset* provision. This is a provision limiting the length of authorization. Congress on occasion enacts a law, or some provisions within a law, that has a predetermined life or deadline after which time the law or the provision is null and void without specific congressional action to extend the law or the sunset provision by reauthorization. Sunset provisions force the authorizing committee and Congress to repass authorization legislation periodically, thereby compelling the executive branch to justify the continuation of the program. The use of the sunset provision gives the authorization committees additional influence over the executive agency or program. Welfare reform, college student financial aid, and federal highway programs are among dozens of "unauthorized" programs where the sunset provision has expired but the programs have not died out of either neglect or congressional interest in avoiding the conflict over them. Such programs continue as long as Congress passes the separate appropriations bills for them, using a House appropriations waiver rule under which such appropriations bills are considered on the House floor (Smith, Roberts, and Vander Wielen 2011: 244–45).

The Changing Role in the Advice and Consent, Treaty Approval, and Appointive Power

Article II, Section 2 specifies the advice and consent powers of the U.S. Senate. It reads:

> He (the president) shall have Power, by and with the Advice and Consent of the Senate, to make treaties, provided two thirds of the Senates present concur; and he shall nominate, and by and with the Advice and Consent of the Senate, shall appoint Ambassadors, other public Ministers and Consuls, Judges of the supreme Court, and all other Officers of the United States, whose Appointments are not herein otherwise provided for, and which shall be established by Law: but the Congress may by Law vest the Appointment of such inferior Officers, as they think proper, in the President along, in the Courts of Law, or in the Heads of Departments.

The President shall have Power to fill up all Vacancies that may happen during the Recess of the Senate, by granting Commissions which shall expire at the End of their next Session.

It is a high hurdle to get the two-thirds of the Senate to approve treaties and appointments of judges and executive branch nominees, especially when the White House is occupied by a president from one party and the Senate is under the control of another party. The executive can sometimes get around a reluctant Senate by use of executive agreements and executive orders, but the latter have their own limitations.

Among the first treaty ratified by the new Congress, in 1796, was the Treaty of Tripoli, which ended the Barbary (or Tripolitan) War. The treaty ended the conflict with the Barbary pirates, who had been harassing U.S. merchant ships out of Tripoli, Lebanon, a predominately Muslim country. It had been negotiated by President John Adams and was ratified unanimously by the Senate on June 7, 1797. Although anti-Catholic sentiment was evident in the Congress at the time, the treaty was ratified by the same Senate that had approved the Bill of Rights. One of the treaty's opening lines is notable: "As the government of the United States is not in any sense founded on the Christian religion . . ." (LeMay 2018: 16). Another early treaty concerned the Louisiana Purchase (1803), which added a sizable number of Catholics to the United States. Spain claimed ownership of the territory of Louisiana, which at the time included 828,000 miles, comprising all or parts of what is today fifteen states between the Mississippi and the Rocky Mountains. France, under Napoleon Bonaparte, had acquired the territory from Spain in 1800 and took possession in 1802. Bonaparte was attempting to put down a slave rebellion in Haiti, which was an important source of grain for the French Empire. President Jefferson sent James Monroe to France to negotiate rights to use of the port of New Orleans. Monroe was authorized to spend up to $10 million. A yellow fever outbreak in Haiti took the lives of half of the French army there, and Napoleon offered to sell the entire Louisiana territory to the United States for $15 million. President Jefferson, and the U.S. Senate, jumped at the opportunity to do so, despite the fact that the treaty added many Catholics to the population, who became citizens by virtue of the treaty (LeMay 2018: 18).

Virtually the same thing happened in 1848 with the Treaty of Guadalupe Hidalgo ending the Mexican-American War. The treaty added a huge number of Catholics to the population, who were former Mexican citizens in the U.S.-acquired territory (what is today all or major parts of California, New Mexico, Arizona, Nevada, Utah, and Colorado) but, by virtue of the treaty, became U.S. citizens unless they declared themselves citizens of Mexico. At the time, Mexicans were not considered to be white and the Constitution specified that only "free-white men" could be native-born or naturalized citizens (LeMay 1999: 25–26). The desire to add so much territory to the western territories overrode any objections to the treaty by the necessary two-thirds of the U.S. Senate.

The desire to add territory was critically important to the Senate ratification of the 1867 treaty to purchase the territory of Alaska from Russia. The treaty was negotiated by William F. Seward, the U.S. secretary of state. Russia had been interested in selling Alaska for some time. The agreement was signed in March 1867 and transferred Alaska to the United States for a payment of $7.2 million, amounting to a bargain-basement price of about 2.5 cents per acre for an area twice the size of Texas. In the Senate, and in the media, criticism of the treaty was high—the treaty was dubbed "Seward's Folly," "Seward's Ice Box," and "Johnson's polar bear garden" (after President Andrew Johnson). But the Senate could not reject the opportunity to acquire so much territory and natural resources, and it ratified the treaty. Seward was vindicated when major gold deposits were discovered in the Yukon in 1896 and Alaska became the gateway to the Klondike gold fields.

Racial considerations and the right to naturalization were at issue regarding the Senate's ratification of the Burlingame Treaty, concluded in 1880, ratified by the Senate in 1881, and proclaimed by President Chester A. Arthur on October 5, 1881. It sought to limit the number of Chinese laborers coming to the United States from China. It promised, among its provisions, that the United States would not enact a law excluding Chinese immigration to the United States in return for China limiting the number of its nationals seeking to immigrate to the United States. The Senate soon, however, passed a law to exclude Chinese labor, and President Arthur vetoed that bill on the grounds that it broke the Burlingame Treaty. Congress got around the veto by passing another law, on May 6, 1882, that "suspended" the immigration of Chinese laborers for a period of ten years, although the law is commonly known as the Chinese Exclusion Act (summarized in LeMay and Barkan 1999: 49–54).

When a president anticipates so much opposition to a treaty under negotiation as to likely fail to be ratified, a president may get around Senate opposition by negotiating an *executive agreement*. Such an agreement is between the heads of state of two or more countries. Since it is not a formal treaty, it does not need a ratification vote in the U.S. Senate. A classic example is the Gentleman's Agreement between President Theodore Roosevelt and the Japanese government in 1907. Roosevelt issued an executive order (Number 589, March 14, 1907) covering the entrance of Japanese and Korean laborers into the United States. In it, Japan agreed to limit emigration from Japan and Korea (then a territory of Japan). The United States agreed not to pass a law excluding Japanese and Korean immigrants. The Gentleman's Agreement, however, illustrates a major flaw in that method to get around Senate opposition. The agreement is only binding while the president who negotiates and signs it remains in office. The next president can nullify it, or the Congress can enact legislation that essentially makes the order moot as it did when it passed the Emergency National

Origins Quota Act of 1921 and the Immigration Act of 1924, the "Johnson-Reed Act," which limited emigration from Japan to a miniscule number (LeMay and Barkan 1999: 100–101, 133–34, 148–51).

The U.S. Senate sometimes outright rejects a treaty. An example of that is the Treaty of Versailles in 1919. It ended World War I and established the League of Nations. The treaty was the signature diplomacy of Democratic president Woodrow Wilson. Wilson called for his Fourteen Points, outlining his vision for a safer world. Negotiated in the Paris Peace Conference by the Big Four (Great Britain, France, Italy, and the United States), ratification of the Versailles Treaty was rejected by the Senate. The opposition to ratification was led by Senator Henry Cabot Lodge (R-MA). President Wilson was a globalist. Senate members of the Republican Party were war-weary isolationists. German Americans opposed the treaty and the United States joining the League of Nations because they felt the treaty dealt too harshly with Germany. Italian Americans felt more territory should have been ceded to Italy. Irish Americans criticized the treaty for failing to address the issue of Irish independence. Even many members of Wilson's party opposed the treaty, and it failed ratification in 1919.

Another flaw in a president's strategy of using an executive order to get around Senate opposition to ratify a treaty is that the next president may nullify it. This is exemplified by President Donald Trump's executive orders nullifying three of President Obama's orders. Republican president Trump, espousing popular nationalism, was determined to oppose any actions of his predecessor, the liberal Democrat president Barack Obama. President Obama had signed the Paris Climate Accord on Earth Day, April 22, 2016. President Trump withdrew from the accord on June 1, 2017 (White House 2017b).

President Obama had begun negotiations for the Trans-Pacific Partnership (TPP), a global trade agreement that upgraded the North American Free Trade Agreement (NAFTA) among Australia, Canada, Japan, Malaysia, Mexico, Peru, the United

States, Vietnam, Chile, Brunei, Singapore, and New Zealand. President Obama signed the TPP on February 4, 2016. It was not ratified by the Senate. The other parties to the agreement tried to revive it in May 2016, but on January 23, 2017, President Trump signed a presidential memorandum to withdraw the United States' signature from the agreement, thereby making its ratification impossible (White House 2017a).

Similarly, President Obama led negotiations involving eight nations to craft an Iranian nuclear deal. Despite numerous studies affirming that Iran was in compliance with the agreement, including one by the Trump administration, President Trump unilaterally withdrew the United States from the deal on May 7, 2018 (Landler 2018).

Conclusion

This chapter has reviewed the constitutional basis for the various functions and powers of the American Congress. It examined how the congressional role in lawmaking evolved and devolved from a primary role in lawmaking to one playing second fiddle to the president in crafting legislative proposals from the legislative branch to the executive branch. The chapter reviewed how the representation function changed as the nation grew from a small collection of thirteen states on the eastern seaboard to fifty states spanning the continent and beyond to Alaska and Hawaii. The enumerated powers specified in Section 8 and the prohibited powers found in Section 9 were discussed.

The war-making powers of the Congress have declined even as the nation grew from a minor power prior to the Civil War to a major player in international affairs by the end of World War I to a superpower after World War II. War powers shifted from the Congress to the White House despite some efforts, such as the War Powers Act of 1974, to curtail the president's power to commit the nation to war without a congressional declaration of war.

Arguably the most expansive of the roles and functions of the Congress, as detailed in this chapter, concern the oversight of the executive branch by the Congress. Congress expanded greatly its committees and subcommittees and their staffs to better enable them to oversee the executive branch using hearings and investigations and requiring reports and internal investigations by the executive branch departments and agencies to self-police. The chapter described two approaches to oversight: the police-patrol and the fire-alarm approaches.

Finally, the chapter reviewed the history of the use of the advice and consent power of the Senate regarding ratification of treaties negotiated by the president and by confirming, or not, appointments of officials to the executive branch and to the federal courts and the U.S. Supreme Court. It discussed examples of the use and limitations of executive agreements to get around the Senate's advice and consent powers.

References

Aberbach, Joel. 1990. *Keeping a Watchful Eye: The Politics of Congressional Oversight*. Washington, D.C.: Brookings Institution Press.

Aldrich, John. 2012. *Why Parties? A Second Look*. Chicago: University of Chicago Press.

Association of Centers for the Study of Congress. n.d. "The 89th Congress." http://acsc.lib.udel.edu/exhibits/show/89th-congress

Bond, Jon R., and Richard Fleisher. 2000. *The President and the Congress in a Partisan Era*. Washington, D.C.: Congressional Quarterly Press.

Budget Counsel Reference. n.d. "Budget and Accounting Act of 1921." https://budgetcounsel.com/public-law-67-13-budget-and-accounting-act-of-1921/

Chambers, William N., and Walter D. Burnham. 1967. *The American Party System: Stages of Party Development*. New York: Oxford University Press.

Chubb, John E., and Paul E. Peterson, eds. 1989. *Can the Government Govern?* Washington, D.C.: Brookings Institution Press.

Davidson, Roger H., Susan W. Hammond, and Raymond W. Smock, eds. 1998. *Masters of the House*. Boulder, CO: Westview Press.

Davidson, Roger, and Walter Oleszek. 1998. *Congress and Its Members*, 6th ed. Washington, D.C.: Congressional Quarterly Press.

Dodd, Lawrence C., and Bruce I. Oppenheimer. 2005. *Congress Reconsidered*, 8th ed. Washington, D.C.: Congressional Quarterly Press.

Farrier, Jasmine. 2004. *Passing the Buck: Congress, the Budget, and Deficits*. Lexington: University Press of Kentucky.

Fenno, Richard, F., Jr. 1966. *The Power of the Purse*. Boston: Little, Brown.

Fisher, Louis. 2000. *Congressional Abdication on War and Spending*. College Station: Texas A&M University Press.

Frisch, Scott A., and Sean Q. Kelly. 2006. *Committee Assignments in the U.S. House of Representatives*. Norman: University of Oklahoma Press.

Gerring, John. 2001. *Party Ideologies in America, 1828–1996*. Cambridge: Cambridge University Press.

Gould, Lewis. 2003. *Grand Old Party: A History of the Republicans*. New York: Random House.

Haas, Garland. 1994. *The Politics of Disintegration: Political Party Decay in the United States, 1856–1900*. Jefferson, SC: McFarland and Company.

Howell, William G., and Jon C. Pevehouse. 2007. *Congressional Checks on Presidential War Powers*. Princeton, NJ: Princeton University Press.

Keith, Robert, and Allen Schick. 2003. *The Federal Budget Process*. New York: Nova Science Publishers.

Kleppner, Paul. 1979. *The Third Electoral System, 1853–1892: Parties, Voters, and Political Cultures*. Chapel Hill: University of North Carolina Press.

Landler, Mark. 2018. "Trump Abandons Iran Nuclear Deal He Long Scorned." *New York Times*, May 8. https://www.nytimes.com/2018/05/08/world/middleeast/trump-iran-nuclear-deal.html

Leip, Dave. n.d. "U.S. Presidential Election Results." https://uselectionatlas.org/RESULTS/index.html

LeLoup, Lance T. 2005. *Parties, Rules and the Evolution of Congressional Budgeting*. Pullman: Washington State University.

LeMay, Michael C., ed. 2013. *Transforming America: Perspectives on U.S. Immigration*. Santa Barbara, CA: ABC-CLIO.

LeMay, Michael C. 2017. *The American Political Party System: A Reference Handbook*. Santa Barbara, CA: ABC-CLIO.

LeMay, Michael C. 2018. *Religious Freedom in America: A Reference Handbook*. Santa Barbara, CA: ABC-CLIO.

LeMay, Michael C., and Elliott Barkan. 1999. *U.S. Immigration and Naturalization Laws and Issues: A Documentary History*. Westport, CT: Greenwood Press.

Library of Congress. n.d. "Topics in Chronicling America—Theodore Roosevelt's 'Great White Fleet.'" https://www.loc.gov/rr/news/topics/greatfleet.html

Loomis, Burdett, and Wendy J. Schiller. 2016. *The Contemporary Congress*, 6th ed. Lanham, MD: Rowman and Littlefield.

Madison, James. 1981. *The Mind of the Founder*. Edited by Marvin Meyers. Hanover, NH: University Press of New England.

Mann, Thomas, and Norman Ornstein. 2013. *It's Even Worse Than It Looks*. New York: Basic Books.

Oleszek, Walter J. 2007. *Congressional Procedures and the Policy Process*, 7th ed. Washington, D.C.: Congressional Quarterly Press.

Pfiffner, James. 1979. *The President, the Budget, and Congress*. Boulder, CO: Westview Press.

Ripley, Randall B. 1967. *Party Leaders in the House of Representatives*. Washington, D.C.: Brookings Institution Press.

Rothman, David. 1969. *Politics and Power*. New York: Athenaeum.

Rubin, Irene S. 2003. *Balancing the Federal Budget*. New York: Chatham House.

Schick, Allen. 1980. *Congress and Money*. Washington, D.C.: Urban Institute.

Schick, Allen. 2000. *The Federal Budget*, 2nd ed. Washington, D.C.: Brookings Institution Press.

Schlesinger, Arthur M., Jr. 1973. *A History of U.S. Political Parties*. New York: Chelsea House.

Shepsle, Kenneth A. 1989. "The Changing Textbook Congress." In *Can the Government Govern?* edited by John E. Chubb and Paul E. Peterson, 238–66. Washington, D.C.: Brookings Institution Press.

Sinclair, Barbara. 1995. *Legislators, Leadership, and Lawmaking*. Baltimore: Johns Hopkins University Press.

Sinclair, Barbara. 2000. *Unorthodox Lawmaking: New Legislative Processes in the U.S. Congress*, 2nd ed. Washington, D.C.: Congressional Quarterly Press.

Sinclair, Barbara. 2006. *Party Wars: Polarization and the Politics of National Policymaking*. Norman: University of Oklahoma Press.

Smith, Steven, Jason M. Roberts, and Ryan J. Vander Wielen. 2011. *The American Congress*, 7th ed. New York: Cambridge University Press.

Stevenson, Charles A. 2007. *The Congress at War: The Politics of Conflict since 1789*. Dulles, VA: Potomac Books.

Thirty-thousand.org. 2006. *The Size of the U.S. House of Representatives and Its Constituent State Delegations*. https://www.thirty-thousand.org/pages/QHA-02.htm

U.S. Naval Academy. n.d. "A Brief History of USNA." https://www.usna.edu/USNAHistory

Van Buren, Martin. 1867. *Inquiry into the Origin and Course of Political Parties in America*. New York: Hurd and Houghton.

Volden, Craig, and Alan E. Wiseman. 2014. *Legislative Effectiveness in the United States: The Lawmakers*. New York: Cambridge University Press.

White House. 2017a. "Presidential Memorandum Regarding Withdrawal of the United States from the Trans-Pacific Partnership Negotiations and Agreement." January 23. https://www.whitehouse.gov/presidential-actions/presidential-memorandum-regarding-withdrawal-united-states-trans-pacific-partnership-negotiations-agreement/

White House. 2017b. "Statement by President Trump on the Paris Climate Accord." June 1. https://www.whitehouse.gov/briefings-statements/statement-president-trump-paris-climate-accord/

Wildavsky, Aaron. 1964. *The Politics of the Budgetary Process*. Boston: Little, Brown.

Witcover, Jules. 2003. *Party of the People: A History of the Democrats*. New York: Random House.

Introduction

The framers of the Constitution developed a unique form of government, a republican democracy, where people (or state legislatures) would elect or appoint representatives to the national legislative body. These founding fathers arguably spent the most time at the Constitutional Convention debating the content of Article I, which laid out the plan for the legislative branch. The discussion at the convention around Congress, as it was to become, also created the most intense disagreement. This intense debate and disagreement, which has surrounded Congress since its inception, continues to be seen today, on nearly every issue.

Why is the world's most powerful and important legislative body so riddled with conflict? Why do voters disapprove of Congress at such high levels but continue to send their own representative back to Congress nearly 90 percent of the time? Why is Congress, which was given the most enumerated powers in the Constitution, riddled with gridlock, stalemate, and polarization?

We argue this was by design, or rather, the institutional foundations of Congress that created this amazing body also create its biggest challenges. The Constitution is not only the basis

---

Senate Majority Leader Harry Reid (D-NV) talks to reporters about the use of the "nuclear option" at the U.S. Capitol on November 21, 2013, in Washington, D.C. The Senate voted 52-48 to invoke the so-called "nuclear option," opting to change Senate rules on the controversial filibuster for most presidential nominations with a simple majority vote. (Chip Somodevilla/Getty Images)

for how Congress operates but also the reason for its conflict-riddled nature. This chapter details a number of the problems and controversies with today's American Congress, beginning with the institutional parameters provided by the Constitution. This chapter will explore the internal workings of Congress and how this can hinder or help lawmaking. It will also address other outside influences on Congress like interest groups, elections, and representation. This chapter also outlines solutions offered by practitioners and political scientists, when appropriate or when they have been offered. This is not an exhaustive discussion of the current problems surrounding Congress but rather a starting place for conversation and study.

The Congressional–Presidential Relationship

The Constitution laid out an intriguing interplay between the legislative and executive branches of government. They were to be completely separate, with their own unique powers. The Constitution states in Article I, Section 1: "All legislative Powers herein granted shall be vested in a Congress of the United States." Similarly, Article II, Section 1 says, "The executive Power shall be vested in a President of the United States of America." In Article II, Section 2, the Constitution stipulates in relation to the president: "he shall take Care that the Laws be faithfully executed."

The two previous sections from the Constitution clearly lay out our separation of powers system of government, where Congress and the president both deal with laws but in very different ways. They work together, or do different aspects, on nearly everything within our federal government. This process can be both collegial and contentious. The arena of legislation creation and execution is one in which they both play but are technically responsible for different features, even if they both try to intervene on the other's playing field.

While each branch had their own distinct powers, the framers of the Constitution also created a system in which they would each be able to check the power of the other. In fact, they were well aware that they were creating a system ripe for conflict. They knew power held in the hands of the few could be dangerous and power must be checked. In "Federalist No. 51," James Madison writes, "But the great security against a gradual concentration of the several powers in the same department, consists in giving to those who administer each department, the necessary constitutional means, and personal motives, to resist encroachment of the others . . . Ambition must be made to counteract ambition. The interest of the man must be connected with the constitutional rights of the place."

This section will outline those constitutionally mandated separate powers, as well as the checks, and how they work in today's political reality.

Legislative Agenda

Constitutionally, Congress is given the sole power to develop legislation (Article I, Section 1) and the legislative agenda. This seems straightforward until we consider how often presidential candidates and presidents themselves discuss policy and legislation. The president is not given a great deal of legislative or lawmaking powers. He is to approve or veto legislation. He is also given the power to provide Congress with the State of the Union (Article II, Section 3), where he presents Congress with a policy platform. Today, we know the modern presidency has greatly expanded its legislative powers; thus, we have two branches of government that, in reality, are legislating.

Throughout the twentieth century, presidents were expanding their legislative powers (Pika, Maltese, and Rudalevige 2017), and as a response, Congress began growing its power by expanding its legislative agenda and legislating on a greater number of topics and policies. The source of the president's legislative power is his power to persuade Congress to do what he wants (Neustadt 1990). This power is not just built upon charm and a good argument; Richard E. Neustadt (1990) says it is also based on the status and authority of the Office of the

President. Some of this power comes from the physical office itself. The president uses his Oval Office to his advantage by inviting members of Congress to the White House to meet with him in the famous office.

A story illustrating this concept involves a senator from the West, who was angry with the White House for refusing to support drought assistance for suffering farmers and ranchers in his state. One evening, after fighting with the president for days, the senator announced he was going to personally "go talk to the man." He got in his car and drove to the White House to meet with the president. Upon returning later that evening, he looked at his staff and reported he had tried to convince the president of his ideas, but it was "damn hard in that office of his." Simply sitting in that office, across from the Resolute desk, can impede a passionate senator's resolve. Members of Congress respect the Office of the President and what it stands for in our government. Presidents are well aware of this status and authority and use it to their advantage.

The power to have a comprehensive legislative agenda, as delivered to Congress in the State of the Union, is much easier for the president than for Congress. The president is the only elected official to represent all Americans; he need only speak for himself. Congress, on the other hand, is made up of 535 individual voting members. They represent 435 diverse and distinct congressional districts and fifty states. They have different ideologies, concerns, and vastly different constituencies. Speaking as one legislative body is impossible; it is even difficult for the two major parties to speak as one organized group. Thus, getting a majority of those members to move in the same direction on policy is, at best, difficult and, at worst, impossible. The president holds the upper hand here, even though it is not his job to formulate policy (see Anderson 1979).

It is easy to see how Congress has difficulty coming up with a cohesive agenda, and when it has difficulty passing an agenda, or when they are simply ignoring the president, the president has another tool at his disposal. That tool is the bully pulpit or the ability to go public (Kernell 2007). This means that rather than going to Capitol Hill to convince members of Congress to support his policies, the president goes directly to the American public (Kernell 2007). He works to convince them of the value of his ideas, and then once they are convinced, voters put pressure on their representatives to pass these laws. We see this through the State of the Union (which is televised across the country), press conferences, interviews, and rallies. Congress can either respond positively to their constituents asking them to act or ignore their requests at their own electoral peril. Often members of Congress are not amused by this; they would prefer that the president comes to them directly rather than indirectly that often feels to them like coercion (Polsby 1978). Modern presidents have increasingly used this power, with President Obama selling his health-care plan through town hall meetings and President Trump holding rallies across the country advocating for his immigration policies. Presidents are fully aware that these actions will harm their relationship with Congress, but they believe that the benefits outweigh the costs.

While not specifically enumerated in the Constitution, presidents argue that the power of executive orders is implied in the Take Care (Article II, Section 3) and Vesting (Article II, Section 1) clauses. This power gives the president legislating abilities. He may issue directives to executive agencies that have the force of law, like when President Obama issued the Deferred Action for Childhood Arrivals directive in 2012 (Department of Homeland Security 2018). Every modern president has issued executive orders, with their first orders usually putting a hold on the previous president's orders (Pika, Maltese, and Rudalevige 2017). The next president who comes along can rescind the executive orders of the previous president, something he cannot do with congressionally passed legislation.

Executive orders, like nearly everything in Washington, are politically charged. Those in Congress who agree with the president see his actions as a necessary way to get around a hostile Congress. Those who disagree see it as a violation of the separation of powers. It cannot be denied that the practice of issuing executive orders can strain relationships with Congress. Their use creates a constant power struggle between Congress and the president.

The final check on legislative power of Congress, and minor control of the agenda, comes in the form of the vice president. According to the Constitution (Article I, Section 3), the vice president is the president of the Senate, which is unique in our separation of powers system of government. The vice president is a member of both branches of government but only elected to one (the executive). The vice president, as president of the Senate, can preside over the Senate at any time. For example, Vice President Joe Biden chose to preside over the Senate vote on the Affordable Care Act on December 24, 2009, as it was a critical piece of legislation for the Obama administration.

The main power of this office, however, is to break ties in the Senate. Depending on the makeup of the Senate, vice presidents can be called upon numerous times during their tenure to break ties, or not at all in the case of Vice President Biden ("Tie Votes," n.d.). As of December 2018, Vice President Mike Pence has been the deciding vote thirteen times in the Senate. While vice presidents cannot introduce bills to the Senate, they can exercise a limited amount of policy power through this vote.

Veto and Override

The veto is one of the most powerful checks the Constitution gives the president on Congress (see Article I, Section 7). If all of his other abilities and persuasive tactics fail and Congress passes a bill he strongly objects to, the president rejects it. This is a tool at the president's disposal that recent presidents have rarely used. Often just the threat of a veto puts Congress on notice that they need to take the president's policy wishes into consideration. The veto, however, is a negative agenda control power. The president can only reject legislation; he cannot introduce it and pass it on his own, save for using an executive order. In this way, Congress has retained most of its legislative powers.

A president can only veto the entire bill; he cannot approve the provisions he likes and reject the ones he opposes (Edwards and Wayne 2014). This process is called the "line-item veto." Congress did pass a legislation in 1996 that gave the president the power to veto specific provisions in a bill and allow the others to go into effect (Line Item Veto Act of 1996, Pub. L. 104–130), but the Supreme Court determined this was unconstitutional (see *Clinton v. City of New York*, 524 U.S. 417, 1998). As Justice John P. Stevens said in the majority opinion, "If the Line Item Veto Act were valid, it would authorize the President to create a different law, one whose text was not voted on by either House of Congress or presented to the President for signature" (*Clinton v. City of New York* 1998).

The Constitution gives Congress the final say in the discussion of vetoes. If a president vetoes a bill, it is sent back to Congress and it can override the veto by a two-thirds vote of both chambers (Article I, Section 7). These supermajorities in Congress are difficult, but not impossible, to attain. President Obama vetoed twelve bills during his two terms as president, and Congress was able to override one of those (Justice against Sponsors of Terrorism Act, Pub. L. No. 114–222). President George W. Bush also vetoed twelve bills, and Congress overrode four of them (U.S. House of Representatives 2019).

President Bush actually vetoed the same bill twice, the 2007 Farm Bill, because of bloated spending. Congress overrode the first veto, creating Public Law 110–234, but then realized that thirty-four pages dealing with foreign aid were missing from the bill. Both chambers then had to pass a new bill, which included the missing pages. President Bush again vetoed the Farm Bill, which was again overridden by Congress and became Public Law 110–246 (CNN 2008).

With enough resolve, Congress, as a body, is able to overcome the veto power, but it is not a common occurrence.

Vetoes and, when they happen, overrides tend to further the political divide between the two branches of government.

War Powers

The Constitution divides war powers between the two branches of government, giving Congress the sole power to declare war (Article I, Section 8) while naming the president as the commander in chief of the army and navy (Article II, Section 2). Congress has only declared war eleven times, in five different wars (Torreon 2015). The last time Congress declared war was for World War II (Elsea and Weed 2014). However, every president since 1798 has committed troops overseas, without congressional approval (Edwards and Wayne 2014; Torreon 2015). President Clinton had over fifty instances of using the U.S. military overseas (Torreon 2015).

Throughout the twentieth century, presidents continued to grow and expand their war powers. Congress did not appreciate the loss of its constitutionally mandated role in war declaration and responded with the passage of the War Powers Resolution on November 7, 1973 (Weed 2017). President Nixon had previously vetoed this legislation, but Congress overrode the veto and this resolution became Public Law 93–148 (Weed 2017). This resolution requires that the president not only notifies and consults Congress before deploying troops but also notifies it within forty-eight hours of committing troops (Weed 2017). The resolution says troops cannot be deployed for longer than sixty days, which can be extended for thirty days, without an official authorization of force or declaration of war by Congress (Weed 2017).

Even with Congress reasserting its power in the area of foreign conflict, there are still controversies and problems. Most modern presidents have been accused of not consulting Congress, not notifying it within forty-eight hours, or violating the sixty-day deadline. For example, when President Obama ordered air strikes on Libya in 2011, many in Congress, including members of his own party, criticized him for violating the

War Powers Resolution (Savage 2011). He responded and argued, as nearly every president has done, that he was following the Constitution and the resolution. Congress views this as lip service and continues its attempt to reassert itself into the area of war powers. Congress is at a disadvantage, though, because the Department of Defense is under the jurisdiction of the president and he is the commander in chief. The president also knows members of Congress, who answer directly to the voters, will not cut off funding for troops in the battlefield and takes advantage of this.

Advice and Consent

One of the most interesting checks Congress has over the president is that of advice and consent (see Article II, Section 2). While the president is the chief executive, which means he is at the top of the entire executive branch of government, he cannot simply choose who he wants to work in these executive branch agencies. At the beginning of a new administration (after a new president is elected), the president must appoint people to head all of the cabinet departments, as well as numerous lower level leadership positions within each department. Unless the president asks them to stay, the previous administration's employees know they are no longer needed. The president nominates qualified individuals to fill thousands of positions in the executive branch. That is not the end, however.

Through the advice and consent power, the U.S. Senate must vote on and approve every one of these people, roughly twelve hundred (see Hogue and Carey 2015). In earlier years, this was a pro forma process, where the Senate would hold hearings on the higher level individuals (cabinet secretaries) but approve them rather quickly. The problem lies again in politics and polarization. As of mid-2018, President Trump's nominees are waiting on average eighty-six days to be confirmed by the Senate (*Washington Post* 2019). President Obama's nominees waited on average sixty-seven days to be confirmed and begin their jobs.

The Senate is not only responsible for confirming executive branch nominees, however. The president also nominates individuals to fill federal judgeship vacancies, including vacancies on the Supreme Court. Federal judges serve life terms (Article III, Section 1); thus, their selection can have lasting effects on court decisions for decades. In recent years, the advice and consent process for federal judges has gotten increasingly more politically charged, arguably due to senators becoming increasingly individualistic (Loomis and Schiller 2016). Additionally, the amount of time it takes to confirm even noncontroversial nominees to the district or circuit federal courts has greatly increased (see McMillion 2012).

In 1992, then Senator Joe Biden (D-DE) was chair of the Senate Judiciary Committee. Regarding a potential vacancy in the Supreme Court, in a Senate floor speech, he said that the president (Bush) should "not name a nominee until after the November election is completed" (DeBonis 2016). If a vacancy occurred and the president nominated a new justice, "the Senate Judiciary Committee should seriously consider not scheduling confirmation hearings on the nomination until after the political campaign season is over. Senate consideration of a nominee under these circumstances is not fair to the president, to the nominee, or to the Senate itself" (DeBonis 2016). This basically advocated for a block of the nominations and ignoring the advice and consent power outlined in the Constitution; however, the Senate Democrats would argue they were simply exercising their constitutional power.

These words would come back to haunt Democrats and the Obama administration in 2016, when there was a vacancy on the Supreme Court with the death of Justice Antonin Scalia. President Obama nominated Merrick Garland, and the Senate Republicans refused to hold hearings on this nomination, citing Biden's own words. In 2018, the retirement of Justice Anthony Kennedy created another vacancy on the Supreme Court. This time, the Democrats used both the Republicans' and Biden's words in their favor.

Filibusters of these nominees greatly increased, until the Senate Democrats invoked the "nuclear option" for all executive branch and lower court nominees in 2013, overcoming Republican filibusters of President Obama's nominees. The Senate Republicans then invoked the same option to overcome an unprecedented filibuster of Supreme Court justice nominee Neil Gorsuch in 2017. By using the "nuclear option," they eliminated the sixty-vote requirement to end a filibuster, instead only requiring a simple majority of fifty-one.

The practice of filibustering presidential nominees, both executive and judicial branch, affects the relationship between the Senate and the president. The president is frustrated with his inability to staff his departments effectively, with people he chooses. The president's relationship with the entire Senate suffers as a lack of trust infuses that relationship. Filibustering also affects the relationships within the Senate itself. Senate leadership must assume that every nominee will be filibustered and plan their strategy accordingly (Theriault 2008). These individualistic senators can hold the Senate hostage, which threatens the collegial atmosphere that has permeated the Senate for two hundred years (Loomis and Schiller 2016).

The Constitution gives the president one more power in the area of appointment, that of recess appointments (Article II, Section 2). This means that if a vacancy occurs while the Senate is in a recess, the president can simply appoint someone to the position until the end of the legislative session. These were originally intended to be a way to fill crucial vacancies in the absence of the Senate, which was originally only in session for a short period every year. They have become a way for the president to bypass the advice and consent power of a polarized and unfriendly Senate. Moreover, it further damages the relationship (Smith, Roberts, and Vander Wielen 2013). The Senate deals with the threat of recess appointments by never adjourning into a recess and instead remaining in pro forma session.

In 2012, President Obama appointed Richard Cordray to be the new chair of the Consumer Financial Protection Bureau as well as three members of the National Labor Relations Board (NLRB). The nominations had been filibustered in the Senate. Thus, President Obama recess-appointed Cordray and the three NLRB members to the positions while the Senate was in a pro forma session. In 2014, in *NLRB v. Noel Canning*, the Supreme Court determined that pro forma meant the Senate was in session and invalidated all 2012 recess appointments (Davidson et al. 2016). This harkens back to our separation of powers system of government. It is not up to the president to determine when the Senate is in session; they determine that themselves. Recess appointments, when not done out of necessity and emergency, are not viewed positively by the Senate, and this further erodes the legislative-executive relationship.

The advice and consent power extends to one more important area, that of international treaty ratification. According to the Constitution (Article II, Section 2), the president and his staff negotiate the treaties with international states, but two-thirds of the Senate must vote to ratify those treaties. The Senate can add amendments to these treaties, which can change the meaning of the treaty and thus require renegotiation with the foreign state (Pika, Maltese, and Rudalevige 2017). Only a handful of treaties have been rejected by the Senate, with the most recent being in 2012 with the Convention on the Rights of Persons with Disabilities ("Treaties," n.d.).

In certain situations, the president needs to move quickly with foreign agreements and, therefore, issues an executive agreement, which holds the force of a treaty without Senate approval. In other situations, he wants to bypass the Senate's constitutional advise and consent power. This happens when the president knows he will not be able to get the two-thirds vote to approve his treaty. Again, going around the Senate only succeeds in making the divide between the Senate and the president deeper and wider.

Impeachment

The final aspect of the congressional-presidential relationship, and arguably the most powerful check Congress has on the president, is that of impeachment. Congress has the power to impeach and remove the president, and any other government official whom the Senate confirms (including judges), for treason, bribery, or high crimes and misdemeanors (Article II, Section 4). The House of Representatives acts first, deciding whether to impeach and under which articles (Cole and Garvey 2015). The Senate then tries the case, and a conviction requires a two-thirds vote of all senators (Cole and Garvey 2015). The chief justice of the Supreme Court presides over the case in the Senate, and the senators act as jurors (Waxman and Fabry 2018).

Congress has only brought forward articles of impeachment against two presidents—Andrew Johnson (1868) and Bill Clinton (1998). (In 1974, President Nixon resigned before the House could vote on articles of impeachment.) In both cases, the House approved articles of impeachment, but the Senate failed to vote to remove the president. This means both presidents were impeached but not removed.

The most recent example is that of President Clinton. The House of Representatives brought forth four articles of impeachment against President Clinton, and the House passed two of them, which charged the president with perjury and obstruction of justice (Mitchell 1998). These charges stemmed from the president's falsified testimony before a federal grand jury relating to his alleged affair with a White House intern (Mitchell 1998). The votes were mostly along party lines, with a handful of members from each party crossing over. The House failed to pass two additional articles of impeachment: perjury in an earlier sexual harassment lawsuit and abuse of power (Mitchell 1998). More Republicans crossed over and voted with Democrats to defeat these measures. The Senate failed to get the two-thirds vote required on either the perjury or obstruction of justice charge. Thus, President Clinton was impeached but was not removed from office.

It is no surprise that impeachment of a president is a serious endeavor. Given the severity, one would guess impeachment resolutions are rarely introduced in the House. That would be false. Numerous articles of impeachment were introduced for President George W. Bush, Vice President Cheney, Defense Secretary Donald Rumsfeld, and Attorney General Alberto Gonzales (Bazan 2010). None of these were voted upon by the full House or even considered by the full House Judiciary Committee.

No articles of impeachment were introduced against President Obama or his administration during his eight years as president. There are numerous impeachment resolutions pending for President Trump (as of summer 2018, for the 115th session of Congress). In fact, the full House of Representatives, as of summer 2018, has twice considered articles of impeachment against President Trump (Garcia 2018). Both votes have been overwhelmingly defeated, with the Democratic leadership opposing them, but the simple fact they have been voted on should say something about the current rancor in Washington.

It should not be surprising to students of Congress that these efforts further strain the tenuous relationship between the Congress and the president. While no solution, per se, is required in the sense that this is an important, and essential, constitutional check Congress has on the president, this tactic should be used with caution. It not only destroys the legislative-executive relationship but it also can undermine an already tenuous public trust in the democratic process.

Institutional Rules, Norms, and Constraints

Many of Congress's current challenges stem from its own rules and the way it operates. What makes this body so unique among the world's legislative bodies also can create tension. This section will examine not only those institutional rules and norms that govern both chambers of Congress and how those can lead to problems but also opportunities and solutions in effective lawmaking.

House–Senate Differences

The House and Senate were designed to be different, two distinct chambers in one branch of government. Initially, the House was the only chamber to be voted into office by the people (Article I, Section 2) and the number of representatives was based on state population. Two senators from each state were to be chosen by state legislatures (Article I, Section 3), thus keeping intact the interests of the smaller states at the Constitutional Convention. The Seventeenth Amendment to the Constitution stipulated the people would elect the state's senators, thus tempering a key component of federalism and state's rights.

The requirements for serving in the House are less onerous than in the Senate (see Article I, Section 2). In the words of James Madison in "Federalist No. 52," "Under these reasonable limitations, the door to this part of the federal government is open to merit of every description, whether native or adoptive, whether young or old, and without regard to poverty or wealth, or to any particular profession of religious faith." One can easily see why the House of Representatives is called the People's House or Chamber. Not only is the number of members per state determined by that state's population but members of the House were also to look like people they represented, share a "common interest with the people" ("Federalist No. 52"), and have an "intimate sympathy with the people" ("Federalist No. 52"). Because the House was more reflective of the population, it was also intended to be more volatile, and more susceptible to public opinion. Because of this plus the fact the House was given a great deal of power in the area of budgeting and taxes (all revenue bills must originate there), the length of a term was limited to two years. Madison said, [T]he greater the power is, the shorter ought to be its duration be protracted" ("Federalist No. 52"). House members can be reelected to serve as many two-year terms as the voters choose.

The Senate was designed to have more strict qualification for service, because as Madison said in "Federalist No. 62," "The propriety of these distinctions, is explained by the nature of the senatorial trust; which, requiring greater extent of information and stability of character, requires, at the same time, that the senator should have reached a period of life more likely to supply these advantages." Due to these requirements and the limited number, the Senate has been called the most exclusive club in the world. The framers wanted senators to be free from foreign influence, due to their important treaty approval powers. Every state has two senators, thus making all states equal in this powerful body. Senators serve six-year terms, because in Madison's words "a continual change even of good measures is inconsistent with every rule of prudence, and every prospect of success" ("Federalist No. 62"). They were concerned with stability overall in the Senate. "No government, any more than an individual, will long be respected, without being truly respectable; nor be truly respectable, without possessing a certain portion of order and stability" ("Federalist No. 62").

It is easy to see why the Senate is also called the world's most deliberative body and a cooling chamber of legislation. The bills that were created and passed in a temperamental, publicly controlled House, would slow down and be thoughtfully considered in the Senate.

In addition to the constitutionally mandated differences, the House and the Senate are governed by their own, very different, rules. The Constitution stipulates each chamber will decide their own rules. The House approves new rules for the chamber at the beginning of each new session of Congress (Gold 2008). The Senate's rules exist from one session of Congress to the next but can be amended (Gold 2008). These very different rules further the individualistic nature of the Senate and the majoritarian nature of the House.

The first of those different rules is the filibuster. In the Senate, individual senators have the power to kill legislation simply by threating a filibuster. No such filibuster tool exists in the House, where the majority party controls nearly everything. In the House, members cannot speak for as long as they want. The length of floor speeches is determined by the powerful House Rules Committee, which also controls the floor schedule, the amendments, and floor debate for individual pieces of legislation. This committee has been called the Speaker's Committee, because the Speaker usually handpicks the majority members of the committee, all of whom will be loyal to him or her and implement the policy preferences of the majority party. The Rules Committee can issue an open rule, which means any member of the House can introduce a germane amendment (directly pertaining to the bill) to any portion of the bill. The Rules Committee very rarely issues an open rule on legislation, with the exception being appropriations bills. An open rule allows the minority party to participate in the majority-controlled House process. It also allows junior members of the majority, who do not sit on the committee of jurisdiction, to offer amendments and have a say in the development of the legislation on the floor. The Rules Committee can also issue a closed rule, which means no amendments can be offered during floor debate. This greatly restricts the ability of the minority party to participate.

During the 111th Congress, when Speaker Nancy Pelosi (D-CA) was in charge, no bills were considered under an open rule on the House floor (Sinclair 2012). This greatly angered the minority party and completely eliminated the Republicans' ability to offer their own legislative ideas during House floor debate. When Speaker John Boehner (R-OH) was elected in 2011, he vowed to return to open rules on appropriations measures, which he essentially stuck to during his tenure. This not only allowed Democrats to participate in the process but also required Republicans take tough votes on contentious amendments. Many in Speaker Boehner's own party became frustrated with the process. This resulted in being forced to get minority support for some legislation as his own party felt the measures were too moderate.

Under Speaker Paul Ryan (R-WI), who was elected Speaker in 2015, the partisan rancor eventually forced him to require all appropriations bill amendments be approved by the Rules Committee (Ferris 2016). He claimed it was because of "poison pill" amendments that the Democrats were adding to appropriations bills (Ferris 2016), using an amendment condemning LGBT discrimination, which was added to the Energy and Water Appropriations bill, as an example (Ferris 2016). This action further deepened the partisan divide in the House and limited the power of the minority to have their policy preferences considered during full House debate.

Unanimous Consent, Holds, and Filibusters

The Senate does not have a similarly empowered Rules Committee. Instead, they use the unanimous consent (UC) agreement tool to place similar constraints on legislation, floor debates, and amendments. The problem is the agreement needs to be unanimous, which is highly difficult in an individualistic Senate. If even one senator objects to the UC, there is no agreement and endless debate and amendments can proceed. Due to the high levels of polarization in the Senate, all UC agreements are negotiated by the majority leader in consultation with the minority leader. UC agreements are often used to hotline noncontroversial items like renaming a post office, congratulating a home state college football team on winning a national championship, or even approving of lower level presidential nominees.

Due to the decentralized power structure in the Senate, individual senators often object to these carefully crafted agreements. These senators are usually members of the minority party, but not always. They object for many reasons: they want to offer amendments, they want to speak, they want to trade their consent for action on another bill, or they are simply trying to halt the majority party from passing a bill. In 2000, when the author was working for a senator from Montana, her boss objected to a UC and put a hold on one of President Clinton's low-level nominees. He did this to get the president's attention on a completely unrelated manner; it worked.

Further, if any one senator is vehemently opposed to a bill or wants to simply block progress, he or she can filibuster the bill. This means no progress can be made on the bill and technically means the bill is being talked to death. However, in the modern Senate, a senator does not have to hold the floor and talk for hours on end (see the movie *Mr. Smith Goes to Washington* for an example of a talking filibuster) to engage in a filibuster (Oleszek et al. 2016). The senator who wishes to stop action on the bill can simply threaten a filibuster, and this can shut down the bill (Loomis and Schiller 2016). Today, all bills brought to the Senate floor are assumed to be under a filibuster threat.

Senate bills face a number of filibuster threats or afford a number of opportunities for minority senators to have input into the legislative process. The first opportunity is on the motion to proceed to the bill, which means the bill cannot even be brought to the floor for debate. The second is the bill itself, which stops all final voting or passage. The third is on any and all amendments to the bill, which stops action on any amendments. In order to stop a filibuster, cloture must be invoked. Cloture can be invoked if sixty senators vote to do so. Once cloture is invoked, thirty hours of debate on the motion remain and all amendments must be germane. In the Senate of today, with small majorities (neither party has a sixty-vote supermajority), cloture is difficult to invoke, requiring the cooperation of at least a handful of minority party members. If cloture must be invoked on the motion to proceed all amendments and the final bill, it is a small wonder anything can get passed in the U.S. Senate.

Who filibusters and why do senators choose to stop progress on a bill? For the most part, senators in the minority party are the ones filibustering and delaying progress on legislation, and previously on judicial and executive branch nominations, to stop a piece of legislation with which they disagree. They use it to get their voices heard on policy. They previously used it to stop contentious or disagreeable presidential nominations.

However, senators also use this tool to make a point about other issues. In 2013, Senator Rand Paul (R-KY) filibustered the nomination of John Brennan to be the Central Intelligence Agency's (CIA) director over his concern with drone strikes (LoBianco 2016). He spoke for thirteen hours and used that opportunity to bring attention to the issue, not necessarily to block the nomination.

In 2003, Senate Democrats, who were the minority party, were filibustering a number of President Bush's judicial nominations over policy differences, most commonly abortion (Toobin 2003). One of the most notable filibusters was against the nomination of Miguel Estrada to the D.C. Circuit Court of Appeals. His personal views on abortion rights were used as justification for the filibuster of his nomination (Toobin 2003). As nearly all filibusters in the modern Senate, this was not a talking filibuster. Democratic Senators were not holding the floor, preventing a vote. In response to the filibuster of four lower court justices, Republican senators decided to make a point and held the floor for over thirty hours, taking turns speaking throughout the night (Dewar 2003). It was almost like a reverse filibuster, in that the majority party was speaking during the minority's actual filibuster. This was a highly choreographed effort, organized to raise public awareness and positive press more than anything, but it did bring attention to the practice of filibustering judicial nominations.

While thirty hours is a very long time to talk, it was undertaken by numerous members of both parties (the Democrats chose to respond to many of the Republican speeches, not wanting to miss the press opportunity). The longest individual filibuster in Senate history is held by Senator Strom Thurmond (R-SC), who held the floor for twenty-four hours and eighteen minutes to stop action on the Civil Rights Act of 1957 (Hickey 2013). The second longest was conducted by Senator Alphonse D'Amato (R-NY) in 1986 as he blocked a military appropriations bills; he held the floor for twenty-three hours and thirty minutes (Cervantes 2012). Senator Wayne Morse (D-OR) held the floor for twenty-two hours and twenty-six minutes in 1953 to voice his displeasure over the Tidelands Oil Bill (Cervantes 2012). Interestingly, the fourth-longest floor speech goes to Senator Ted Cruz (R-TX), who held the floor speaking against the Affordable Care Act (commonly known as Obamacare) for twenty-one hours and nineteen minutes (Blake 2013). This is notable because he was not actually blocking or stopping progress on anything; he simply held the floor to speak against the legislation.

The effects of the filibuster are obvious; it serves to halt progress on a piece of legislation. In some situations, the threat of a filibuster can serve to gain the minority party certain concessions from the majority. However, when every piece of legislation is assumed to be under a filibuster threat, it loses its power. Instead, the working relationship between the two parties is frayed, and the collegial nature of the Senate of the past is all but extinct. Polarization in the chamber increases, while public trust and approval numbers for the Senate, and Congress as a whole, decrease.

There have been numerous efforts to reform the filibuster process within the U.S. Senate, as it is not outlined in the Constitution and really has only been in use since 1841 (MacNeil and Baker 2013). Senators introduce legislation each session to amend the Standing Rules of the Senate in relation to the filibuster. Some of these ideas include decreasing the number of votes needed to invoke cloture to fifty-five or ratcheting down the requirements on subsequent cloture votes (Strand and Lang 2017). A second reform would require those senators who wish to block a bill to actually conduct a live, talking filibuster on the floor (Strand and Lang 2017).

Of course, the rules governing the filibuster do not require legislation and can be amended from the Senate floor. In 2013, the Senate Democratic Majority Leader Harry Reid (D-NV), in response to the Republicans filibustering President Obama's nominations, invoked what has been called the nuclear option for all executive branch and lower court judicial nominations

(Loomis and Schiller 2016). This Senate rule eliminates the sixty-vote requirement to invoke cloture, instead requiring fifty-one votes to stop a filibuster, essentially ending the filibuster as a threat for these nominations. Once the door was opened, it was only a matter of time before the sixty-vote requirement was eliminated for the final remaining nominee category—the Supreme Court. That happened in 2017 during the debate on President Trump's nomination of Neil Gorsuch to the Supreme Court. Now, it takes fifty-one votes to invoke cloture for any presidential nominee. The sixty-vote requirement still exists for filibusters on legislation and motions to proceed.

Both parties have been in favor of filibuster reform, and subsequently against it, as control of the chamber changes from Republican to Democrat and back again. When Senator Harry Reid eradicated the sixty-vote cloture requirement in 2013, he said, "It is manifest we must do something to change things. In the history of our country, some 230 plus years, there have been 160 filibusters of executive and judicial nominations. Half of them have occurred during the Obama Administration" (C-SPAN 2013). He was speaking of unprecedented filibusters by Senate Republicans. Then Minority Leader Mitch McConnell (R-KY) said, "I think it's a time to be sad about what's been done to the United States Senate" (Peters 2013).

Fast forward to 2017 and the tables turned. The Democrats were holding up a vote on President Trump's nominee Neil Gorsuch. Now Senate Majority Leader McConnell said, "This is the latest escalation in the left's never-ending judicial war, the most audacious yet. And it cannot and it will not stand. There cannot be two sets of standards: one for the nominees of the Democratic president and another for the nominees of Republican presidents" (Flegenheimer 2017). The Democratic Minority Leader Chuck Schumer (D-NY) said, "When history weighs what happened, the responsibility for changing the rules will fall on the Republicans' and Leader McConnell's shoulders" (Flegenheimer 2017). While the sides change with each election, it should be clear to readers that the responsibility for this lies with both parties in the Senate.

The solutions to the problem of rampant filibusters are not simple or even obvious. Each party has changed the Senate rules to eliminate the threat of the filibuster for all presidential nominees. The sixty-vote cloture requirement still remains for legislation. Many who watch the Senate believe it is only a matter of time before the filibuster is eliminated for good. This would change the institution in monumental ways. No longer would it be the highly individualistic body, able to be brought to its knees by one senator, by one small state. It, instead, will look more like the House of Representatives, highly majoritarian, with more partisan centralized power. Some find this to be positive, to make the Senate more democratic, where even small majorities rule. Others find it as the end of a great and mighty institution where minorities and small states have a big say in policy and the direction of the country.

The only clear solution is a return to collegiality in the Senate, to a time when civility ruled. Disagreement and debate were important, but so were relationships. Further, civility in politics must also return, where the branches of government are not constantly at odds. If the Senate can return to this, the extensive use of the filibuster might lessen. Might.

Additional Differences

In the Senate, members can offer any type of amendment to any piece of legislation; there is no general germaneness rule. When Senator Edward Kennedy (D-MA) was still alive, members and staff alike would wait patiently on the Senate floor for him to offer his federal minimum wage increase amendment, to every single piece of legislation.

Furthering the individual versus majority nature of the chambers, the House has an electronic voting system, where members have voting cards that they insert into voting machines on the House floor. Electronic boards light up on the walls and show how every member has voted. In the Senate, no such electronic system exists. During recorded roll call votes, senators vote in person on the Senate chamber; their votes are recorded by hand by clerks sitting in the well of the Senate floor.

The chamber differences were rarely starker than when analyzing the efforts to repeal Obamacare. The House of Representatives, with its majoritarian rules and centralized power structure, voted to repeal the law over sixty times between 2011 and 2017 (Cowan and Cornwell 2017). The Senate, with its individually empowered members and dilatory tactics, never voted to repeal the bill in a binding way. Both the chambers were controlled by Republicans during two of those years (2015–2017), and still the Senate was not able to repeal the bill, despite the fact that the majority party wanted to do so. The Senate did vote on a resolution to instruct committees to begin drafting legislation to repeal the bill in 2017 (Cowan and Cornwell 2017).

While the House and the Senate are two parts of the same branch of government, they have many differences. The framers intended this; the two chambers of the legislative branch were meant to operate differently, with distinct powers and components. This system created a legislative body that, on one hand, has the ability to respond quickly to public demand or emergency and, on the other, responds more deliberately. This can be an asset, when legislation should be purposefully considered. However, when time is of the essence or when the American people demand quick action, this system is frustrating at best and at worse is a detriment to the running of a good government.

Drafting, Considering, and Passing Legislation

The main power and duty of the legislative branch is to legislate. The only constitutional stipulation is that bills must pass both chambers in identical versions before going to the president for his signature and to become a law. Each chamber has filled in the details on how that occurs.

Any member of Congress can write and introduce a bill on any subject at any time. Any member can cosponsor any other piece of legislation. In the Senate, members can introduce as many amendments as they deem appropriate. In fact, most members take advantage of this and introduce and cosponsor countless pieces of legislation during an average session of Congress. To illustrate this, during the 114th session of Congress (2015–2016), over seven thousand pieces of legislation were introduced in the House and over four thousand in the Senate. These included bills and all types of resolutions. Three hundred twenty-nine of these were signed by the president and became law, which is about a 3 percent success rate. Over five thousand amendments were introduced in the Senate and one thousand in the House.

With the low success rate, one wonders why members introduce so many pieces of legislation in the first place. The answer is both simple and complicated, and the following reasons do not all apply to each member, but at least one of them applies to each instance of a bill being introduced. The first reason is the member is interested in making good policy for the country. The member might be chair of a committee or subcommittee and has the expertise and staff power to make good policy. The second reason is they are trying to represent their states or districts; the bill is important for their constituents. These bills often correspond to important campaign issues or are used in reelection campaigns. These efforts can sometimes get crossways with the party leadership, but the members are willing to anger their leaders in order to adequately represent their constituents or get reelected. In these cases, the leadership often overlooks the perceived party disloyalty, because of reelection concerns. A third reason is to simply make a statement on an issue. The member might seek national attention on an issue, be running for a higher office, or wanting to make the other party or other members look bad.

In the same vein, the ideas for legislation come from many different places. The first is necessity, events, or an emergency, in the home state or district or to a national level. Necessary legislation can sometimes be predicted, especially in the case of reauthorizations or sunsets. Members know exactly when these laws expire, and they can prepare for them. For instance, the Farm Bill (as it is commonly known in Congress and among the agricultural community alike) authorizes all programs within the Department of Agriculture (USDA) for five years at a time. Beginning at least a year before it expires, USDA and Congress begin working on writing a new bill. This process does not always go smoothly. The Federal Aviation Administration, which is also usually authorized for five years at a time, failed to be reauthorized for two whole sessions of Congress and had to be extended numerous times (Elias 2011). An even more stark example of delayed reauthorizations is that of the Endangered Species Act (ESA), which was first passed into law in 1973; its authorization for appropriations expired in 1992 (Corn and Wyatt 2016). Congress has been unable, for many often politically charged reasons, to reauthorize the funding for this program. They do, however, continue to fund the ESA without authorization, which is administered primarily by the Fish and Wildlife Service within the Department of the Interior. John Kingdon (2003) argues ideas become policies or laws only when their time has finally come, when the policy window, as it were, opens and the idea can get through. It is possible the time for ESA reauthorization just has not arrived yet.

In the case of events or emergencies, members of Congress cannot predict when these will arise. They include terrorist attacks and natural disasters. The bills often provide funding and expansion of emergency services to the affected areas.

There are numerous sources for ideas on legislation: campaign promises and constituent demands, party priorities and change in partisan control of one or more chambers of Congress or the White House, presidential priorities and administration officials, and interest groups or other organized interests.

Who writes these pieces of legislation? For the most part, members and their staff draft the legislation in coordination with the Legislative Counsel office in each chamber. Executive branch officials often offer drafting assistance, especially when they are the policy experts and the proposed legislation affects their departments. In certain situations, interest groups, citizen groups, or other outside groups (i.e., think tanks and policy research groups) assist in drafting legislation. Another place where legislation is drafted is by congressional, presidential, or joint commissions or task forces.

After a bill is introduced, the next step is consideration by the committee of jurisdiction. Committees begin by holding hearings on the bill, hearing testimony from witnesses chosen from both the majority and the minority (although the minority party gets far fewer witnesses). Witnesses voice their support or opposition to the bill; they share with members how this bill will affect their area of expertise or businesses. This can occur either in a subcommittee or in the full committee.

After the hearings are held, the next step is to mark up the bill. This is when all members of the committee have an opportunity to have a say in the text of the legislation. They can offer amendments and debate the bill. However, members of the minority have less of an opportunity as their amendments usually do not pass, unless they are acceptable to at least a small number of the majority members on the committee. After a final vote on the amended bill in the markup session, the bill is reported out of the committee. In the House it is referred to the Rules Committee, where again the majority party rules. In the Senate, it is placed directly on the Senate Calendar and can be considered at any time on the Senate floor.

In the House, the process of considering bills is controlled heavily by the majority party leadership, which includes committee chairs and the Rules Committee. The majority leadership sets the legislative priorities at the beginning of each new session of Congress, and unless an emergency or unforeseen event occurs, those priorities will be followed for the next two years. The most important bills are given the first numbers, usually 1–20. These bill numbers are reserved for the Speaker. If a bill is listed as H.R. 1, or even 10, you can assume it is a priority for the majority party for that session. Otherwise, all bills are numbered in accordance with their order of introduction.

Rank and file members (those not in the leadership) can expect their bills to receive consideration only if they serve on the committee of jurisdiction, if their issue becomes a priority for the leadership, if the member starts to get national attention, or if they are in a tight reelection race. If they are not on the committee of jurisdiction as a voting member, the odds of that bill being considered even by a subcommittee are slim to none, unless of course it becomes a priority for the leadership. It can become a priority if the issue gains some notoriety or if the member trades a hearing for a vote or other action important to the leadership.

In a majoritarian body like the House, how do rank and file, or even minority party, members get a say in the legislative process? There are a few procedural tools at their disposal. The first is the discharge petition, which is a motion to remove a bill from the committee and get it on the Discharge Calendar (Oleszek et al. 2016). The petition must have the signatures of 218 members of the House to be eligible, and once it has sat on the Calendar for seven days, it can be voted upon (Oleszek et al. 2016). If the discharge motion passes, any member who signed the petition can move to immediately consider the bill (Oleszek et al. 2016). If it is voted down, it cannot be considered again during that session of Congress.

The discharge petition is a rarely used, but important, tool. It gives minority members a chance to raise issues they feel important; it gives rank and file members of the majority a chance to bring attention to their issues, which may not align with their leadership's priorities. However, members rarely use the discharge, as it supersedes committee authority; bills have not gone through the regular order of hearings and markups. Members do not want their own committee's authority to be thwarted at a later time, so they use the discharge power sparingly. Further, it does not endear members to the leadership, especially if the petition is filed by junior members of the majority. If it is filed by the minority, polarization and partisan bickering could get even worse. Between 1931 and 2014, 646 petitions were filed, and only 19 were actually discharged from committee and passed by the House (Oleszek et al. 2016). Three of those became law, the most prominent being the Bipartisan Campaign Reform Act (BCRA) of 2002, commonly known as the McCain-Feingold bill (Oleszek et al. 2016). In the summer of 2018, a number of discharge petitions were filed on immigration-related legislation. These efforts all failed, and Speaker Ryan (R-WI) said, "Obviously, we don't like discharge petitions" (Golshan 2018). He cited the fact that control of the House floor is lost when these petitions are filed and voted upon.

No similar process exists in the Senate; a senator can simply ask for UC to discharge a bill from the committee (Gold 2008). If no senator objects, the bill is discharged and can be placed on the Calendar. In addition, Rule XIV of the Standing Rules of the Senate can be invoked, which means that a senator can object to the bill being referred to a committee in the first place and it is then placed on the Calendar for consideration (Riddick's Senate Procedure 1992). These are all tools usually employed by the minority party in the Senate to bring bills up for consideration.

The second procedural tool at the disposal of House members relates to the Rules Committee and the rule that accompanies all legislation that reaches the floor. As discussed earlier, all bills on the House floor have a rule that accompanies them. This rule establishes when it will be debated, how the bill will be debated, and how many, if any, amendments can be offered. Before the bill can be considered, the rule must be approved by a floor vote. Members can vote against the rule, and if it is defeated, no rules govern the discussion of the bill. At this point, the Speaker would likely pull the bill from consideration (Oleszek et al. 2016). The rule very rarely ever fails, even though its approval is usually by straight party line. The defeat would be a huge blow to both the Rules Committee and the Speaker's authority (Oleszek et al. 2016).

A third tool is suspension of the rules. This is exactly as it sounds; no rules accompany the bill. It is used on important or noncontroversial bills (Oleszek et al. 2016). Two-thirds of all House members must vote to suspend, and then there is only forty minutes of debate allowed (Oleszek et al. 2016). It greatly speeds up the legislative process.

As is evident, there are a number of tools and powers at the disposal of individual members of Congress to get their policy ideas considered. However, it still takes a majority of members in both chambers to pass legislation. On noncontroversial legislation or legislation that has been crafted with input and consultation from both parties, members of the minority party vote with the majority party to pass legislation. For controversial bills, few, if any, members of the minority will vote with the majority. As polarization gets stronger, legislation becomes less bipartisan. A notable recent example was the tax bill passed in late 2017. Not a single Democrat voted for this bill in the House or the Senate (Kaplan and Rappeport 2017). Republicans are not the only ones guilty of passing partisan bills. In 2009, the House Democrats passed the $800 billion stimulus package without any Republican votes (Calmes 2009). In 2010, the Affordable Care Act (Obamacare) notoriously passed without a single Republican vote in either the House or the Senate. With a country whose citizens are all over the political spectrum, passing legislation without any votes from the minority party seems ill-advised, especially when one considers how often party control of both chambers of Congress changes. It is little wonder why approval of Congress remains low in opinion polls.

The Budget

The Constitution gives Congress the enumerated power of passing appropriations bills to authorize money be spent from the Treasury (Article I, Section 9) and all tax (or revenue as they are called in the Constitution) bills shall originate in the House, with the Senate able to amend them (Article I, Section 7). The

Congressional Budget Act (CBA) of 1974 requires the annual passage of a budget resolution (Heniff and Murray 2011). It also lays out a timeline for when certain aspects of the budget should be completed. This section will outline how Congress establishes a federal budget and spending bills.

The first step in this process is the president submits his budget proposal to Congress by the first Monday in February, but Congress has the power to provide him an extension (Streeter 2010). This budget proposal is for the upcoming fiscal year; thus, the president presents the proposal roughly eight months before that fiscal year starts. His proposal is far from the final say in the matter. In fact, Congress can disregard the president's wishes, but it must rely on the president and his Office of Management and Budget for accurate numbers and budgetary projections.

After receiving the president's budget proposal, the House and Senate Budget Committees then draft their own budget resolutions. These are frameworks, which outline revenues and spending (Schick 2007). They are concurrent resolutions, however, and are not signed by the president; hence, they are not binding (Schick 2007). The budget resolution does not provide specific details for how federal dollars will be spent—just overall totals in twenty different categories (Schick 2007). Both chambers pass their own bills, which must be conferenced together to form one bill, and that final bill must pass both chambers. According to the CBA, the budget should be complete by April 15. Since the budget is not binding, there is no penalty for not completing work by April 15 or not passing a budget resolution at all (Streeter 2010).

The budget resolution provides the House and Senate Appropriations Committees with the total amount they can appropriate for the upcoming fiscal year. These are called 302(a) allocations. The full appropriations committees then give each subcommittee their individual allocations for how much they can spend. These are called 302(b) allocations. The subcommittees can then begin drafting their individual bills.

Each subcommittee reports out a bill, which is then considered by the full committee, and then it can go to the floor for a vote by the full House (or Senate). These appropriations bills, unlike the budget resolution, are binding on all aspects of government and, as such, are signed by the president. Under the CBA, the House should be finished with all of their appropriations bills by June 30. The Senate should follow. All appropriations bills should be passed and signed by the president by the end of the fiscal year on September 30.

In a perfect congressional world, this is how the budget would be formulated by Congress every year. However, we know from recent events this is not what happens. In many recent years (2003, 2005, 2007, 2010, 2011, 2012), Congress did not pass a final budget resolution. This means no framework exists for Congress to write spending bills. Further, in recent years, we have seen upheaval surrounding the inability to pass individual appropriations bills, which leads to omnibus spending bills and government shutdowns. This is no way to fund a national government the size of the United States.

However, was this the way the framers intended it to work? The very nature of the House, which is run by the majority party, allows them to pass a budget resolution, pass most of the appropriations bills out of committee, and seek approval on the full House floor. However, the individualistic Senate, with its filibuster and dilatory tactics, passes far fewer individual appropriations bills out of committee, even fewer through the full Senate floor, and this is assuming they can even pass a budget resolution. These problems stem from the very nature of the two bodies, the institutional rules that govern them, and the types of people able to serve in each body. While funding a government is one of Congress's most important powers, it might seem the way it was designed created the problems we now see.

Why can Congress not pass its spending bills on time? The nature of the bodies discussed earlier is one major reason. Polarization, and the subsequent gridlock, is another. The third reason is more controversial; it is the elimination of the earmark. According to the Congressional Research Service (CRS), an earmark is difficult to define and differs based on what bill it refers to. In common terms, it includes "funds set aside within an account for a specified program, project, activity, institution, or location" (CRS Team 2006: 2). These earmarks are requested to be included in the bill by specific members of Congress. Often these projects are for their district or state and will help them in representation or in reelection. In some cases, these projects are suggested to members by lobbyists or interest groups.

Until Speaker Boehner (R-OH), and eventually the Senate Democrats, outlawed them in 2011, earmarks were prevalent on every appropriations bill that passed Congress. Earmarks allowed members of Congress to designate where tax dollars would be spent. Proponents, or defenders of the process, argued elected officials should be deciding where these dollars were spent, not unelected bureaucrats in the executive departments. Opponents pointed to the seemingly wasteful spending. Every year Senator John McCain (R-AZ) would go to the Senate floor and list what he considered the worst earmarks in each appropriations bill (Phillips 2009). Senator Tom Coburn (R-OK) picked up this argument and also fought against earmarks, providing a list of the most memorable examples of waste. One was the $500,000 to the National Science Foundation to study shrimp on treadmills (Coburn 2014). Another was possibly the most notorious and one that most likely was the death knell for all earmarks: the $452 million "Bridge to Nowhere" in Alaska (Coburn 2014). Additional ethical concerns swarmed around the process, as members of Congress and their staff were sentenced to federal prison time for accepting bribes for including earmarks in legislation (Ferris 2018).

It might seem like a good idea to eliminate earmarks, especially when one considers out-of-control government spending. However, earmarks never accounted for more than 1 percent of the total federal budget (Roll Call 2014). The ban has not changed how much money is spent. That money is still being appropriated and spent; it is just now allocated to specific places or programs by federal agency bureaucrats instead of members of Congress (Roll Call 2014). Some argue this violates the constitutional requirement that Congress decides how money from the Treasury is spent. It also ends transparency in how these decisions are made and eliminates even the indirect voice of voters (Roll Call 2014).

So why cannot Congress pass its spending bills on time? Proponents of the earmark theory say it is because of their elimination. With earmarks, leadership in both chambers could trade funding for an important project in a member's state or district for a vote on an important piece of legislation. Without this logrolling, members have little incentive to support spending bills, or any bills for that matter.

Leadership

Only three positions in Congress are outlined in the Constitution: the Speaker of the House, the president of the Senate, and the president pro tempore. All other officers of both chambers are left up to them. The Speaker is the leader of the House (Article I, Section 2). He or she is elected by the full House on the first day of the legislative session, which means not only that the majority party wins the speakership but also that the leader of the minority receives a number of votes in the speaker race.

Besides the Speaker, each party will elect their own leadership with secret ballots done in party meetings. The next highest position is the majority leader. This person is the floor leader, a strategist and spokesperson for the party (Davidson et al. 2016). The minority leader does the same job for the minority party, with one exception. They are to be the chief critic of the majority party and their policies. The next position is that of majority and minority whip. They count votes and try to get all of the members of their party moving in the same direction. Whips must be able to gain the trust of members and know what each small faction is thinking. They must also work closely with the other members of the leadership team.

The Speaker of the House has not only a great deal of power but also responsibility. They are the face of the House, for better or worse. They get the credit when things go well but also get punished when things go bad. They must appease their members while also working with the minority to pass legislation. These two tasks are often at odds, with the Speaker never being able to please everyone, and in the end pleasing no one. This is more evident in recent years when the Speaker must pacify the extreme members of his or her own party, who are not aligned with the rest of the House (readers interested in this topic will enjoy Alberta 2017).

In the House, recent years have seen the rise of splinter or extreme groups. These are especially prevalent within the Republican Party. 2010 saw the rise of the Tea Party, and the 2010 midterm elections ushered in a number of like-minded members of Congress. Many of them formed the Tea Party Caucus within the House, which faded away between 2015 and 2016. In 2015, a new group formed, the House Freedom Caucus, composed of ideologically far-right conservative members of the Republican Party. These members were partly responsible for the resignation of former Speaker Boehner, and their opposing certain government funding, such as Planned Parenthood, has contributed to government shutdowns. The Freedom Caucus does not disclose their membership, but according to Pew Research, there are thirty-six members who have self-identified as members of the group (Desilver 2015).

With the Republican Party holding a slim majority in the House, if those thirty-six members decide to oppose the Speaker on legislation, the Speaker must look elsewhere for votes. This means both former Speaker Boehner and Speaker Ryan had to court the Democrats for votes on certain bills, particularly spending bills. This means the bills were more moderate than they would have been had the Freedom Caucus supported them. In essence, their presence and hard-line position on bills were moderating legislation rather than moving them to the right.

This happens whenever there are far-right or far-left groups in either party. It also means the Speaker's and the minority leader's jobs are much harder than they would be without these groups. Arguably the most vocal group on the Democratic side is the Congressional Black Caucus, whose membership is predominantly Democrat but is also open to black Republican members.

While these caucuses are largely informal groups on the Hill, they can have a great deal of sway and power. Often they are focused on a specific policy area or public awareness (Davidson et al. 2016) and are bipartisan. They also provide a response to the centralized House, allowing members to cater to constituent interests (Loomis and Schiller 2016). There are approximately six hundred caucuses on Capitol Hill, with members from both chambers and parties (Loomis and Schiller 2016). They run the gamut of interests and issues, from the Americans Abroad Caucus to the Tuberculosis Elimination Caucus (House Administration Committee 2018).

As stated earlier, the vice president serves as president of the Senate, but his only official job is to break tied votes in the Senate and preside over the Senate. His informal duty is to swear in all new and reelected senators. The president pro tempore of the Senate is to preside in the absence of the president, which is essentially all the time. However, the pro temp is traditionally the longest-serving member of the majority party and hence cannot sit in the presiding chair all day. Therefore, his or her office schedules senators to preside for two-hour stints. These members are usually the junior members who need to learn the rules of the Senate.

The Senate majority party is led by a majority leader, who is elected by secret ballot in party caucus meetings. The minority is led by a minority leader, elected similarly. Both of these positions are seen as the floor leaders of their respective parties. Both parties also elect a whip, whose job is similar to that in the House.

Due to the individualist nature of the Senate, the leadership team has a difficult task of getting consensus or even a simple majority on legislation. The two leaders in the Senate have historically worked out more agreements than their counterparts in the House, due to the unique rules of the Senate, specifically the UC and filibuster. The Senate leadership also has fewer tools at their disposal to bring members into line. They do not remove members from committees, nor do they have a Rules Committee to control amendments and floor debate. This requires more strategy and problem-solving skills. It also means the Senate leadership has a harder time passing even simple legislation.

Committee Structure

Congressional committees are called little legislatures, because often this is where the real legislative work occurs. They are an example of the decentralized power structure within Congress, which gives legislative agenda-setting power to the individual committees and numerous leaders on the committees and subcommittees. In the House, the Speaker and the leadership teams of both parties not only still exert a great deal of pressure over the committees but also give them a good deal of authority. In the Senate, leadership plays less of a heavy-handed role in controlling the committees, leaving it up to the individual committee leaders.

In the House, there are twenty-one standing committees. There is a hierarchy of committees, with members wanting to be on the more important or prestigious committees. In the House, the Appropriations, Energy and Commerce, Rules, and Ways and Means are considered "A" committees. Members strive to be on one of these committees. In the Senate, there are seventeen standing committees and three that are called Select Committees but are standing committees in all but name (Aging, Ethics, and Intelligence). Hierarchy exists here as well, with Appropriations, Armed Services, Finance, and Foreign Relations being considered Super "A" Committees.

Agriculture; Banking, Housing, and Urban Affairs; Commerce, Science, and Transportation; Energy and Natural Resources; Environment and Public Works; Health, Education, Labor, and Pensions; Homeland Security and Governmental Affairs; and Judiciary are considered "A" committees. Rules and Administration, Small Business, Veterans Affairs, and Budget are "B" committees. Indian Affairs is classified as a "C" committee. Senate rules stipulate members cannot serve on more than one Super A, two in the A category, which includes Super A, and only one in the B category (Davidson et al. 2016).

All of the committees except for the two respective appropriations committees are called authorizing committees. These authorizing committees make policy in their specific area as well as provide oversight to executive branch programs under their jurisdiction. Appropriations committees decide how much money will be spent in every aspect of government. Each authorizing committee has a specific jurisdiction—for example, the Agriculture Committee in both chambers handles all agriculture-related issues as well as provides oversight and investigation into the USDA.

In the Senate, these authorizing committees also hold the nomination hearings for all presidential appointments within their jurisdiction. For example, the Senate Armed Services Committee will conduct the background investigation, hold the hearings, and make recommendations to the full Senate for all presidential nominations to the Department of Defense. Similarly, all nominations to the federal courts are handled by the Senate Judiciary Committee.

In the case of overlapping jurisdictions, there can often be turf wars. In 2002, when the legislation creating the all new Department of Homeland Security (DHS) was being debated, many of the committees did not want to give up control of their respective intelligence gathering agencies, even though putting them all in one agency was the point of the new department. For instance, the members of the Judiciary Committee did not want to give up the Federal Bureau of Investigation (FBI) to the new department. Due to these turf wars, DHS does not contain any of the intelligence gathering agencies like FBI, CIA, or Defense Intelligence Agency (DIA). They remained in their respective departments, and those committee chairs got to retain control of them.

Committees are controlled in a partisan manner, with the majority party having more seats on every standing committee. There are a few exceptions to this. The Senate Ethics Committee, the Joint Economic Committee, the Joint Committee on the Library of Congress, and the Joint Committee on Printing all have equal numbers of Republicans and Democrats.

Each committee is headed by a committee chair, who is the leader of the majority party on that committee. The leader of the minority party is called the ranking member. The chair sets the agenda for the committee, which includes which bills will be considered and on what issues the committee will focus. The chair also hires the majority committee staff and organizes hearings. The ranking member not only offers policy alternatives but also works with the chair to make sure the minority's views are incorporated into committee bills. He or she also hires the minority staff and chooses minority witnesses for hearings.

The respective parties each choose which of their members will fill seats on the individual committees. Each chamber and party have their own rules for how many committees a member can serve on, who chooses committee membership, and who leads the committees. For instance, the Senate Republicans have a term limit of six years for committee chairs, while the Senate Democrats do not have term limits (Davidson et al. 2016). Members can request specific committees, and they request committees that are important either to their state or district or with which they have experience or are interested in. Members are rewarded for loyalty and being a good committee member by being placed on their desired committees (Davidson et al. 2016). Expertise, geographic area of constituency, campaign considerations, and gender are also all considered when making committee assignments (Davidson et al. 2016).

Conversely, members can also be punished for disloyalty and be removed from their committees. In 2012, three Republican House members were removed from their committee assignments by Speaker Boehner when they voted against budget legislation (Wyler 2012). Members can also be removed from their committee assignments due to serious misconduct. In 2018, Speaker Paul Ryan removed Representative Patrick Meehan (R-PA) from the House Ethics Committee for sexual misconduct reasons (Reuters 2018). In early 2019, House Republican leadership removed Representative Steve King (R-IA) from the House Agriculture and Judiciary Committees because of a comment King made regarding white supremacy (Gabriel, Martin, and Fandos 2019).

Congressional Staff

While members are the ones who serve on committees, represent their constituents, offer amendments, and vote on bills, they are assisted in nearly every aspect of their job by congressional staff. These individuals are often what Kingdon (2003) called the hidden players, but if you ever visit Capitol Hill and the Senate or House offices, you will soon realize Washington is run by those not elected to office.

These individuals serve on the staffs of every member of Congress as well as on every committee and in every leadership office. There are currently about seventeen thousand congressional staffers, with the House having almost twice as many as the Senate (Petersen, Reynolds, and Wilhelm 2010). Historically, staff members were only employed by the standing committees, serving as clerks (Fox and Hammond 1977; Malbin 1980). Members began hiring personal staff in the late nineteenth century, with the biggest jump in staff numbers occurring in the 1970s (Malbin 1980; Petersen 2008).

Who are these people? They are overwhelmingly young, with the majority of staffers in their twenties or thirties (Fox and Hammond 1977; Hagedorn 2015). Staffers are well educated, with over 60 percent of all staff having a graduate degree of some sort (Hagedorn 2015). Men outnumber women in the highest positions, but women have gained considerable traction since the 1970s, filling 28 percent of the congressional chiefs of staff positions and 30 percent of the committee staff director roles (Hagedorn 2015). These individuals are ambitious, have a great deal of policy expertise, are committed to their jobs and bosses, often share the same ideology as their boss, have numerous layers of accountability, and work long, hard, unpredictable hours (Fox and Hammond 1977; Hagedorn 2015; Romzek 2000; Romzek and Utter 1997). Due to the last two characteristics, these individuals have short careers in Congress, creating a great deal of staff turnover (Hagedorn 2015; Salisbury and Shepsle 1981).

In committees, staff members play large roles in policy development, drafting legislation and amendments and investigating the executive branch either for oversight purposes or for presidential nominations. They meet with constituent groups and lobbyists (Price 1971). They are the true policy experts, able to focus on a vast majority of their time on a very specific policy area (Hagedorn 2015). Each party has their own staff, each headed up by a staff director, chief of staff, or clerk (the title differs depending on the committee). Other positions include counselors (legal team), press secretaries and communications directors, professional or research staff (policy staff), and executive or staff assistants. These staffers are housed in their own committee offices within the Capitol complex in Washington, D.C., separate from the individual member offices.

Each member of Congress also has their own personal staff, which handle all their individual needs as a member, which include policy and press. These staff members are split between the home state or district and Washington. A major purpose of the personal staff is to help serve the constituents, with a number of them solely responsible for casework and constituency services. These staffers also become policy experts, but many are not able to specialize like committee staffers, simply because of time constraints. Each personal staff is led by a chief of staff or administrative assistant. Other positions include legislative directors, legislative assistants and correspondents, communications director and press secretary, office manager, and staff assistants. All personal offices also employ interns for the summer or during a school year semester.

It is widely understood among political scientists and political observers alike that congressional staff members are important to the policy process and are often policy leaders (DeGregorio 1994; Hagedorn 2015; Hall 1993; Hammond 1990). They are the true policy experts in many cases, as the members of Congress do not have the time or resources to devote to truly being an expert on every issue they oversee. Thus, they delegate much of this to their staffers. The possibly contentious aspect of congressional staffers is they are often setting the agenda in their offices (Hagedorn 2015). These unelected individuals are coming up with policy ideas and writing legislation. They are negotiating policy on behalf of their bosses. They write and develop the communication plans. They hire and fire more staffers to do the same. Outsiders might find all of this troubling.

However, is this problematic? It is, if the staff member is striking out on his or her own, going beyond the member's policy preferences and speaking incorrectly on the member's behalf. If the staffer is staying within the member's preferences and acting as a good agent to his or her boss, this can actually help representation. The staffer is often from the same state or district as the member of Congress—therefore dedicated to helping his or her home. The staffer also has more time to devote to learning the problems and intricacies of the issues, thus ensuring better policies. Further, the more staff members there are, the more they can help the member's constituents with problems, furthering good representative government.

Outside Influences

The Perpetual Campaign

According to the requirements laid out in the Constitution, House members are up for reelection every two years, while senators are up every six years. This should mean at the very least, members are concerned about reelection every other year. This is not how things work in reality, however. Members not only agonize over every vote and how it will impact their reelection efforts, but every statement both public and private and even what their staffers and families say and do. They think about reelection constantly, and in an age of twenty-four-hour news and social media, average Americans are able to take down the reelection hopes of any member of Congress. Once the current election is over, the media immediately begins making predictions about the next election. Congressional campaigns are now perpetual.

There are many aspects of the congressional campaign. The first of these features occurs long before any campaigning can take place, but it is vital to the overall process. It is the process by which the number of House seats is divided among the fifty states. This is called reapportionment and is outlined in the Constitution (Article I, Section 2). A census is taken by the federal government every ten years, and these numbers are used to determine how many of the 435 total seats in the House of Representatives each state receives. Each state must have at least one (Montana, South Dakota, North Dakota, Wyoming, Alaska, Vermont, Delaware), and states can gain and lose seats every ten years. Generally speaking, in the past twenty years, states in the South and West have gained seats, while those in the East and Midwest have lost seats (Jacobson 2009). This can change the face of the House of Representatives and also affects campaigns as members might suddenly find they no longer have a seat in which to run. Additionally, when states receive an additional seat, there is another campaign to run and opportunities for those interested in public service.

After reapportionment, the next step is redistricting. This is the process by which the new district lines are drawn within a state. Every congressional district must be reasonably equal in population size to match with the original intention of the House of Representatives (see *Wesberry v. Sanders*, 376 U.S. 1, 1964). Today, districts contain approximately seven hundred thousand people. Redistricting can occur when a state gains, loses, or simply has a population shift. For instance, Colorado did not gain or lose seats following the 2010 census but had to redraw its congressional districts to align with population shifts. Additionally, districts cannot cross state lines, and the Supreme Court has determined districts should be reasonably compact, but this requirement is often overlooked.

Redrawing the lines is where politics first enters into this process. Whoever controls the drawing process controls who will represent that district, and this is rarely done without politics. Each individual state's constitution or laws determine how the district lines will be drawn. In some states, a commission takes on the task; the commission can be political or independent, elected or appointed. In other states, the state legislature handles the task, usually with gubernatorial approval. In a number of cases, the district lines are challenged in state courts by whichever group feels they have suffered, and these cases have found their way to the Supreme Court in recent years.

Gerrymandering is the process by which district lines are drawn to benefit a certain party, group, or individual. Communities of similar interests (parties, race, geography, etc.) can either be packed together or cracked apart. There are three main types of gerrymandering: partisan, incumbent, and racial.

Partisan gerrymandering is the drawing of district lines to benefit or hurt a certain party. The individuals who redraw the lines can put majorities of the same party into districts so they control those districts. They can also dilute the voting power of the minority party so as to keep them from having their own representation. This usually happens when commissions or state legislatures are controlled by a certain party and is an example of the old adage "to the victors go the spoils."

Some contend partisan gerrymandering is causing the fluctuations in House control over the past twenty years. It is definitely a possible cause. However, an interesting counterargument must be considered. The districts that created the Democrat takeover of the House in 2006 were the same districts that caused the largest changeover in seats in House history by the Republicans in 2010. The Census had occurred, but the new districts had yet to be drawn.

Others debate whether partisan gerrymandering is causing increased polarization in Congress. More and more congressional seats are in fact becoming less competitive; however, over the same time period, counties are also becoming less competitive (Enten 2018). While some researchers say gerrymandering is causing polarization (Blake 2013), others contend it has nothing to with it (Masket, Winbur, and Wright 2012; McCarty, Poole, and Rosenthal 2009). Many political scientists contend voters are sorting themselves, which means they are moving to counties or congressional districts where they share political and ideological views with the majority; they want to be among friends, at least politically speaking (Dews 2017). These same political scientists say gerrymandering, therefore, is not causing the increased polarization. The districts are organically becoming more liberal or conservative.

The second main type of gerrymandering is incumbent, which is redrawing the lines to protect incumbents and ensure reelection. It is similar to partisan, as it usually benefits a particular party. Incumbents are reelected 95 percent of the time, but some researchers have found redistricting is actually decreasing incumbent reelection rates (Friedman and Holden 2009). California follows this method; between 2002 and 2010, only one incumbent, out of a total of fifty-three members of Congress, lost reelection (Davidson et al. 2016).

The final type of gerrymandering is racial. Districts created to either benefit a racial minority or put all racial minorities into the same district are called majority-minority districts. The Supreme Court has decided district lines cannot discriminate against minorities, which many have interpreted as a requirement to give minorities their own districts when numbers justify it (Jacobson 2009). This has resulted in some uniquely shaped districts, even with the court's reasonably compact requirement. The other requirement in redistricting states, which have majority-minority districts is nonretrogression. This means after redrawing the lines, racial minorities cannot have fewer districts than they did before, if the numbers warrant it.

Gerrymandering has received a great deal of voter and media attention in recent years, both positive and negative. Efforts are underway in numerous states to overhaul the redistricting process. For example, in 2018 in Colorado, two measures appeared on the November ballot, which will do just that. Both of these measures received the requisite number of votes to amend the state constitution and will be implemented during the next round of redistricting. One measure will require that independent voters are represented on the commission to redraw the lines and that eight of the twelve members must approve the new plan, eliminating the chance the two major parties would gang up on the independents and keep politicians from being able to choose their constituents. Members of both parties supported this effort called Fair Maps Colorado. They argued these measures will bring fairness and credibility into elections (Eason 2018).

A similar concept regarding politicians choosing their own constituents is carpetbagging. This is when a politician moves to a state or district to run for office. The Constitution's rules absolutely allow this, and numerous famous politicians have taken advantage of it. One well-known example is Hillary Clinton. While still First Lady, she bought a house in New York State so she could run for the open Senate seat. She had not previously lived in New York but was elected their senator in 2000 and served until she was nominated to be secretary of state in 2009. Former presidential candidate and governor of Massachusetts Mitt Romney is another example. In 2018, he announced his candidacy for an open Utah Senate seat and won that election in November 2018. While this example was less egregious (as he owned a vacation home there, his mother was originally from Utah, and he was the CEO of the 2002

Olympic Winter Games in Salt Lake City), it is still an example of carpetbagging.

A second major component of the perpetual campaign is fundraising. Once the districts have been redrawn and a candidate decides to enter the race, he or she must raise enough money to be competitive. If the candidate is the incumbent in the race, either Senate or House, he or she will have an easier time raising money due to the incumbency advantage. As stated elsewhere in this chapter, incumbents are reelected 95 percent of the time (Jacobson 2009). This is due to their higher name identification; privileges of the office such as voting on legislation, constituency services, and franking (the ability of members of Congress to send mail to their constituents for free); and an easier time raising money (Jacobson 2009).

Even with the incumbency effect in place, congressional campaigns have become more expensive, with the average cost of a House race being $1 million and a Senate race costing on average $10 million (Jacobson 2009). These numbers obviously vary greatly, with the record currently held by former Senator Jon Corzine (D-NJ), who raised $63.3 million—$60.2 million of which was a personal loan he made to his campaign (Herrnson 2012).

Overall, $4 billion was spent on all congressional races in 2016. That total includes all money given to candidates and expenditures on behalf of the candidates, from individuals, political action committees (PACs), and the political parties.

Candidates must constantly be raising money in order to be competitive. This requires a great deal of time and effort. In odd-numbered years, members focus on fundraising; in even-numbered years, they are raising money in addition to constant in-person campaigning. The House and Senate leadership are well aware of this, and they often craft the congressional calendar to accommodate their members' campaign schedules. During an average week, the Senate usually gavels into session on Monday afternoon and will adjourn on Friday afternoons. The

House operates on a Monday through Thursday or Tuesday through Friday schedule to accommodate member travel.

About once a month, Congress takes a one-week recess, which it calls "state work periods." These usually correspond to a major holiday. Both chambers are in recess during the entire month of August. They both usually adjourn for most of October so members can campaign. After Election Day, Congress will go back to Washington to wrap up unfinished business. Interestingly in 2018, Senate Majority Leader McConnell (R-KY) announced he was canceling the August recess in an effort to keep Democrat senators from campaigning (Everett and Schor 2018). August is normally a time for members to spend the entire month campaigning, and fundraising, for reelection. While this move might hurt Democrats running in states where President Trump won, it also served to hurt Republicans running in moderate states. It also did nothing to improve decreased civility and increased partisanship in the Senate.

There are federally designated limits to how much money candidates can *receive* from individuals, PACs, and parties, but there are no *spending* limits. As outlined in the Bipartisan Campaign Reform Act (BCRA) of 2002, and adjusted for inflation, an individual may give $2,700 to a candidate per election (Federal Election Commission 2018). This means you can give $2,700 during the primary election and another $2,700 in the general election, for a total of $5,400 to any congressional candidate. Individuals are the largest contributors to congressional candidates (Jacobson 2009). PACs can contribute $5,000 per election to a federal candidate, for a total of $10,000. Political parties are also limited to $5,000 per election to each candidate.

Super PACs have grown in notoriety since 2010 and have acquired both respect and disdain. There are numerous super PACs on all sides of the political spectrum, with groups supporting candidates in both parties. Contrary to popular understanding, they cannot give money directly to candidates. Instead, they spend money on their own independent efforts to either defeat or support a candidate. These efforts, which often involve professionally run campaigns, cannot be coordinated with any candidate. This can raise concern with the actual candidates they support, who are carefully formulating their campaign message and tone. They have no control over what the super PAC is saying about them, and therefore, candidates often claim they do not want the support of these groups.

Super PACs can be one person, company, organization, or a group of all of them. In 2014, a total of 1,285 super PACs raised $696 million and spent $345 million on congressional races. The top two spenders during that election cycle were both designated as liberal (opposing Republican candidates or supporting Democrat candidates). They were the Senate Majority PAC, which spent $46 million, and the House Majority PAC, which spent $29 million.

The amount of money in politics concerns many citizens and watchdog groups. According to a 2015 *New York Times* poll, 84 percent of Americans think money plays too big of a role in politics (*New York Times* 2015). The Supreme Court, in *Citizens United v. Federal Election Commission* (2010), said money is speech, and under the First Amendment to the Constitution, corporations and unions can spend their money supporting, or denouncing, candidates for federal office but cannot give money directly to candidates (SCOTUSblog.com, n.d.). This decision increased the amount of money spent on electioneering in this country. Many citizens find this, the amount of money in campaigns, to be a major problem in today's political world.

However, can we limit the amount of money spent on politics? The Supreme Court says no and is not likely to change that precedent in the near future. We must ask ourselves if those messages put out by all the outside groups are changing voters' minds. Are voters that impressionable? Should they instead be researching candidates on their own? The solution to more money in politics, if one finds it offensive, is more education. The more we know about political issues and candidates, the more we are able to tune out the noise and make our own decisions.

Representation Conflicts

In a republican form of government like we have, voters do not engage in direct democracy at the federal level. They do not vote on the latest budget amendments; they do not vote to approve treaties; they do not provide oversight of the administration. Instead, they elect House and Senate members to do these things for them. In turn, the members of Congress are to represent the policy preferences of their constituents, which is called substantive representation. However, in large diverse states, a senator's constituents do not agree on every issue or even any issues. This creates almost immediate conflict, because the needs of a member's state or district can conflict with the needs of the nation as a whole. Further, constituents are not privy to all of the information at a member's disposal, thus do not always fully comprehend the intricacies of legislation. This sets up a constant internal battle for members of Congress— how to represent their constituents—while also making good policy (see Fenno 1978).

There are three main types of representation in Congress. Substantive representation has already been mentioned. This is when the member of Congress votes with, or shares policy preferences with, a majority of his or her constituents or even a subset of the constituents. An example of this is a member of Congress who represents the Big First District of Kansas (the nickname given to this large west Kansas congressional district), voting for the Farm Bill and increased farm subsidy rates. Partisan gerrymandering can actually increase substantive representation, as like-minded individuals are in the same district and thus are more easily represented. However, if you are a minority in your homogenous district, you will most likely never be substantively represented by your member of Congress.

The second type of representation is descriptive. This is when the member of Congress shares a descriptive characteristic with a number of his or her constituents. This can include education, occupation, race, gender, sexual orientation, or religion. The member looks like the constituents. We see this most often in the discussion of majority-minority districts, where the racial minority in the district is able to elect a racial minority member of Congress. The debate is whether you can have both. Can a nonracial minority member of Congress substantively represent that minority? Many researchers say yes—that descriptive representation is not essential for substantive representation (Cameron, Epstein, and O'Halloran 1996; Swain 1993).

A third type of representation is collective. This is when the member represents individuals who might not be in their state or district. These often include such things as race, gender, or sexual orientation. For example, with the small number of members of Congress who are LGBTQ, organized groups of these individuals often seek these members out for representation.

Members can be classified as trustee or delegate representatives (Miller and Stokes 1963). Trustee members are those who vote on issues based on their own preferences and understanding of the issues. Delegate members of Congress vote based on what a majority of their constituents want, placing no independent judgment into the decision (Miller and Stokes 1963).

Members of Congress engage in a number of activities to represent their constituents. The easiest and most visible is voting on legislation both on the floor and in committee. They can also sponsor or cosponsor legislation that represents their constituents' needs and interests. Members help their constituents with casework or problems they are having with federal agencies. For instance, if a constituent is a veteran and having problems with Veterans Affairs (VA) benefits, she can contact her member of Congress for assistance. The member then contacts the VA on the constituent's behalf and helps her navigate the bureaucratic red tape. The members also hire staff members in the state or district who meet with constituents, conduct casework, and attend meetings. The members also seek out media attention, especially from their local media, as a way to communicate with their constituents. This is a double-edged sword as members cannot control what type of coverage they receive. It is an important tool for constituents to ensure their member is doing what they want.

The question with representation is whether the member of Congress is actually representing his or her constituents' interests in Congress. Clearly, the member has many competing influences upon what he or she does (voters, party leaders, interest groups, president, committees), and he or she will never make everyone happy. Many political scientists believe that members do respond to a change in public opinion on issues (Jones and Baumgartner 2004; Stimson, MacKuen, and Erikson 1995) and that they respond more right before an election or right after a mandate election (Peterson et al. 2003). With the incumbency rate, we can see voters like the job their own member of Congress is doing. While voters disapprove of the overall legislative body, they tend to approve of their individual member of Congress and believe he or she should be reelected.

Interest Groups and Lobbyists

Recently, lobbyists and interest groups have been surrounded by negative references in American politics. Few other influences on congressional action garner more debate. Interest groups are people and companies who share a policy agenda. They can include grassroots organizations (e.g., the Environmental Working Group, the National Education Association, and the National Rifle Association) or professional associations (e.g., the American Medical Association and the American Farm Bureau Federation). All of these groups, along with most corporations, have business and interests before Congress. They all have lobbyists to represent them before Congress.

According to opensecrets.org, a government watchdog site, there were eleven thousand registered federal lobbyists in 2017. The total amount all of these groups spent on lobbying in 2017 (not including campaign contributions) was $3.34 billion. In 2016, lobbyists spent about $31 million on campaign contributions. Unless they are forming super PACs, the contributions must abide by the individual donation limits established in BCRA.

It is well known in political science that these contributions do not lead to changed votes or policy positions (Baumgartner et al. 2009). Instead, these groups are buying access to members of Congress to show their members they are representing their interests. Members of Congress, in addition, are concerned with representation and reelection (Mayhew 1974) and thus are granting access to the groups from their states or districts (Hall and Wayman 1990). Members of Congress know exactly which groups represent large numbers of constituents and who provides them with reliable information (Hansen 1991). This is the other important piece of the interest group puzzle. These groups and lobbyists are policy experts themselves, often with a great deal of experience in the area they represent. Thus, they can provide valuable policy analysis to the members and their staff.

It is hard to argue with citizens' right to organize and influence their government. It is also hard to argue with an organization's or company's right to do the same. However, there is corruption in lobbying. The most egregious case in recent years is that of Jack Abramoff. He was a lobbyist for numerous wealthy Native American tribes. He exchanged campaign donations from these tribes, and favors from himself, to members of Congress and their staff for earmarks and favorable treatment in Congress and within the executive branch (*Washington Post* 2007). These favors included trips on private planes to the Super Bowl, golfing in Scotland, meals at his restaurant, and box seats at every major sporting event. Even though what Abramoff did in his dealings with Congress sounds outrageous, some was not illegal at the time. He was finally sentenced to five years in prison for defrauding lenders in his purchase of gambling boats (*Washington Post* 2007). Additionally, more than twenty congressional and executive branch staff members were convicted of such things as bribery, perjury, obstruction of justice, and conspiracy, all relating to Abramoff (*Washington Post* 2007). Representative Bob Ney (R-OH) was convicted of conspiracy and making false claims, while former House Majority Leader Tom Delay (R-TX) was indicted on campaign finance charges (*Washington Post* 2007). Many members of Congress lost their reelection bids in 2006 in part because of their ties to Abramoff.

Congress passed the Honest Leadership and Open Government Act of 2007 in response to these scandals, which prohibits senators from lobbying Congress for two years and House members for one year after leaving Congress. High-level staff members also face similar restrictions. Members and staff are now prohibited from accepting any meals, gifts, or lobbyist-funded travel, which is a direct response to Abramoff. As a result of this law, there are fewer deals made over dinner and drinks at Washington's watering holes and restaurants. There are also fewer relationships made, both with interest groups and with fellow members and staff. This means staff and members rarely socialize with those across the aisle. One could argue this law, while possibly adding additional transparency to the lobbying process, is furthering partisanship and polarization.

Partisan Considerations

Political parties were not mentioned in the Constitution and certainly not in Article I, which outlined the legislative branch. However, organization and passing legislation required some collective action, so parties soon emerged in Congress. Today, they are one of the most important ways Congress organizes itself. The majority party plays a significant role in every aspect of the working Congress, from who sits on what committee to what bills are considered. Even in the individualistic Senate, the majority leader plays a key role in the Senate agenda, and the committee chairs (who are chosen from the majority party) play an equally important role in policy agenda setting.

Political scientists have a number of theories for explaining the effect parties have on Congress and the role they play in both chambers. The first of those is the Conditional Party Government (CPG) theory first proposed by David Rohde (1991). This theory focuses on positive agenda power or the ability to pass legislation in Congress, either through committees or on the floor. CPG occurs when the members of the majority party in Congress are all aligned with the same policy interests, and those interests differ from those of the opposing party (Aldrich and Rohde 2000; Rohde 1991). This means polarization is present. When the members of the party all agree with the leadership (because the interests are all homogenous), they delegate more authority to their leaders; they can trust them to bring up and pass legislation they support, although the legislation is decidedly skewed (Aldrich and Rohde 2000; Rohde 1991). The party leadership then uses this power and authority to twist arms and pass legislation in their favor.

Similar to this is the Cooper–Brady (1981) argument, where party leaders are empowered by the rank and file and they are empowered more when the opposing party is strongly aligned and led (strong polarization exists). When there are factions within the party, party leadership is not trusted or followed (Cooper and Brady 1981). Contrary to CPG, under this argument, polarization, not policy alignment, leads to strong leadership.

Other theories of party control focus on negative agenda control, or cartel politics, which is the idea that majority party leaders only bring forward policies that the majority of their party favors; they then kill or stall all other policies or legislation (Cox and McCubbins 1993, 2005). The cartel is trying to protect members of the majority from taking difficult votes and subsequently suffering electorally (Cox and McCubbins 1993,

2005). Leadership will not offer up bills that will hurt members of their majority, which could pose a threat to them keeping the majority. In this cartel situation, there are a number of veto points (places where legislation can be halted), and all of these points are controlled by the majority party. These points include the committee chairs, the Rules Committee, and the Speaker of the House (Cox and McCubbins 1993, 2005).

None of these theories fully captures the current situation in Congress. The majority party's power to pass skewed or one-sided legislation, in a party consisting of similar policy interests (CPG), is not fully coming to pass. The parties today are fractured, and the far-right Freedom Caucus often opposes the legislation proposed by the Republican leadership; policy interests are not homogenous. Exceptions might be the 2017 tax bill or the 2010 Affordable Care Act, both of which relied heavily on strong party leaders and a caucus working in lockstep to pass them.

The Cooper–Brady (1981) argument comes the closest to explaining current conditions. Polarization is present, which means party leaders should be empowered, but they have not been. Factions also exist, which means party leaders will not be trusted, which does correspond with present conditions, but it still does not account for the effect of polarization.

As far as using negative agenda control (cartel), Speaker Boehner did not use this as much as expected; instead he relied on moderate minority party members to pass important legislation. This was forced upon him by the factions within his own party. Speaker Ryan is finding a similar situation, especially with fiscal issues.

While questions remain how partisan considerations play out in the real world of Congress, we are also left to ask what is causing the polarization. It is not up for debate whether Congress is polarized; it is. Some argue this is an inevitable outcome of divided government, where the branches are warring with each other (Binder 2003), while others argue divided government has no effect on legislative effectiveness (Mayhew 1991).

However, when one looks at the polarization levels, it is evident it is on the rise, no matter if there is unified or divided government.

Other potential causes of polarization in Congress include gerrymandering of House districts, increased partisanship and polarization in the electorate, increasingly powerful and partisan party leaders in Congress (Theriault 2008), ideological House members moving to the Senate and taking their polarized politics with them to their new chamber (Theriault 2008), the increasing ideological distance between the two chambers even when they are controlled by the same party (Binder 2003), and the changing agenda of Congress with a focus on more contentious issues (Lee 2009). It is at once all of these in combination, and none of them alone.

A final cause of polarization could be the constant change in chamber control we have seen in the past twenty years. Democrats controlled the House from 1955 until 1995, while they had control of the Senate from 1955 until 1981 and then from 1987 until 1995. This relative stability in party control of Congress has ended in recent years. Control of the House switched again in 2007 (from Republican to Democrat) and in 2010 (to Republican, one of the biggest gains of House seats in congressional history at sixty-three). The Senate has also changed control a number of times in recent years. It changed from Republican to Democrat in 2001 after a member of the Republican Party (Senator Jim Jeffords of Vermont) switched his party affiliation to Democrat. It changed again after the 2002 elections (back to Republican), in 2007 (to Democrat), and, most recently, in 2014 (to Republican). We can assume upcoming elections will have similar effects on partisan control of Congress.

The change in control of Congress seems a natural result of voter preferences and satisfaction or dissatisfaction with the status quo. It would appear, however, voters are not getting what they want from Congress. If they were, we would not see these drastic changes in seats and control. The ultimate check on members of Congress is reelection and the voters; but to what end? Does this constant changing further polarization? It could be argued it does. Many things switch when control changes. Committee chairs change, leadership changes, staff people lose or gain jobs, and office space drastically changes for members moving up or down on the hierarchy. Those now in the minority may be bitter; those in the new majority may want to punish the new minority for ills they suffered while in that spot. While the change in power is always peaceful, which sets our legislative body apart from others around the world, it can still leave residual hard feelings among members.

While the causes are up for debate, many of the effects of polarization are not. When polarization is high, productivity decreases. Both chambers are mired in stalemate and gridlock, and little gets done. There are arguments to be made that moderate levels of polarization can lead to increased legislative output (Mayhew 1991), but we have not seen moderate levels of polarization in either chamber for quite a while.

Another effect of high polarization is low approval numbers. While this may not seem to be a serious issue, it does lead to lower trust in government and overall apathy to the political process. If the polarization leads to low enough approval, voters might conversely be energized and engaged to vote. Voters then vote out incumbents, leading to more turnover in Congress. Some argue this is a positive outcome, while others worry about a chamber with no institutional knowledge or policy expertise, save for the unelected staff members. In response to this threat, members of Congress might introduce different types of legislation, meant to appease voters, with a more populist slant.

Parties, and the rise of organizing Congress along party lines, might not be major problems in and of themselves, but the outcomes of polarization and gridlock are definitely inhibiting a productive Congress. Some maintain Congress is better when it is doing less, while others argue Congress should at least be completing its enumerated tasks such as establishing laws of naturalization, providing advice and consent for presidential nominations, and passing yearly budgets and appropriations bills. With the current levels of polarization, even these most basic of congressional tasks are not getting completed in a timely fashion or at all.

We cannot rid American politics of parties altogether, and those who claim we just need a strong third party are not paying attention to Duverger's law, which says we will always have two strong parties because of our institutions. Our rules maintain only two main parties will be dominant in politics. It does not keep third parties from forming or even supplanting one of the existing parties, but it does mean there will always be two main ones.

Similar to what Madison wrote about factions (parties can be considered factions as he described) in "Federalist No. 10," something must be done about the effects of partisanship, which currently is polarization. One solution is the return to a respectful and civil body. The House was always a place for spirited debate but where historically the members of both parties respected each other. The Senate has long been a collegial body, filled with mutual respect. That has changed. Members of opposite parties rarely speak to each other, let alone socialize together outside of the Capitol. The lack of civility rears up not only on the Senate and House floors but also in the office halls and on traditional and social media. Members of Congress seem to have real disdain for their colleagues across the aisle. This is also seen in the public realm among voters, who think just because someone is of a different party or ideology, they must be wrong, or worse, a bad person.

These problems of polarization and lack of civility did not happen overnight and are not going to be fixed overnight. It must change, however, or we are faced with an indefinite future of a polarized, gridlocked Congress that produces one-sided legislation. This one-sided legislation makes one side of the spectrum happy but is contrary to what the other half of the voters want. One should ask oneself if this is what a republican democracy is about.

Civility must return to politics, which begins with all social discourse in this country, not just at the highest levels but in everyday conversations among voters as well. Politicians represent what their voters want. If voters want their members to fight and argue on the Senate or House floor, they will. If they want them to stick to their policy views no matter what, demanding the other side must compromise, that is not going to work. Both sides must give a little; both must make an effort to mend fences and work together.

Women and Minorities in Congress

While the presence of women and minorities in Congress is not a problem, the lack of their presence is seen by many to be a problem. Specifically, it is argued women and racial minorities should be represented in Congress at or near the same rate as they are seen in the citizen population.

Jeannette Rankin (D-MT) was the first female elected to Congress in 1916 (Manning and Brudnick 2018). This occurred before women even had the right to vote. The first woman to serve in the Senate was Rebecca Felton (D-GA), who was appointed and who served for one day in 1922. The first female senator to be elected to her own six-year term was Hattie Caraway (D-AR) in 1932 (Manning and Brudnick 2018). Since then, 329 women have served in Congress. In the 116th Congress (2019–2021), there are 131 women in Congress, with 106 in the House and 25 in the Senate (Panetta and Lee 2019). This is a new record for female service.

The numbers for racial minorities in Congress are closer to being representative of the larger population. In the 116th Congress, there are fifty-four African American voting members of the House and three in the Senate (Panetta and Lee 2019). In the House that is 12.4 percent, with the overall population being 12.3 percent, according to the U.S. Census Bureau. There are forty-two Hispanic members in the House (9 percent, when their actual percentage in the overall U.S.

population is 12.5 percent) and four in the Senate (Panetta and Lee 2019). Fifteen House members and three senators are Asian Americans, and there are four Native American House members (Panetta and Lee 2019).

Women's impact on policy in Congress is similar to that of men, with many saying they feel women and minorities provide a unique perspective to the policy process (Swers 2002). Women serve on nearly every committee and hold leadership roles on numerous committees, as well as in party leadership (Arnold and King 2002). In 2007, Nancy Pelosi (D-CA) was the first female to be elected Speaker, the highest position in Congress. Female members of Congress bring new issues to the congressional agenda and feel a certain responsibility to focus on issues of importance to women like breast cancer research, equal pay, and sexual assault in the military (Dodson 2006; Herrick 2017; Kedrowski and Sarow 2002; Swers 2002).

Racial minorities also play a critical role in congressional policy. A great deal of discussion focuses on the effects of substantive and descriptive representation and majority-minority districts. These districts do usually elect minority representatives, thus providing them with descriptive representation (Lublin 1999). In terms of actual policy, black and Hispanic members of Congress are more involved with oversight of minority policy issues (Minto 2009). Black members have been found to be just as effective as white members in terms of getting their bills passed (Canon 1999). As one might expect, Hispanic members are more likely to introduce pro-Hispanic legislation than non-Hispanic members (Wilson 2010). It should not be assumed, however, that all racial minority members of Congress are concerned with the same policy issues, just like female members are not all concerned with the same issues. Other factors play large roles, such as party and district or state concerns (Herrick 2017).

Women and minorities are effective at representing their constituents in Congress; so why are there so few of them? For racial minorities, it might be due to a concept called voter dilution, which means separating minority communities into different districts so they cannot elect a minority representative to Congress (Herrick 2017). These candidates also have a hard time gaining name recognition outside their own communities and raising the necessary funds. For women, the explanation is a bit more involved. When women do run, they win just as often as do men, but they are less likely to run in the first place (Lawless and Fox 2008). Jennifer L. Lawless and Richard L. Fox (2008) have found women have a natural aversion to political campaigning, get recruited less than men, feel less qualified than men to run, and are usually the ones who care for the home and children, which leaves little time for running for office.

Solutions to getting more women and minorities to run, and serve, in Congress are numerous. Women and minorities need to be recruited and encouraged to run. To overcome their aversion to politics, women are being encouraged to run as women, as themselves (Zernike 2018). In 2018, Liuba Grechen Shirley, a Democratic candidate for Congress in New York, petitioned the Federal Election Commission (FEC) to allow her to use campaign funds to pay for a babysitter for her young children (Zauzmer 2018). The FEC agreed. Changes like these will allow more women to run for office.

Congressional Ethics

Public approval of Congress has hit all new record lows in recent years. Americans have a real distrust and dislike of their elected officials; much of this can be attributed to the wrongdoings of members themselves. In recent years, we have seen numerous ethical charges against members of Congress, many dealing with illegally taking gifts, or campaign contributions, from businesses or organized interests.

According to the Constitution, members have the ability to remove one of their own. The last time this happened was in 2002, when the House of Representatives voted to remove Representative Jim Traficant (D-OH) from office for receiving bribes (Smith, Roberts, and Vander Wielen 2013). Most members choose to resign or not seek reelection in similar circumstances. In 2005, Duke Cunningham (R-CA) resigned after he accepted over $2 million in bribes relating to defense contracts. In 2006, William Jefferson (D-LA) was defeated for reelection after $90,000 in bribe money was found in his freezer. Other scandals involve more indecent activities. Representative Mark Foley (R-FL), Senator Larry Craig (R-ID), and Representative Anthony Weiner (D-NY) are just a few of the examples of members who resigned or did not seek reelection due to extramarital affairs, soliciting sexual favors, or sexual harassment. The 2017–2018 #MeToo movement uncovered numerous instances of sexual harassment in Congress, such as Senator Al Franken (D-MN) and Representative Blake Farenthold (R-TX), both of whom resigned from office.

Both the House and Senate have Ethics Committees that are charged with investigating any members accused of ethical charges or violating the House or Senate rules (Loomis and Schiller 2016). In 2018, Senator Robert Menendez (D-NJ) was investigated by the Senate Ethics Committee, which admonished him for accepting thousands of dollars in illegal gifts but did not recommend his removal from the Senate (Killough 2018). This came after the Department of Justice dropped their charges against the senator following a mistrial in federal court (Killough 2018).

The Office of Congressional Ethics (OCE) was created in 2008 and allows the general public to request ethics investigations (Loomis and Schiller 2016). The Office investigates and makes recommendations to the House Ethics Committee (Loomis and Schiller 2016). In 2017, House Republicans attempted to defund and take away the OCE's power, but public backlash forced them to abandon their plan (Cheney and Bresnahan 2017).

Solutions to the problem of congressional ethics violations or the seemingly lack of any ethical behavior in Congress are few and far between. The Ethics Committees in both chambers need to have real investigative powers as well as the ability to do more than simply reprimand members. Voters need to be also more aware of who is representing them in Congress and respond with electoral repercussions.

Solutions

The problems and controversies surrounding Congress are many, and solutions are varied. It is an amazingly dynamic body, capable of impressive action, even in its inaction.

Still many continue to be disillusioned with Congress, even as it stands as one of the most impressive legislative bodies in the world. As long as voters continue to send the same people to Washington and ignore any indiscretions, violations will continue. Voters must demand better but also then allow members to do their jobs. Constantly deriding the good members will ensure we only get the bad. If we want good people to run for office, we must allow them to do their jobs. Civility must not just be present in our conversations with each other but in our treatment of our elected officials.

References

Alberta, Tim. 2017. "John Boehner Unchained." *Politico*, December. https://www.politico.com/magazine/story/2017/10/29/john-boehner-trump-house-republican-party-retirement-profile-feature-215741

Aldrich, John H., and David Rohde. 2000. "The Republican Revolution and the House Appropriations Committee." *Journal of Politics* 62: 1–33.

Anderson, James. 1979. *Public Policy Making*. New York: Holt, Rinehart, and Winston.

Arnold, Laura W., and Barbara M. King. 2002. "Women, Committees, and Institutional Change in the Senate." In Vol. 4 of *Women Transforming Congress*, edited by Cindy

Simon Rosenthal, 284–315. Norman: University of Oklahoma Press.

Baumgartner, Frank R., Jeffrey M. Berry, Marie Hojnacki, David C. Kimball, and Beth L. Leech. 2009. *Lobbying and Policy Change: Who Wins, Who Loses, and Why*. Chicago: University of Chicago Press.

Bazan, Elizabeth. 2010. "Impeachment: An Overview of Constitutional Provisions, Procedure, and Practice." Congressional Research Service, December 9.

Binder, Sarah. 2003. *Stalemate: Causes and Consequences of Legislative Gridlock*. Washington, D.C.: Brookings Institution Press.

Blake, Aaron. 2013. "Where Ted Cruz's Marathon Speech Stands in History." *Washington Post*, September 25.

Calmes, Jackie. 2009. "House Passes Stimulus Plan with No G.O.P. Votes." *New York Times*, January 28.

Cameron, Charles, David Epstein, and Sharyn O'Halloran. 1996. "Do Majority-Minority Districts Maximize Substantive Black Representation in Congress?" *American Political Science Review* 90 (4): 794–812.

Canon, David T. 1999. *Race, Redistricting, and Representation: The Unintended Consequences of Black Majority Districts*. Chicago: University of Chicago Press.

Cervantes, Bobby. 2012. "Longest Filibusters in History." *Politico*, December 5.

Cheney, Kyle, and John Bresnahan. 2017. "What Is the Office of Congressional Ethics and Why Does It Matter?" *Politico*, January 3.

CNN. 2008. "Congress Passes Farm Bill over Bush Veto." June 18. http://www.cnn.com/2008/POLITICS/06/18/farm.bill/index.html

Coburn, Tom. 2014. "The 10 Most Outrageous Government Boondoggles I Ever Saw." *Politico*, February 5.

Cole, Jared P., and Todd Garvey. 2015. "Impeachment and Removal." Congressional Research Service, October 29.

Cooper, Joseph, and David W. Brady. 1981. "Institutional Context and Leadership Style: The House from Cannon to Rayburn." *American Political Science Review* 75: 411–25.

Corn, M. Lynne, and Alexandra M. Wyatt. 2016. "The Endangered Species Act: A Primer." Congressional Research Service, September 8.

Cowan, Richard, and Susan Cornwell. 2017. "House Votes to Begin Repealing Obamacare." Reuters, January 13.

Cox, Gary, and Mathew McCubbins. 1993. *Legislative Leviathan: Party Government in the House.* Berkeley: University of California Press.

Cox, Gary, and Mathew McCubbins. 2005. *Setting the Agenda: Responsible Party Government in the U.S. House of Representatives.* New York: Cambridge University Press.

CRS Team. 2006. "Memorandum: Earmarks in Appropriation Acts: FY1994, FY1996, FY1998, FY2000, FY2002, FY2004, FY2005." January 26.

C-SPAN. 2013. "Harry Reid Nuclear Option. Senate Debate on Filibuster Rules." C-span.org, November 21. https://www.c-span.org/video/?c4474510/harry-reid-nuclear-option

Davidson, Roger H., Walter J. Oleszek, Frances E. Lee, and Eric Schickler. 2016. *Congress and Its Members*, 15th ed. Thousand Oaks, CA: Congressional Quarterly Press.

DeBonis, Mike. 2016. "Joe Biden in 1992: No Nominations to the Supreme Court in an Election Year." *Washington Post*, February 22.

DeGregorio, Christine. 1994. "Congressional Committee Staff as Policy Making Partners in the U.S. Congress." *Congress & the Presidency* 21: 49–66.

Department of Homeland Security. 2018. "Deferred Action for Childhood Arrivals (DACA)." https://www.dhs.gov/deferred-action-childhood-arrivals-daca

Desilver, Drew. 2015. "What Is the House Freedom Caucus, and Who's in It?" Pew Research, October 20.

Dewar, Helen. 2003. "An All-Nighter in the Senate." *Washington Post*, November 13.

Dews, Fred. 2017. "A Primer on Gerrymandering and Political Polarization." The Brookings Institute, July 6.

Dodson, Debra L. 2006. *The Impact of Women in Congress*. New York: Oxford University Press on Demand.

Eason, Brian. 2018. "Colorado Lawmakers Send Anti-Gerrymandering Reforms to November's Ballot." *Denver Post*, May 16.

Edwards, George C., III, and Stephen J. Wayne. 2014. *Presidential Leadership: Politics and Policy-Making*. Stamford, CT: Cengage.

Elias, Bart. 2012. "Federal Aviation Administration (FAA) Reauthorization: An Overview of Legislative Action in the 112th Congress." Congressional Research Service, August 9.

Elsea, Jennifer K., and Matthew C. Weed. 2014. "Declarations of War and Authorizations for the Use of Military Force: Historical Background and Legal Implications." Congressional Research Service, April 18.

Enten, Harry. 2018. "Ending Gerrymandering Won't Fix What Ails America." FiveThirtyEight, January 26. https://fivethirtyeight.com/features/ending-gerrymandering-wont-fix-what-ails-america/

Everett, Burgess, and Elana Schor. 2018. "McConnell Cancels Most of August Recess." *Politico*, June 5.

Federal Election Commission. 2018. "Contribution Limits for 2017–2018 Federal Elections." https://transition.fec.gov/pages/brochures/contriblimitschart.htm

Fenno, Richard F. 1978. *Home Style: House Members in Their Districts*. Boston: Little, Brown.

Ferris, Sarah. 2016. "Ryan Changes Rules for Spending Bills." *The Hill*, June 8.

Ferris, Sarah. 2018. "House GOP Mulls Lifting a Ban on Earmarks." *Politico*, January 9.

Flegenheimer, Matt. 2017. "Senate Republicans Deploy 'Nuclear Option' to Clear Path for Gorsuch." *New York Times*, April 6.

Fox, Harrison W., and Susan W. Hammond. 1977. *Congressional Staffs: The Invisible Force in American Lawmaking*. New York: The Free Press.

Friedman, John N., and Richard T. Holden. 2009. "The Rising Incumbent Reelection Rate: What's Gerrymandering Got to Do With It?" *Journal of Politics* 71: 593–611.

Gabriel, Trip, Jonathan Martin, and Nicholas Fandos. 2019. "Steve King Removed from Committee Assignments over White Supremacy Remark." *New York Times*, January 14.

Garcia, Eric. 2018. "House Votes to Table Trump Impeachment." *Roll Call*, January 19.

Gold, Martin B. 2008. *Senate Procedure and Practice*. Lanham, MD: Rowman and Littlefield.

Golshan, Tara. 2018. "House Members Are Demanding a Vote on Immigration—and Leadership May Not Be Able to Stop Them." Vox.com, May 18.

Hagedorn, Sara L. 2015. *Taking the Lead: Congressional Staffers and Their Role in the Policy Process*. Unpublished manuscript.

Hall, Richard D., and Frank W. Wayman. 1990. "Buying Time: Moneyed Interests and the Buying of Mobilization of Bias in Congressional Committees." *American Political Science Review* 84: 797–820.

Hall, Richard L. 1993. "Participation, Abdication, and Representation in Congressional Committees." In *Congress Reconsidered*, edited by Lawrence C. Dodd and Bruce I. Oppenheimer. Washington, D.C.: Congressional Quarterly Press.

Hammond, Susan W. 1990. "Committee and Informal Leaders in the House." In *Leading Congress: New Styles, New Strategies*, edited by John J. Kornacki. Washington, D.C.: Congressional Quarterly Press.

Hansen, John M. 1991. *Gaining Access: Congress and the Farm Lobby, 1919–1981*. Chicago: University of Chicago Press.

Heniff, Bill, Jr., and Justin Murray. 2011. "Congressional Budget Resolutions: Historical Information." Congressional Research Service, April 4.

Herrick, Rebekah. 2017. *Minorities and Representation in American Politics*. Thousand Oaks, CA: Sage/Congressional Quarterly Press.

Herrnson, Paul S. 2012. *Congressional Elections: Campaigns at Home and in Washington*, 6th ed. Thousand Oaks, CA: Sage/Congressional Quarterly Press.

Hickey, Walter. 2013. "The Longest Filibuster in History Lasted More Than a Day—Here's How It Went Down." *Business Insider*, March 6.

Hogue, Henry B., and Maeve P. Carey. 2015. *Appointment and Confirmation of Executive Branch Leadership: An Overview*. Congressional Research Service, June 22.

House Administration Committee. 2018. "Congressional Member and Staff Organizations." https://cha.house.gov/member-services/congressional-memberstaff-organizations

Jacobson, Gary C. 2009. *The Politics of Congressional Elections*, 7th ed. New York: Pearson.

Jones, Bryan D., and Frank R. Baumgartner. 2004. "Representation and Agenda Setting." *Policy Studies Journal* 32 (1): 1–24.

Kaplan, Thomas, and Alan Rappeport. 2017. "Republican Tax Bill Passes Senate in 51–48 Vote." *New York Times*, December 19.

Kedrowski, Karen, and Marilyn Stine Sarow. 2002. "The Gendering of Cancer Policy: Media Advocacy and Congressional Policy Attention." In *Women Transforming Congress*, edited by Cindy Simon Rosenthal, 240–59. Norman: University of Oklahoma Press.

Kernell, Samuel. 2007. *Going Public: New Strategies of Presidential Leadership*, 4th ed. Washington, D.C.: Congressional Quarterly Press.

Killough, Ashley. 2018. "Sen. Bob Menendez 'Severely Admonished' by Senate Ethics Committee." CNN, April 26.

Kingdon, John. 2003. *Agendas, Alternative, and Public Policies*, 2nd ed. New York: Harper Collins.

Lawless, Jennifer L., and Richard L. Fox. 2008. "Why Are Women Still Not Running for Public Office?" *Brookings Institution Issues in Governance Studies* (May).

Lee, Frances E. 2009. *Beyond Ideology: Politics, Principles, and Partisanship in the U.S. Senate*. Chicago: University of Chicago Press.

LoBianco, Tom. 2016. "Five Politically Important Recent Filibusters." CNN Politics, June 16.

Loomis, Burdett A., and Wendy J. Schiller. 2016. *The Contemporary Congress*, 6th ed. Lanham, MD: Rowman and Littlefield.

Lublin, David. 1999. *The Paradox of Representation: Racial Gerrymandering and Minority Interests in Congress*. Princeton, NJ: Princeton University Press.

MacNeil, Neil, and Richard A. Baker. 2013. *The American Senate: An Insider's History*. New York: Oxford.

Malbin, Michael J. 1980. *Unelected Representatives: Congressional Staff and the Future of Representative Government*. New York: Basic Books.

Manning, Jennifer E., and Ida A. Brudnick. 2018. *Women in Congress, 1917–2018: Service Dates and Committee Assignments by Member, and Lists by State and Congress.* Congressional Research Service, May 17.

Masket, Seth E., Jonathan Winburn, and Gerald C. Wright. 2012. "The Gerrymanderers Are Coming! Legislative Redistricting Won't Affect Competition or Polarization Much, No Matter Who Does It." *PS: Political Science and Politics* 45: 39–43.

Mayhew, David. 1974. *Congress: The Electoral Connection.* New Haven, CT: Yale University Press.

Mayhew, David. 1991. *Divided We Govern: Party Control, Lawmaking, and Investigations 1946–1990.* New Haven, CT: Yale University Press.

McCarty, Nolan, Keith T. Poole, and Howard Rosenthal. 2009. "Does Gerrymandering Cause Polarization?" *American Journal of Political Science* 53: 660–80.

McMillion, Barry J. 2012. *Length of Time from Nomination to Confirmation for "Uncontroversial" U.S. Circuit and District Court Nominees: Detailed Analysis.* Congressional Research Service, September 18.

Miller, Warren, and Donald Stokes. 1963. "Constituency Influence in Congress." *American Political Science Review* 57: 45–56.

Minto, Michael D. 2009. "Legislative Oversight and the Substantive Representation of Black and Latino Interests in Congress." *Legislative Studies Quarterly* 34: 193–218.

Mitchell, Allison. 1998. "Impeachment: The Overview." *New York Times*, December 20.

Neustadt, Richard E. 1990. *Presidential Power and the Modern Presidents.* New York: The Free Press.

New York Times. 2015. "Americans' Views on Money in Politics." *New York Times*, June 2. https://www.nytimes.com/interactive/2015/06/02/us/politics/money-in-politics-poll.html

Oleszek, Walter J., Mark J. Oleszek, Elizabeth Rybicki, and Bill Heniff Jr. 2016. *Congressional Procedures and the Policy Process*. Thousand Oaks, CA: Congressional Quarterly Press.

Panetta, Grace, and Samantha Lee. 2019. "This Graphic Shows How Much More Diverse the House of Representatives Is Getting." *Business Insider*, January 12.

Peters, Jeremy W. 2013. "In Landmark Vote, Senate Limits Use of the Filibuster." *New York Times*, November 21.

Petersen, R. Eric. 2008. *Legislative Branch Staffing, 1954–2007*. Congressional Research Service, Report R40056, October 15.

Petersen, R. Eric, Parker H. Reynolds, and Amber Hope Wilhelm. 2010. *House of Representatives and Senate Staff Levels in Members, Committee, Leadership, and Other Offices, 1977–2010*. Congressional Research Service, Report R41366, August 10.

Peterson, David A. M., Lawrence J. Grossback, James A. Stimson, and Amy Gangl. 2003. "Congressional Response to Mandate Elections." *American Journal of Political Science* 47: 411–26.

Phillips, Kate. 2009. "McCain Returns to Familiar Battles over Earmarks." *New York Times*, March 2.

Pika, Joseph A., John A. Maltese, and Andrew Rudalevige. 2017. *The Politics of the Presidency*, 9th ed. Los Angeles: Congressional Quarterly Press.

Polsby, Nelson W. 1978. "Interest Groups and the Presidency: Trends in Political Intermediation in America." In *American Politics and Public Policy*, edited by Walter Dean Burnham and Martha W. Weinberg, 41–54. Cambridge: MIT Press.

Price, David E. 1971. "Professionals and 'Entrepreneurs': Staff Orientations and Policy Making on Three Senate Committees." *Journal of Politics* 33: 316–36.

Reuters. 2018. "Republican Congressman Removed from Ethics Committee." January 20.

Riddick's Senate Procedure. 1992. Public Law 99–75. https://www.govinfo.gov/app/details/GPO-RIDDICK-1992

Rohde, David. 1991. *Parties and Leaders in the Postreform House*. Chicago: University of Chicago Press.

Roll Call. 2014. "The Congressional Earmark Ban: The Real Bridge to Nowhere Commentary." July 30.

Romzek, Barbara S. 2000. "Accountability of Congressional Staff." *Journal of Public Administration Research and Theory* 2: 413–46.

Romzek, Barbara S., and Jennifer A. Utter. 1997. "Congressional Legislative Staff: Political Professionals or Clerks?" *American Journal of Political Science* 41: 1251–79.

Salisbury, Robert, and Kenneth A. Shepsle. 1981. "U.S. Congressman as Enterprise." *Legislative Studies Quarterly* 6: 559–76.

Savage, Charlie. 2011. "Attack Renews Debate over Congressional Consent." *New York Times*, March 21.

Schick, Allen. 2007. *The Federal Budget: Politics, Policy, and Process*, 3rd ed. Washington, D.C.: Brookings Institution Press.

SCOTUSblog.com. n.d. "Citizens United v. Federal Election Commission." https://www.scotusblog.com/case-files/cases/citizens-united-v-federal-election-commission/

Sinclair, Barbara. 2012. *Unorthodox Lawmaking: New Legislative Processes in the U.S. Congress*. Washington, D.C.: Congressional Quarterly Press.

Smith, Steven S., Jason M. Roberts, and Ryan J. Vander Wielen. 2013. *The American Congress*, 8th ed. New York: Cambridge.

Stimson, James A., Michael B. MacKuen, and Robert S. Erikson. 1995. "Dynamic Representation." *American Political Science Review* 89 (3): 543–65.

Strand, Mark, and Tim Lang. 2017. "The U.S. Senate Filibuster: Options for Reform." The Congressional Institute, September 25.

Streeter, Sandy. 2010. *The Congressional Appropriations Process: An Introduction.* Congressional Research Service, December 2.

Swain, Carol. 1993. *Black Faces, Black Interests: The Representation of African Americans in Congress.* Cambridge, MA: Harvard University Press.

Swers, Michele L. 2002. *The Difference Women Make: The Policy Impact of Women in Congress.* Chicago: University of Chicago Press.

Theriault, Sean M. 2008. *Party Polarization in Congress.* New York: Cambridge.

"Tie Votes." n.d. U.S. Senate. https://www.senate.gov/pagelayout/reference/four_column_table/Tie_Votes.htm

Toobin, Jeffrey. 2003. "Advice and Dissent: The Fight over the President's Judicial Nominations." *New Yorker*, May 26.

Torreon, Barbara S. 2015. "Instances of the Use of United States Forces Abroad, 1798–2015." Congressional Research Service, October 15.

"Treaties." n.d. U.S. Senate. https://www.senate.gov/artandhistory/history/common/briefing/Treaties.htm

U.S. House of Representatives. 2019. "Presidential Vetoes." https://history.house.gov/Institution/Presidential-Vetoes/Presidential-Vetoes/

Washington Post. 2007. "Unraveling Abramoff: Key Players in the Investigation of Lobbyist Jack Abramoff." *Washington Post*, June 26.

Washington Post. 2019. "Tracking How Many Key Positions Trump Has Filled So Far." https://www.washingtonpost.com/graphics/politics/trump-administration-appointee-tracker/database/Waxman, Olivia B., and Merrill Fabry.

2018. "From an Anonymous Tip to an Impeachment: A Timeline of Key Moments in the Clinton-Lewinsky Scandal." *Time*, May 4.

Weed, Matthew C. 2017. *The War Powers Resolution: Concepts and Practice*. Congressional Research Service, March 28.

Wilson, Walter C. 2010. "Descriptive Representation and Latino Interest Bill Sponsorship in Congress." *Social Science Quarterly* 91: 1043–62.

Wyler, Grace. 2012. "John Boehner Has Started Purging Fiscal Hawks from House Committees." *Business Insider*, December 4.

Zauzmer, Julie. 2018. "Candidate Can Use Campaign Funds to Pay for Babysitter, FEC Rules." *Washington Post*, May 10.

Zernike, Kate. 2018. "Forget Suits: Show the Tattoo. Female Candidates Are Breaking the Rules." *New York Times*, July 14, 2018.

This chapter presents eight original essays on the topic of the American Congress. It includes essays written by established scholars of the topic, by scholars at the beginning of their professional careers, and by former staff members of Congress. Collectively, these essays provide insights and a perspective different from the expertise of the authors. They are presented in alphabetical order of the contributor's last name.

Preparing for the Senate Confirmation Process
Chad Calvert

"What's a murder board?" he wanted to know. "Sounds bad."

"You will do just fine," I responded. "We make the murder board as painful as possible to help you figure out how to answer the questions."

This dialogue didn't happen at Gitmo; it was a common question I got from people nominated by the president of the United States as I helped them with their confirmation in the U.S. Senate. The "murder board" is just another step in the process for these nominees who are being considered for

---

Senator Charles Grassley (R-IA) gets some paperwork from a staffer before the start of the Senate Finance Committee markup of the nominations of Jacob "Jack" Lew to be Treasury secretary, William Schultz to be Health and Human Services general counsel, and Christopher Meade to be Treasury general counsel followed by an organization vote including subcommittee assignments on February 26, 2013. (Douglas Graham/CQ Roll Call/Getty Images)

the senior-most executive branch positions. The road for a presidential appointment with Senate confirmation, a PAS nominee, can be a long one. And the murder board, or mock Senate confirmation hearing, comes near the end.

During my three-year tenure as a political appointee in the Congressional Affairs office at the U.S. Department of the Interior, I assisted with or managed the confirmations of at least twenty-three PAS nominees, including all the subcabinet posts at least once—sometimes more than once as people came and went. For many nominees, this is their first direct encounter with the U.S. Senate, and for even the most seasoned of public officials, it is one of the most intense processes of their careers.

And that's where the "Sherpa" comes in. "Sherpa" is the Tibetan term for the guy who carries all the bags, knows the trail, and makes sure the climber doesn't get lost or fall off the mountain. It's the term commonly used in Washington, D.C., to describe the person who helps a PAS nominee through the process. As a Sherpa, I never lost a climber, but we did occasionally get stuck in the ice for a while.

People nominated to Senate-confirmed roles—the secretaries, deputy secretaries, undersecretaries, assistant secretaries, administrators, bureau directors, ambassadors, and so on—are sorted and selected by the Office of Presidential Personnel (OPP). There are roughly twelve hundred PAS positions in the U.S. government for the president to fill, and through a variety of channels, OPP finds the people for the president to consider. The OPP's prenomination process includes a thorough background check and other means of vetting people's histories and policy views. Due to the rigor of OPP's background check, and the unpredictable and lengthy professional limbo into which a person can fall, lots of people drop out at this stage—both voluntarily and involuntarily.

If a hopeful nominee can make it through vetting and be formally nominated by the White House, then his or her paperwork is sent to the U.S. Senate, where it is directed to the standing committee with jurisdiction over that department or agency. At this point, the White House typically hands off management of the nomination process for most subcabinet nominees to the department-level political staff to manage.

The Sherpa's first job is to contact the majority and minority staff of the committee to discuss the nomination. Most committees will ask a nominee to fill out a questionnaire and deliver any writings that have been published, official decisions or opinions, and a variety of other documents that provide insight into the policy views of the nominee. It is up to the Sherpa, working with the White House and the nominee, to make sure all these documents are complete and delivered in a timely fashion.

The next step is to prepare the nominee for their "Hill" visits, a colloquial term for courtesy meetings with senators on Capitol Hill. The Sherpa works with the nominee and White House to set up these meetings with the chairman and ranking member of the relevant committee, other members of the committee on both sides of the aisle, and senators from the home state of the nominee. For high-profile nominees, Republican and Democrat leadership of the full Senate might want to meet with them.

Most of these meetings will be substantive, to discuss policy views and background, but sometimes more parochial interests come up like, "Will you help me get the National Park Service to allow dogs on my favorite trail?" and so on. It is very important for the Sherpa to help the nominee perfect the art of acknowledging a senator's interests without making policy commitments that might be contrary to the president's agenda. This is a tricky dance where the nominee must make a lot of promises to work diligently with every senator on issues important to them, without making any promises to change policies. It is a dance that will continue throughout the confirmation hearing.

The next step is to schedule the Senate confirmation hearing. This involves making sure all the documents have been delivered and all the committee staff questions have been answered and then working to get time on the calendar. Any controversy related to the nominee can slow down this process, especially if the opposition party controls the committee.

With a hearing date finally on the calendar, we set up the murder board. The Sherpa identifies ten to fifteen people, usually within the department, who have special subject matter knowledge. These people are often a mix of political appointees and career officials. A mock hearing room is created, and each person stands in for a member of the Senate Committee. There is usually a dais, nameplates, a hearing table, and microphones. There are low chairs for the nominee, so they feel small. High chairs are used for the mock senators, so the nominee feels even smaller. And then you hit the nominee with tough questions for four to five hours. The tougher you can make the murder board, the more prepared a nominee is for unanticipated hostility or trick questions in the actual confirmation hearing.

The day of the confirmation hearing can be great—with the nominee's family dressed like it's Easter, with friendly faces all around, and expectations of an early lunch. Or it can go badly—with expectations of one set of unanswerable questions after another; the family's Easter clothes covered in tears, and unabated tension for hours on end.

And then the hearing is over. Often, members of the committee will submit written questions for the record and a small team of policy experts and the Sherpa will work with the nominee to help him or her answer all the questions and get him or her returned to committee staff within forty-eight hours. Again, the trick is to be responsive without locking in the nominee to policy decisions that could be contrary to the president's agenda. Sometimes nominees receive only a handful of written questions, and sometimes they get hundreds of pages.

The next phase of the process can be tough for nominees. Their lives are effectively on hold both professionally and personally. Decisions about work, about a spouse's work, where to live, and whether to move a family or enroll children in a new school are all paused, pending the business of the Senate that can be painstakingly slow. The committee might take a couple of weeks to report out the nomination—usually following a review of the written question responses and any necessary follow-up—and then the nomination is placed on the Executive Calendar of the full Senate.

Once on the Executive Calendar, the Sherpa works with Senate leadership staff and the White House to move the nomination by "unanimous consent." Unanimous consent (UC) is an important procedural mechanism that can clear the path for a unanimous voice vote, as long as no single member objects. To find out whether there are objections to a request for UC, the majority leader will "hotline" the item, which means sending a message out on a special telephone to all Senate offices saying that the majority leader intends to call up and pass something by UC—in this case your nomination. The message further asks that if any senator wishes to object to the UC request, he or she should contact the majority leader's office. At this point, any senator can object anonymously, effectively putting a "hold" on the nomination. Now begins the game called "whack-a-mole." The White House and the Sherpa work to find out who has the hold and what they need to do to remove the hold. Often as soon as one hold is removed, another pops up and you start again.

The power of the hold lies in the power of the filibuster. The "holding" senator is saying that he or she would object to a motion to proceed to the nomination, thereby possibly forcing a cloture vote on the motion. A cloture vote only requires a simple majority for nominees, but once "cloture" is obtained, there follows as many as thirty hours of debate before the Senate can move to a final roll call vote. And because the Senate has limited calendar time for these kinds of delays, "holds" are usually honored as if they were actual filibusters. The White House is encouraged to work out the issues with the "holding" senator so that the Senate can proceed with UC and a voice vote.

These issues to be worked out are often unrelated to the person. For example, I have seen holds placed on nominations to the Department of Energy because someone wanted to protect a naval shipyard. I have seen holds placed on nominees to the Department of Agriculture because someone wanted a water project funded and holds on a Commerce nominee because of a highway project. This phase can become highly political and add many frustrating months to the process.

And finally, if the nominee is not confirmed before the end of the congressional session (which lasts two years), then it drops off the Executive Calendar. The nomination is returned to the White House, and the whole congressional confirmation process must begin anew.

But sometimes the stars align, the "hotline" triggers no objections, and the nominee is confirmed expeditiously on a voice vote. The nominee finally gets a swearing-in ceremony, and the Sherpa moves on to the next nominee.

Chad Calvert is a former political appointee at the Department of the Interior. He also worked in both the House and the Senate. He is currently manager of governmental relations and external affairs for Noble Energy.

Refocusing on Policy Dynamics
Adam Cayton

I first became interested in the causes of policy change during the 2008–2009 financial crisis and the subsequent recession. In the fall of 2008, I was beginning my senior year of college, majoring in political science, and imagined that I knew a fair amount about the government and economy. Then the financial crisis arrived. I realized that I did not understand the relationship between the economy and the political system, nor did I understand what drives the United States (or other countries) to adopt particular policies at particular times. I had no idea what policies had created the structural problems that revealed themselves in a dramatic fashion that year, why they were adopted, or what explained the response. The following year I took a job at a nonprofit consumer credit counseling organization that, in addition to providing credit counseling and financial education, negotiated with mortgage lenders on behalf of borrowers to secure loan modifications, and participated in state and federal grant programs related to financial counseling, education, and borrower assistance. This organization interacted regularly with lenders, borrowers, and bureaucrats at different levels of government, giving me insight into how economic policy was unfolding on the ground.

I was struck by the disconnect between how politicians and reporters portrayed the American economy, the firsthand accounts I was hearing of what had caused people's financial hardship, and their experiences trying to navigate debt and income loss. Most striking was that the problems politicians treat as separate (health care, unemployment, banking regulation, social welfare policy) were deeply intertwined in people's paths into crisis. For instance, a huge proportion of our clients would have been able to continue paying mortgages and meeting other financial obligations had their savings not been spent on medical bills in the years prior to the recession. Mortgage lenders, whose profit motive should protect them from bad financial decisions, were nonetheless foreclosing on properties only to sell them at a loss when they had borrowers perfectly willing to continue making payments on the underwater mortgage, if only they could have some modification that would reduce their monthly payment. Politicians and their staff were likely hearing the same things we were (many referrals came from the office of our representative); so how did they translate this complexity into specific policies both in this case and in general?

As a graduate student looking for answers to these questions, I found that the field of congressional studies shares my confusion. There is no clear, testable explanation of policy dynamics in the United States that allows us to predict when and how policy will change with any specificity. Even if not totally attainable, this should be the central research problem in legislative studies. Until we can explain the content of the decisions reached by Congress, and ideally other legislatures, we do not have satisfactory theories of those institutions.

To be sure, congressional scholars can say a lot about policy dynamics. For instance, we know much about the legislative agenda (Baumgartner and Jones 1993), the timing of policy change (Kingdon 1984), and who gets to control the agenda (Cox and McCubbins 2005). We can explain whose proposals are more likely to pass (Krehbiel 1998; Volden and Wiseman 2014) and when public policy is more likely to move based on public opinion (Stimson, Mackuen, and Erikson 1995).

So what's missing? Even if we add all this work together, congressional scholars do not have a clear explanation, or even a theoretical conjecture, of how the law will change. Legislative scholarship supplies no theory for the content of legislation and the timing of specific policy changes. "Content" means a statement about what actions a law would require, who the targets of those actions are, and what problem it addresses. This is more informative than simply saying that policy moved "left" or "right," leaving the reader to imagine what that means.

For a start, we need measures of the content of legislation, going beyond the topics it addresses to explain the tools used to achieve policy goals. Once we have a way to compare what different bills would do, we can explain why they are proposed and why some pass and others do not. To do this it is important to think systematically about how members of Congress try to influence public policy. Why do they sometimes offer material inducements and sometimes create rules and enforcement mechanisms? Why do some actors need regulation, while others should be granted more discretion? When do they think a problem deserves study, and when do they not?

To start addressing this puzzle, I am working to create a database of the policy tools included in congressional legislation. Despite the fundamental importance of what the government does to address policy, no one has measured this dimension of bill content. So far, the data show substantial and predictable differences between the parties. For instance, between 2007 and 2012, Republicans introduced only 27 percent of spending bills but 67 percent of spending cuts. Democrats introduced 66 percent of new regulations and 77 percent of welfare bills. Using these data scholars can analyze the exceptions to the pattern to see what else, besides ideology and partisanship, influence bill content. We can also uncover the circumstances that lead different kinds of bills to pass. This kind of work should be a starting point for more direct study of policy dynamics.

References

Baumgartner, Frank R., and Bryan D. Jones. 1993. *Agendas and Instability in American Politics*. Chicago: University of Chicago Press.

Cox, Gary W., and Mathew D. McCubbins. 2005. *Setting the Agenda: Responsible Party Government in the U.S. House of Representatives*. Cambridge; New York: Cambridge University Press.

Kingdon, John W. 1984. *Agendas, Alternatives, and Public Policies*. Boston: Harper Collins.

Krehbiel, Keith. 1998. *Pivotal Politics: A Theory of U.S. Lawmaking*. Chicago: University of Chicago Press.

Stimson, James A., Michael B. Mackuen, and Robert S. Erikson. 1995. "Dynamic Representation." *American Political Science Review* 89 (3): 543–65.

Volden, Craig, and Alan E. Wiseman. 2014. *Legislative Effectiveness in the United States Congress: The Lawmakers*. Cambridge; New York: Cambridge University Press.

Adam Cayton is an assistant professor at the University of West Florida. He specializes in Congress, legislative institutions, and campaign effects. He received his MA and PhD in political science from the University of Colorado.

The Importance of Increasing Women's Representation in the U.S. Congress
Kathleen Dolan

While most Americans understand that women are under-represented in the American Congress, it is unlikely that they are fully aware of how dramatic this underrepresentation is. Women, who make up 51 percent of the U.S. population, are only 23 percent of the members of Congress (U.S. Census Bureau 2018). As a result of the 2018 midterm elections, there are 24 women senators and 105 women in the House of Representatives (Center for American Women and Politics 2018). Internationally, the United States ranks 104 out of 193 countries in terms of the percentage of the national legislature that is female (Inter-Parliamentary Union 2018). And we have to keep in mind that this 20 percent figure is an all-time high, achieved after decades of slow progress since Jeannette Rankin became the first woman to serve in Congress in 1916. If women's representation in Congress continues to increase at the current rate, it could take another one hundred years to reach gender parity.

Reaching gender parity in Congress, however long it takes, should be a goal for our nation and for our political system. Although women are in the minority in Congress, their presence matters and results in unique and tangible benefits both in terms of legislation crafted and resources delivered to their constituents. Perhaps the first, and most basic, reason that women's presence in Congress matters is that it signals a free, open, and democratic process that is the hallmark of a healthy democracy. For much of our history, women were excluded by both formal legal barriers and informal social and cultural norms. In the contemporary period, however, legal hurdles have been dismantled and social and cultural bias against women has been largely overcome (Dolan 2014; Hayes and Lawless 2015). Our democracy becomes more democratic when it is open to all and can represent the voices of all people in our society.

Reaching gender parity in Congress is also an important goal because there is significant evidence that women members of Congress do the job differently than do their male colleagues. Political scientists talk about members of Congress providing their constituents with two forms of representation: descriptive and substantive. Descriptive representation focuses on the degree to which elected officials "look like" the people they represent. It is probably hard for young girls and women to aspire to serve in Congress if they don't see any members who look like them. Women members of Congress serve as important role models for women and girls in our country, sending the message with their presence that there is a place for women in the body and in the political world. This role model effect has been seen to increase women's engagement in politics in many countries (Wolbrecht and Campbell 2007).

Substantive representation addresses the tendency legislators have to work on issues that represent the needs of particular groups or constituencies. Here we also see women members of Congress providing an important representational function. While all women members of Congress do not take the same positions on every issue, there is a substantial body of evidence that demonstrates that women legislators are more likely to take up issues that are more directly central to women's lives than are their male colleagues. For example, women members of Congress are more likely than male members to sponsor legislation that deals with sexual harassment, equal pay, family leave, sexual assault in the military, reproductive policies, and health care for women (Dodson 2006; Swers 2002). There are important differences here based on the political party of the women members, with Democratic women being much more likely than their Republican women colleagues to focus attention on gender-related policy issues and, obviously, propose more liberal policies to address these issues. Democratic and Republican women are most likely to join forces on women's health and childcare issues (Swers 2013).

Beyond the substance of the legislation they pursue, evidence suggests that women members of Congress are also more effective and active legislators than their male colleagues. For example, women members of the House bring, on average, 9 percent more federal spending to their districts than do male members and are more likely to sponsor and cosponsor legislation and make more floor speeches addressing their legislative agenda (Anzia and Berry 2011; Pearson and Dancey 2011). So it is clear that there are benefits to constituents when they are represented by these hardworking members of Congress.

Women's integration as members of Congress has been relatively slow, but the pace has increased since 1992. In most election years, we see an increase in the number of women who stand as candidates for Congress and an increase in the number of women elected. This was clearly the case in the 2018 election. In reaction to the gendered nature of the 2016 presidential election, the #MeToo movement, and President Trump's treatment of women's issues, women were motivated to run in historically high numbers. In the 2018 midterms, 476 women filed to run for the House of Representatives, a 60 percent increase over the previous record of 298 women who ran in 2012. The 53 women who filed to run for the Senate was a 33 percent increase over the 40 women who ran in 2016. Almost half of these declared candidates won their primary elections, resulting in 235 women running in the general election for the House and 22 running for the Senate. In the end, women were 23 percent of the candidates for Congress in 2018 and are now 23 percent of the membership of the 116th Congress.

While the election of 2018 was an important one for increasing women's representation in Congress, there are two important realities to recognize. First, there is a significant and problematic partisan gap among women candidates for Congress. Among the 257 women who ran in general elections for the two chambers, 77 percent did so as Democrats. Of the 125 women serving in the current 116th Congress, 105 are

Democrats. That women candidates and officeholders are overwhelmingly Democrats is a reality we have seen for many years now. There is a good deal of evidence to suggest that Republican women have a harder time winning primary and general elections than do Democratic women. Republican Party leaders and voters are still less supportive of women candidates than are Democratic Party officials and voters. This is a serious problem for the goal of increasing women's representation because it inhibits the opportunities for Republican women. Women can only achieve so much if they can only be truly competitive in one of the two major political parties.

The second reality about women's representation in Congress is that, even in years when the number of women candidates reaches historic levels, women candidates are still swamped by the number of men who run for Congress. Ironically, in 2018, a record number of men ran for Congress, almost 30 percent more than ran in 2016. So, while the absolute number of women who ran in 2018 increased, their proportion of the total candidate pool was the same as in recent elections. Women can't be expected to become a larger proportion of the members of Congress if they aren't a larger proportion of the candidate pool.

Indeed, the key to increasing women's representation in any elected body is increasing the number of women who are willing to run (Lawless and Fox 2010). So efforts to recruit, train, and fund more women candidates are the keys to making the American Congress a more diverse and representative institution.

References

Anzia, Sarah, and Christopher Berry. 2011. "The Jackie (and Jill) Robinson Effect: Why Do Congresswomen Outperform Congressmen?" *American Journal of Political Science* 55: 478–93.

Center for American Women and Politics. 2018. *Women in U.S. Congress 2018*. Eagleton Institute of Politics, Rutgers University.

Dodson, Debra. 2006. *The Impact of Women in Congress*. New York: Oxford University Press.

Dolan, Kathleen. 2014. *When Does Gender Matter? Women Candidates and Gender Stereotypes in American Elections*. New York: Oxford University Press.

Hayes, Danny, and Jennifer Lawless. 2015. "A Non-Gendered Lens? Media, Voters, and Female Candidates in Contemporary Congressional Elections." *Perspectives on Politics* 13: 95–118.

Inter-Parliamentary Union. 2018. *Women in National Parliaments*. http://archive.ipu.org/wmn-e/classif.htm

Lawless, Jennifer, and Richard Fox. 2010. *It Still Takes a Candidate: Why Women Don't Run for Office*. New York: Cambridge University Press.

Pearson, Kathryn, and Logan Dancey. 2011. "Speaking for the Underrepresented in the House of Representatives: Voicing Women's Interests in a Partisan Era." *Politics & Gender* 7: 493–519.

Swers, Michele. 2002. *The Difference Women Make: The Policy Impact of Women in Congress*. Chicago: University of Chicago Press.

Swers, Michele. 2013. *Women in the Club: Gender and Policy Making in the Senate*. Chicago: University of Chicago Press.

U.S. Census Bureau. 2018. *Quick Facts: United States*. https://www.census.gov/quickfacts/fact/table/US/LFE046216

Wolbrecht, Christina, and David Campbell. 2007. "Leading by Example: Female Members of Parliament as Political Role Models." *American Journal of Political Science* 51: 92139.

Kathleen Dolan is a distinguished professor and chair of the Department of Political Science, the University of Wisconsin–Milwaukee. She earned her PhD in political science from the

University of Maryland. She specializes in Congress, election and voting, and women and politics. She is author of When Does Gender Matter? *(Oxford University Press, 2014) and* Voting for Women *(Westview Press, 2004).*

Effective Tribal Advocacy: Sovereignty + Grassroots + Substance + Money
Danna R. Jackson, Esq.

If You Can Afford It, Work on the Hill

That was the career advice given to me—a young Indian lawyer—by a prominent Indian lawyer—who had already bought the "partner house" in a lovely suburb of Washington, D.C., and secretly longed for grittier times. Shortly thereafter, I caught my break. Senator Tim Johnson (D-SD) sought a lawyer to handle his committee work for the Senate Committee on Indian Affairs and was kind enough to hire me. I had a front-row seat to sausage making.

My prominent Indian lawyer friend had given me great advice—my tenure on the Hill was a blast. I was personally and professionally fulfilled. But alas! I had my first child, and I needed to find a job where I could afford to pay off my student loans plus contemplate saving for my baby's future. After three and a half years, I landed at a large law firm where I represented tribes. It is from both these perspectives that I provide my view.

Indian Tribes—Not Just Another Interest Group

When distinguishing interest groups, the most fundamental concept to understand about tribes is that they are sovereign governments that possess powers of self-government that pre-existed the United States. When interpreting the meaning of tribal sovereignty, Chief Justice John Marshall of the U.S. Supreme Court held that tribes have full jurisdiction over on-reservation activities, to the exclusion of state law (see *Johnson v. M'Intosh* 21 U.S. 543, 1823). In separate decisions, Marshall found that tribes' sovereign powers are retained unless relinquished through treaty or expressly limited by the plenary power of the American Congress (*Cherokee Nation v. Georgia*, 30 U.S. 1, 1831; *Worcester v. Georgia*, 31 U.S. 515, 1832). Marshall also described tribes as "dependent, domestic nations," and in so doing, the Court established the trust relationship between the United States and tribes.

So, while tribes have governments, their own laws, and court systems, tribal authority, status, and jurisdiction continue to be amended and evolve through congressional acts, executive orders, and court decisions.

Indian people are also racially distinct, but that is not what defines an Indian person under the law. An Indian person belongs to a political body—a tribal nation (*Morton v. Mancari*, 417 U.S. 535, 1974).

Thus, when a tribal nation representative requests a meeting on the Hill, protocol demands that a staffer approach it with the respect it deserves—as a government-to-government engagement.

Observations of Effective Lobbying by Tribes and Tribal People

As described earlier, tribes have a distinct status that should, on its own, provide them a leg up when vying for attention on the national stage. From my experiences, the most effective lobbying efforts do not just rely on tribes' status as a sovereign. To be effective, tribes also must engage in other ways: with grassroots efforts, with reliable substance, and through political giving.

Grassroots Power Can Lead the Way

Tribal grassroots organizers may or may not have resources to lobby Congress directly. But grassroots members can instigate a flood of constituent letters and/or request in-state meetings with members and staff. Also, grassroots members are very good at finding other organizations and allies to forward the message. Additionally, grassroots members vote. Critically important, grassroots members lobby their tribal heads of state. Individuals can influence Congress, but if a tribal governmental representative is carrying the same message in a government-to-government context, the effort is compounded exponentially.

For example, the Violence Against Women Act (VAWA) was reauthorized in 2013 (Pub. L. No. 113–4). Included in this act was an Indian title that provides a number of tools that enable law enforcement, courts, prosecutors, and advocates get at the problem of domestic violence in Indian country. Grassroots tribal victim advocates effectively launched an informational campaign. But only after tribal victim advocates demanded that their tribal governments make violence against women a priority, and the tribal heads directly told Congress and other federal representatives of that priority, did laws and policy change. VAWA 2013 is the most prosovereignty legislation that I have seen in modern times. For example, VAWA 2013 authorizes tribal courts to assert jurisdiction over non-Indian perpetrators of domestic violence. This means that for the first time in decades, tribes can handle certain felonies and crimes of domestic violence in their own systems and on their own turf.

Substance Matters

Grassroots energy is critical to an effective lobby effort but only if it is paired with substantive information and data. An effective lobby effort is armed with "white sheets." The white sheet may be accompanied by reports and data, but good information, distilled into a concise one or two-page report, may be the only thing the member of Congress has time to digest. An effective lobbyist knows what type of information needs to be transmitted to the Hill and when it needs to land. It is critical that the transmitter (lobbyist) be a trusted, honest, and reliable source. To that end, an effective lobby effort knows the detractors and is candid about the barriers.

As a lawyer or lobbyist, I knew when I needed to bring in a tribal leader to have the government-to-government meeting or ask the grassroots allies to engage, but I also stood ready to produce any amount of substantive and credible information on which lawmakers could comfortably rely.

Monetary Contributions

Finally, I cannot write about Washington without writing about money. In recent years, tribes have become powerhouses in the world of political contributions (Center for Responsive Politics, n.d.). According to Open Secrets, in the 2018 election cycle, tribes have contributed over $11 million—a remarkable sum given that 2018 is not a presidential year. Most of the contributions are given to individuals. Not dissimilar to a Fortune 500 company, tribes are giving at epic levels. Why should tribes give at this level?

"History has demonstrated time and time again that failure to engage politically results in catastrophic policies against Native people and our inherent tribal rights," said Pechanga tribal chairman Mark Macarro (Sultan 2017). In other words, some tribal leaders do not want to leave policy to chance.

Not all tribes want or can participate in the political process through monetary contributions, nor should they. Similarly, not all tribes have the ability to benefit from a grassroots effort. Good outcomes can come even if tribes do not have all the elements of effective lobbying, listed earlier. But in a perfect scenario, sovereignty + grassroots energy + substantive data + money = better political outcomes for tribes.

References

Center for Responsive Politics. n.d. "Indian Gaming." https://www.opensecrets.org/industries/indus.php?ind=G6550

Sultan, Niv M. 2017. "Tribal Battles Make for Well-Fed Lobbyists." Center for Responsive Politics, May 31. https://www.opensecrets.org/news/2017/05/tribal-battles-well-fed-lobbyists/

Danna R. Jackson, Esq., is chief legal counsel, Montana Department of Natural Resources and Conservation. She earned her law degree from the Montana School of Law. She previously served in the U.S. Attorney's Office and as a U.S. Senate staffer.

The President and the Congress
Joshua Kennedy

"It's going to be so easy," then candidate Donald Trump said of replacing the Affordable Care Act (ACA) during the 2016 campaign (Lanktree and Lillywhite 2017). A central plank of the Republican agenda since the passage of the ACA in 2010, the new president immediately took aim at the law upon his inauguration, and with Republicans in control of Congress, fulfilling this promise seemed eminently attainable. But within a month, President Trump had quickly changed his tune from the one he carried during the campaign. "Nobody knew that health care could be so complicated," he lamented in February 2017. No repeal followed, and two years into his administration, the president's prospects of fulfilling this pledge, and that of the Republican Party, were no brighter.

President Trump may be unique among American presidents because of his lack of governmental experience prior to assuming the office, but frustration in dealing with Congress is a phenomenon to which all modern presidents can relate. Of course, having legislative majorities helps (especially in an era where the parties are increasingly polarized), but even this is not a guarantee of success; its partisan motives aside, Congress is a unique institution with its own preferences, and these do not definitionally line up with the president's preferences, even when the same party controls both institutions (e.g., Moe 1989; Pfiffner 1988). The president's veto helps too; it can serve as a powerful tool of bargaining leverage under the right circumstances (e.g., Cameron 2000).

But presidents have another advantage over Congress: their ability to dominate news coverage and draw public attention. The "bully pulpit" that Theodore Roosevelt so famously referenced provides unique opportunities to the occupant of the White House to exert leverage over the other branches of government. This practice is known among political scientists as the art of "going public," which Samuel Kernell (2007: 1–2) defines as "a strategy whereby a president promotes himself and his policies in Washington by appealing directly to the American public for support."

The logic is straightforward: because members of Congress are principally motivated by a desire to be reelected (e.g., Mayhew 1974), if the president can win public support for his program, legislators should feel more pressured to assent for the sake of their seats. But how effective are these efforts? Is going public truly a means of winning support for an agenda, or is it mostly a distraction from the more formal aspects of the presidency that contribute most directly to success?

The Bully Pulpit and the Limitations of Going Public

The link between public approval and presidential support in Congress appears clear, but a closer read of events and research cast doubts on the viability of this strategy. President Clinton's famous pledge to veto any health-care reform bill that failed to meet his stated goals ultimately led to no bill at all, despite initial public support (e.g., Kernell 2007). President George W. Bush made reform of Social Security a principal plank of his second-term agenda and immediately moved forward with an extensive push based around "going public" early in 2005, but as with Clinton's health-care initiative, the push was unsuccessful (e.g., Kernell 2007). Following the tragic school shooting in Newtown, Connecticut, that killed twenty-six (twenty of whom were children), public support for expanded background checks topped 90 percent (*Washington Post* 2013), but President Obama's efforts to shepherd such legislation through Congress ultimately ended in failure.

Indeed, much political science research buttresses these anecdotal claims. For one, the strategy seems to depend in large measure on being able to move public opinion in the first place, but evidence that presidents have such influence is lacking (e.g., Edwards 2003). Other research has used presidential approval as a proxy for whether public support of the administration pushes legislators to be more inclined to support the president, with only weak or marginal results (e.g., Bond and Fleisher 1990; Edwards 1989; Kennedy 2016).

Given these findings, wouldn't it make sense for presidents to drop the strategy altogether? After all, results would suggest that this is an ineffective method for moving public opinion or for swaying the votes of members of Congress. And yet there are certain advantages conferred by going public that are more indirect, and which speak to the utility of the strategy as a method for influencing Congress even in the absence of broad shifts in public opinion.

Brandice Canes-Wrone (2006) has written what is perhaps the definitive account of how going public matters from an operational perspective. Her research posits that previous conceptions of the effects of going public on presidential success in Congress are too broadly focused or not mindful enough of how additional factors complicate the relatively straightforward process, which makes the notion of the bully pulpit so appealing. As such, Canes-Wrone's theory argues that, for a given issue, both salience (i.e., how prevalent is this issue in the minds of the public?) and preexisting sentiment (i.e., is this an issue the public already supports?) condition the degree to which going public can serve as an effective strategy.

The gist of her findings is this: presidents are most effective at using public sentiment as leverage in negotiating with Congress when the White House strategically focuses on those items for which there is some degree of underlying enthusiasm in the broader citizenry already. This is not equivalent to "leading by the polls"; presidents are not required to change their opinions to match public sentiment but rather are incentivized to pick those issues that *both* they and the broader citizenry care about. By doing so, presidents put Congress on the defensive and force them to either go against broader public sentiment or back down and support the president. If we think of politics as a "game" in the theoretical sense, this represents an opportunity for the president to make the first move, and moving first to force your opposition into a defensive posture is critically effective in politics (and a host of other types of "games," of course).

Indeed, the picture Canes-Wrone paints largely fits in with existing conceptions that what makes a president successful is the ability to adopt an appropriate strategy for the circumstance (e.g., Edwards 2009; Pfiffner 1988). While many are predisposed to assume that presidents are powerful simply by definition (they are the president, after all), Richard Neustadt ([1960] 1990: 11) captured the reality when he famously asserted that "presidential power is the power to persuade." But persuasion comes in many forms, and if presidents find that traditional methods of bargaining with Congress are not yielding fruitful results, they can, in the right instance, bring the public into the arena on the side of the White House. Like presidential power broadly, how presidents interact with Congress is a complex and multifaceted process, and the circumstances determine the winning strategy.

References

Bond, Jon R., and Richard Fleisher. 1990. *The President in the Legislative Arena.* Chicago: University of Chicago Press.

Cameron, Charles M. 2000. *Veto Bargaining: Presidents and the Politics of Negative Power.* New York: Cambridge University Press.

Canes-Wrone, Brandice. 2006. *Who Leads Whom? Presidents, Policy, and the Public.* Chicago: University of Chicago Press.

Edwards, George C., III. 1989. *At the Margins: Presidential Leadership of Congress.* New Haven, CT: Yale University Press.

Edwards, George C., III. 2003. *On Deaf Ears: The Limits of the Bully Pulpit.* New Haven, CT: Yale University Press.

Edwards, George C., III. 2009. *The Strategic President: Persuasion & Opportunity in Presidential Leadership.* Princeton, NJ: Princeton University Press.

Kennedy, Joshua B. 2016. "Does Congress Care about the President's Popularity? Limitations on Presidential Prestige and the Power of Persuasion." *White House Studies* 13 (3): 269–84.

Kernell, Samuel. 2007. *Going Public: New Strategies of Presidential Leadership.* Washington, D.C.: Congressional Quarterly Press.

Lanktree, Graham, and James Lillywhite. 2017. "Watch Donald Trump Change His Tune from Easy to Difficult on Repealing Obamacare." *Newsweek*, July 20. https://www.newsweek.com/easy-difficult-watch-donald-trump-change-his-tune-repealing-obamacare-639782

Mayhew, David R. 1974. *Congress: The Electoral Connection.* New Haven, CT: Yale University Press.

Moe, Terry. 1989. "The Politics of Bureaucratic Structure." In *Can the Government Govern?* edited by John E. Chubb and Paul E. Peterson, 267–329. Washington, D.C.: Brookings Institution Press.

Neustadt, Richard E. (1960) 1990. *Presidential Power and the Modern Presidents.* New York: The Free Press. Page reference is to the 1990 edition.

Pfiffner, James P. 1988. *The Strategic Presidency: Hitting the Ground Running.* Chicago: The Dorsey Press.

Washington Post. 2013. "Q: Would You Support or Oppose a Law Requiring Background Checks on People Buying Guns at Gun Shows?" April 12. https://www.washingtonpost.com/page/2010-2019/WashingtonPost/2013/03/12/National-Politics/Polling/question_10030.xml?tid=a_inl_manual

Joshua Kennedy is an assistant professor of political science at Georgia Southern University. He specializes in American politics with a particular focus on the presidency. He received his PhD in political science from the University of Colorado.

Ideology in Congress
Verlan Lewis

Perhaps the most striking characteristic of the contemporary American Congress is its historically low approval ratings. Since 1973, Gallup has surveyed Americans on whether they have a "great deal," "quite a lot," "some," "very little," or no trust in a variety of American institutions, including banks, the medical system, the military, newspapers, public schools, "big business," organized labor, organized religion, the presidency, the Supreme Court, and Congress. Among these institutions, Congress has by far the lowest approval rating: just 11 percent of Americans expressed a "great deal" or "quite a lot" of trust in Congress in 2018 (Gallup, 2018).

The social scientists and journalists who have tried to explain this phenomenon often point to ideological polarization in Congress as a key source of its declining popularity. According to this narrative, party polarization has led to extreme policies and the erosion of democracy (Hacker & Pierson, 2005), socioeconomic inequality (McCarty, Poole, & Rosenthal, 2006), dysfunctional politics (Mann & Ornstein, 2008), and gridlock and institutional failure (Mann & Ornstein, 2012). Beyond the polarization literature, congressional scholars, in general, have increasingly turned to ideology as the key concept in a new "master theory" of political science (Hacker & Pierson, 2014). As Frances Lee has documented, almost half of all major political science journal articles, and over 80 percent of articles on Congress, refer to ideology (Lee 2009). Unfortunately, political scientists, in general, fundamentally misunderstand what ideology is and what it does. As a result, an entire superstructure of political science research is seriously flawed. This essay will show how political scientists currently misunderstand the role of ideology in Congress and point to how we can improve our understanding of it.

The Liberal Conservative Myth and the American Congress

The problem with the congressional party polarization literature is that it is based on the Liberal Conservative Myth (LCM). The LCM is the mistaken view held by many people that political history can be meaningfully described as the movement of individuals and groups, including political parties, on an ideological, spatial spectrum frozen in time. This spatial spectrum consists of static ideological dimensions that run from "liberal" to "conservative," or "left" to "right," and whose meanings are fixed and unchanging. This view came to prominence among social scientists in the 1950s with the publication of Anthony Downs's *An Economic Theory of Democracy* (1957). However, it took forty years, until the creation of DW-NOMINATE by Keith Poole and Howard Rosenthal, to make this approach to the study of Congress ubiquitous (1997). Once political scientists could assign, so they thought, a numeric value to the ideological preference point of each member of Congress (values range from the most liberal, –1, to the most conservative, +1), they decided to try to explain more and more congressional behavior using their index of ideology scores. It was only a matter of time until political scientists and journalists, alike, were using DW-NOMINATE scores to explain congressional gridlock and dysfunction: if members of Congress were voting increasingly lockstep with their copartisans, and rarely crossing the aisle, this must be a result of increasingly polarized ideological preference points. The contributions of Downs, Poole, and Rosenthal have caused congressional scholarship to be dominated by a rational-choice, or political economic, approach. While applying the methodological lens of economics to the study of Congress has yielded many important insights, the development of a monolithic methodological approach has created some blind spots as well (Bensel 2016; Caughey and Schickler 2016; Lee 2009, 2016).

For example, the congressional party polarization literature claims that, on average, Democrats in Congress have moved to the "left," and Republicans in Congress have moved, even farther, to the "right" since the 1930s and that this causes gridlock, dysfunction, and institutional failure. In reality, this is a confusing way to describe the political history of Congress because, over this same time period, the very meanings of "liberalism" and "conservatism" ("left" and "right") themselves have changed significantly. In the postwar era, the "liberal" and "conservative" issue positions on foreign policy, tax policy, racial policy, military spending, trade policy, and virtually every other issue area have changed significantly—sometimes multiple times. Thus, it makes no sense to claim that the Democratic Party in Congress has become more "liberal" or that the Republican Party in Congress has become more "conservative" in recent decades (Lewis, 2019). This blind spot in the scholarly literature undermines the vast congressional party polarization literature because it is largely built upon a shaky foundation. Congressional scholars can improve our understanding of ideology in Congress by drawing on insights from other disciplines and methodologies, including intellectual history, social psychology, and historical institutionalism.

Uncivil Agreement in Congress

One important recent finding from the social psychology literature has shown that, over the past half century, the American electorate has experienced behavioral, but not issue-based, polarization (Mason, 2018). In other words, even though Americans today do not hold more extreme issue positions than they did in previous decades, they do harbor, and act upon, more hostility toward their partisan and ideological opponents. If we apply this idea to the American Congress, we find the same thing. DW-NOMINATE scores notwithstanding, members of Congress do not hold more extreme issue positions than they did in previous decades. However, they do act in more hostile ways toward their partisan opponents. Thus, rational-choice scholars have confused increasingly partisan roll call voting behavior with increasingly extreme ideological preference points.

As my own historical, institutional, and intellectual history research has shown, because the very meanings of "liberalism" and "conservatism" have changed drastically over the past fifty years, it makes no sense to describe the Democratic Party in Congress as moving to the "extreme left" and the Republican Party in Congress as moving to the "extreme right." If we actually look at the content of the roll call votes that DW-NOMINATE calculates, we find that Democrats today are not calling for higher tax rates than Democrats in the 1940s, Republicans today are not calling for lower federal spending levels than Republicans in the 1940s, Democrats today are not calling for more corporate regulation than Democrats in the 1950s–1960s, Republicans today are not calling for more traditional marriage laws than Republicans in the 1990s, and so on. It is not that issue positions have become more extreme in recent decades, but that behavior has become more uncivil.

Conclusion

Once we move beyond the LCM, and once we distinguish between issue-based and behavioral polarization, we can better understand how ideology actually operates in Congress. Once we understand that issue positions have not become more extreme in Congress over time, then we can recognize that ideological tribalism is the source of misbehavior by members of Congress rather than ideological preference points. As long as political scientists and journalists focus on "extreme" issue positions, they will miss the real source of problems in Congress, and members of Congress will never change their behavior in the way that reformers wish. However, if we can recognize the pathologies caused by ideological tribalism and the LCM, then we might just have some success in rehabilitating Americans' trust in their national legislature.

References

Bensel, R. 2016, October. "Lost in Translation: An Epistemological Exploration of the Relation between Historical Analysis and the NOMINATE Algorithm." *Studies in American Political Development* 30 (2): 185–201.

Caughey, D., and E. Schickler. 2016, October. "Substance and Change in Congressional Ideology: NOMINATE and Its Alternatives." *Studies in American Political Development* 30 (2): 128–46.

Downs, A. 1957. *An Economic Theory of Democracy*. New York: Harper and Row.

Hacker, J. S., and P. Pierson. 2005. *Off Center: The Republican Revolution and the Erosion of American Democracy*. New Haven, CT: Yale University Press.

Hacker, J. S., and P. Pierson. 2014, September. "After the 'Master Theory': Downs, Schattschneider, and the Rebirth of Policy-Focused Analysis." *Perspectives on Politics* 12 (3): 643–62.

Lee, F. E. 2009. *Beyond Ideology: Politics, Principles, and Partisanship in the U.S. Senate*. Chicago: University of Chicago Press.

Lee, F. E. 2016, October. "Patronage, Logrolls, and 'Polarization': Congressional Parties of the Gilded Age, 1876–1896." *Studies in American Political Development* 30 (2): 116–27.

Lewis, V. 2019. *Ideas of Power: The Politics of American Party Ideology Development*. New York: Cambridge University Press.

Mann, T. E., and N. J. Ornstein. 2008. *The Broken Branch: How Congress Is Failing America and How to Get It Back on Track*. New York: Oxford University Press.

Mann, T. E., and N. J. Ornstein. 2012. *It's Even Worse That It Looks*. New York: Basic Books.

Mason, L. 2018. *Uncivil Agreement: How Politics Became Our Identity*. Chicago: University of Chicago Press.

McCarty, N., K. T. Poole, and H. Rosenthal. 2006. *Polarized America: The Dance of Ideology and Unequal Riches*. Cambridge: MIT Press.

Poole, K. T., and H. Rosenthal. 1997. *Congress: A Political-Economic History of Roll-Call Voting*. New York: Oxford University Press.

Verlan Lewis is an assistant professor of political science at the University of Colorado, Colorado Springs. He specializes in American political parties. He is author of the forthcoming book: Ideas of Power *(Cambridge University Press, 2019).*

A Legacy of Women on Capitol Hill: Legislation and Leadership
Summer Mersinger

At a baby shower for a friend, I found myself in a discussion with a group of women—some mothers, others not, but all who either work or had worked in Congress—discussing a recent moment in the U.S. Senate heralded in the press as history in the making. On April 19, 2018, Senator Tammy Duckworth (D-IL) carried her infant daughter to the Senate floor during a confirmation vote for the new NASA administrator. Previously children were barred from visiting the Senate floor, something the House of Representatives allows, and this seemingly minor act of carrying a baby into the Senate Chamber became a symbol for the evolution of women serving in this institution (Hamedy and Diaz 2019).

As momentous as this event seemed, the discussion among the group of women that day actually revolved around alternative options available so that the baby was not present for the Senate vote. While it seems a group of women, some even mothers, might embrace this as a major development and see it as a huge step forward for women, many in the group wondered what was the point and why did it signify some sort of victory for women.

We all held very similar views on the matter, including those women who had their own children. The Senate floor is the place where the great debate of equality occurred and where women's suffrage led to the creation of the Nineteenth Amendment to our Constitution allowing women to vote in our great democracy. So why should we, as women, celebrate someone bringing their infant to the Senate floor? Was that really some sort of victory for women?

Setting aside those questions and the entire matter of a baby in the Senate, I think we would all agree that Senator Duckworth's accomplishments should not be defined by being the first woman to bring an infant to the Senate floor. Rather her more important legacy includes being one of the first women to fly combat missions as a helicopter pilot in the Iraq War during which time she suffered severe injuries after her Blackhawk was shot down, resulting in the loss of her legs. Overcoming any setback from her injuries, she went on to pursue a career in the government focusing on our veterans and eventually launched her political career first as a member of the U.S. House of Representatives and eventually as a U.S. senator. Senator Duckworth speaks three languages, has a PhD, still flies planes as a civilian, and is a mother to two daughters ("About Tammy," n.d.). At the end of the day, bringing her infant daughter onto the Senate floor pales into insignificance when compared to her other notable accomplishments.

Let's not forget the fact that Senator Duckworth is one of twenty-three women serving the U.S. Senate ("Women in the Senate," n.d.). This number is not at all representative of the

50 percent of the female population in the United States (actu-ally the 2010 U.S. Census showed that number as 50.8 percent female versus 49.2 percent male) (Howden and Meyer 2011). However, this number has definitely increased throughout the history of the Senate, with almost half of the total num-ber of female senators currently serving in the 115th Congress ("Women in the Senate," n.d.).

Female senators are not the only trailblazers in the institu-tion. In a traditionally male-dominated field, female staffers likewise hold a number of high-level, senior positions of lead-ership in Congress. Working day to day in buildings where women are still fighting for restroom equity (McKeon 2011), the expansion of female influence in the halls of Congress is a notable development in our recent history.

If someone did a study on personality traits of senior female staff in congressional offices, I think they would find a number of similarities. These women are not only assertive and per-sistent but also reasonable and caring. They are mentors and teachers—finding the talent in those around them and using that talent for the good of the organization. There are women not afraid to tackle a tough issue and gracefully accept the credit they deserve, but those same women quickly acknowledge the contributions of others sharing the credit. These women have high expectations for those they work with day to day but not as high as the expectations they place on themselves. They do not waste time with unnecessary compliments but provide pos-itive feedback when earned and constructive feedback when warranted. They face issues head-on, do not run away from the conflict, and constantly make compromises, expecting those around them to do the same. Party affiliations aside, many of the senior female staff in Congress share these characteristics.

It is not unusual for me to receive an email or a call from a young woman on Capitol Hill in a senior position who is start-ing a family. The question is always the same: "How did you do it?" By "it" they are referring to the fact that I managed to give birth to (and keep alive) four children while serving in a senior position for a U.S. senator. As these young women anticipate hearing advice that is the holy grail of balancing a career and motherhood, my usual response is probably closer to "I still have no idea how I did it." I'm probably not the only female Senate staff member with children who feels this way.

Yet many women in these senior positions not only survive the struggles of balancing family life and work life but, more importantly, they also thrive while being held to the same standards and expectations as their male counterparts. It is not always easy and often requires some quick, and creative, actions and decisions, as well as a willingness to ask for help when needed.

Case in point, returning from maternity leave after the birth of my third child in 2010, a major piece of legislation harmful to an important company in my home state was on the Senate floor for debate. Senate offices are relatively small, lacking privacy of any kind, so pumping breast milk for my babies involved walking to another location in a different building from my office. As a sidenote here, the first room designated solely for breastfeeding in the U.S. Senate office buildings was completed in 2006 just in time of the birth of my first child (Linderman 2017). Every day, I made my pilgrimage to and from the "spa," as my coworkers had coined the designated lactation rooms, at least three times a day.

This particular morning I had a narrow window between meetings to visit the lactation room. About five minutes after arriving and getting setup, my cell phone rang. I was needed on the Senate floor as soon as possible. Acting quickly, I "unhooked," grabbed my stuff to leave the lactation room, and asked another staff member to meet me near the door to the Capitol with my staff ID. Once at the meeting point, she handed me my ID, and I, in turn, handed her a small black cooler quickly blurting out "Here, take my breast milk." Without question, she grabbed the bag and headed back to the office while I started jogging (while wearing heels) to the Senate floor.

In hindsight, I could have sent someone else familiar with the issue to the Senate floor or maybe even just told the senator that it was not a good time. However, at the time I did not hesitate. The senator requested my presence on the floor, so that is where I needed to be at that moment. While I refused to ask someone else to go to the Senate floor in my place, I was not afraid to ask for help with something as personal as transporting my breast milk.

Over the years, I often joked that I could run circles around my male colleagues with little more than three hours of sleep. I learned to be efficient, how to delegate, and how to prioritize. While others in the office might spend an hour or more reading the daily news, I had it down to twenty minutes. If it took someone a couple of hours to write a speech, I could crank one out in thirty minutes or find someone to help so my part only took thirty minutes. I was always determined to keep up regardless of the constraints on my time both in and out of the office. I know many other women in senior positions on Capitol Hill approach their work in the same way.

Recently I had the privilege of hearing Justice Ruth Bader Ginsburg speak about her career and her time as a Supreme Court justice. She made so many profound statements and shared numerous stories about landmark gender equality cases. However, the most amazing statement she made was while discussing the collegial working relations on the Supreme Court. In her fight with colorectal cancer, she mentioned that she never missed a day of hearings. She made this statement in reference to the late chief justice William Rehnquist who she said went out of his way to accommodate her during treatment. Yet, it was a piece of advice she received from Justice Sandra Day O'Connor that truly epitomized the grit of these two pioneering women on the Supreme Court. Justice O'Connor, a breast cancer survivor, told Justice Ginsburg to schedule her chemotherapy for Fridays so that she could deal with the side effects over the weekend and be back to work on Monday.

Maybe Senator Duckworth bringing her infant daughter to a vote on the Senate floor is a monumental event worth documenting in our history books. But to me, it was just an example of how women working in the halls of Congress operate, always finding a way to make things work and taking the initiative to ask for help and doing things differently in order to succeed.

References

"About Tammy." n.d. U.S. Senate. https://www.duckworth .senate.gov/about-tammy/biography

Hamedy, Saba, and Daniella Diaz. 2019. "Sen. Duckworth Makes History, Casts Vote with Baby on Senate Floor." CNN Politics, April 20. https://www.cnn.com/2018/04/19/ politics/tammy-duckworth-baby-senate-floor/index.html

Howden, Lindsay H., and Julie A. Meyer. 2011. "Age and Sex Composition: 2010." U.S. Census Bureau, 2010 Census Briefs, May.

Linderman, Juliet. 2017. "How Women in Congress Have Fought for Equal Treatment within the Hall of Capitol Hill." *Christian Science Monitor*, November 3.

McKeon, Nancy. 2011. "Women in the House Get a Restroom." *Washington Post*, July 28.

"Women in the Senate." n.d. U.S. Senate. https://www.senate .gov/artandhistory/history/common/briefing/women_ senators.htm

Summer Mersinger is senior vice president of the Smith-Free Group. She was a top staff aide for fifteen years to U.S. Senator John Thune (R-SD). She previously served as director of government relations at the D.C. law firm Arent Fox. She earned her JD from Columbus School of Law, Catholic University, and a BA in political science from the University of Minnesota.

The Marginalization of Congress
Christina G. Villegas

On the eve of the ratification of the Constitution, James Madison (1788) declared that "in republican government, the legislative authority necessarily predominates." In fact, Congress enjoyed such high public esteem that Madison worried that the nation—without the implementation of proper checks and balances—would succumb to legislative tyranny. It is, thus, quite remarkable that the country's most representative institution has deteriorated into the most loathed branch of the federal government. Low public approval ratings now perpetually plague Congress as a whole, and members of Congress, themselves, frequently express disgust at their own collective inability to pass a budget or forge meaningful compromise on issues like health care, immigration, entitlement reform, and government spending.

Mainstream scholars most commonly attribute Congress's institutional failures and its decline in esteem to ideological polarization and hyperpartisanship, which they contend result in incivility and gridlock. Such scholars tend to place most of the blame on congressional Republicans, arguing that in recent years the party's standard bearers have become "ideologically extreme; contemptuous of the inherited social and economic policy regime; scornful of compromise; unpersuaded by conventional understanding of facts, evidence, and science; and dismissive of the legitimacy of its political opposition" (Mann and Ornstein 2016: xxiv). Recent polling data suggest, however, that both parties have moved away from the center and that the deep ideological division within Congress mirrors the fact that voters themselves are becoming more reliably conservative and liberal (Kiley 2017).

While the deepening ideological divide among the public at large has undoubtedly contributed to incivility and gridlock within Congress, congressional scholar Frances Lee (2009) nevertheless observes that—aside from the 1960s and 1970s when congressional consensus was maintained by Democratic supermajorities—"intense partisan conflict has been the norm" (19–20). Thus, it seems that partisan polarization is not solely responsible for Congress's lessening influence in the constitutional constellation and its declining image in American public opinion. Over the past half century, two additional factors have contributed to the growing marginalization of Congress: the demotion of Congress from a lawmaking institution into an organ of the administrative state and the corresponding rise of executive prominence.

The conversion of Congress from the central branch of government into just another component of the administrative state can be traced back to the mid-twentieth century when theorists and politicians alike embraced the view that Congress is ill suited to respond to the regulatory demands of modern life. Consequently, members of Congress began passing vaguely defined objectives delegating widespread legislative authority to achieve those objectives to executive departments. While abdicating its lawmaking authority in one sense, Congress simultaneously empowered itself to supervise and oversee administrative departments by decentralizing power into committees and subcommittees that specialize in the policy areas executive agencies were authorized to regulate (Postell and Postell 2018). The delegation of lawmaking power to agencies, combined with the creation of jurisdictionally specific committees, has enabled members of Congress to avoid responsibility for unpopular legislative actions and to engage in valuable reelection activities such as holding public hearings, political grandstanding, and influencing agency actions on behalf of interest groups and constituents. As a result, however, Congress has become inept at fulfilling its constitutional duty. Instead of deliberating and making tough legislative decisions on behalf of the American public, members of Congress delegate responsibility for the nation's most vexing political problems to the executive branch. This practice has contributed to a collective aversion to decision-making that has inadvertently weakened Congress's ability to influence the very bureaucracy it created. For instance, in recent decades, members of Congress have lost the will to formulate budgets, impose spending controls, and pass program reauthorizations. Such incompetence and lack of financial responsibility may serve the self-interest of individual incumbents seeking reelection, but as Christopher DeMuth (2018) observes, it is a chief cause of the declining popular legitimacy of Congress as an institution.

Another side effect of congressional relinquishment of legislative authority to executive departments has been the dramatic rise of the president as the focal point of American politics and policy making. Through the use of signing statements, executive orders, and other tools of direct authority, presidents can now single-handedly influence a wide array of domestic and foreign policy. Political scientist Greg Weiner (2018) illustrates this point by explaining how Congress, acting under its constitutional power to enact a "uniform rule of naturalization," has "passed immigration laws so broad that these measures managed to accommodate both President Barack Obama's executive decision not to enforce them in a defined class of cases—thus the Deferred Action for Childhood Arrivals program—and the Trump administration's zero-tolerance policy of enforcing laws every time." In each of these instances, Congress granted deference to the president and the courts rather than responding legislatively—by rescinding Deferred Action for Childhood Arrivals or ending family separation, for example. Thus, rather than attempting to persuade one another and their fellow citizens through reasoned speech and meaningful debate, congressional representatives instead align themselves based on their support or opposition to whichever president happens to be in office. This abdication of duty effectively exacerbates existing political divisions because, as Weiner (2017) points out, "In a membership of 535, Congress more fully represents the richness of U.S. politics than the presidency, a binary institution with which, at a given moment, one either agrees or does not."

Maintaining the status quo may serve the election goals of incumbent members of Congress, but without a revival in its lawmaking authority, Congress runs the risk of becoming increasingly unpopular and eventually obsolete. In order to reclaim its central and esteemed position in the constitutional order, Congress must, in the words of Philip Wallach (2018), "understand its proper purpose again." As Madison notes in "Federalist 51," however, "a dependence on the people is, no doubt, the primary control on the government." Thus, restoring public trust in Congress will ultimately require that voters themselves reward representatives who take their constitutional legislative responsibilities seriously.

References

DeMuth, Christopher. 2018. "The Difference Congress Makes." *Claremont Review of Books* XVIII (3). Accessed December 4, 2018. https://www.claremont.org/crb/article/the-difference-congress-makes/

Kiley, Jocelyn. 2017. "In Polarized Era, Fewer Americans Hold a Mix of Conservative and Liberal Views." Pew Research Center, October 23. Accessed December 3, 2018. http://www.pewresearch.org/fact-tank/2017/10/23/in-polarized-era-fewer-americans-hold-a-mix-of-conservative-and-liberal-views/

Lee, Frances E. 2009. *Beyond Ideology: Politics, Principles, and Partisanship in the U.S. Senate.* Chicago: University of Chicago Press.

Madison, James. 1788. "Federalist No. 51." Accessed November 30, 2018. http://press-pubs.uchicago.edu/founders/documents/v1ch10s16.html

Mann, Thomas E., and Norman J. Ornstein. 2016. *It's Even Worse Than It Was: How the American Constitutional System Collided with the New Politics of Extremism.* New and Expanded Edition. New York: Basic Books.

Postell, Joseph, and Samuel Postell. 2018. "Role of Congress as Representative Government and the Rise of the Progressive Administrative State." Accessed November 30, 2018. https://constitutingamerica.org/role-congress-representative-government-rise-progressive-administrative-state-guest-essayists-joseph-postell-samuel-postell/.

Wallach, Philip. 2018. "Congress Indispensable." *National Affairs* Fall (37). Accessed November 30, 2018. https://www.nationalaffairs.com/publications/detail/congress-indispensable

Weiner, Greg. 2017. "It's All about the President Now." *Washington Post*, October 26. Accessed November 30, 2018. https://www.washingtonpost.com/opinions/its-all-about-the-president-now/2017/10/26/e7f0e77e-b9cd-11e7-9e58-e6288544af98_story.html?utm_term=.d389b3e97881

Weiner, Greg. 2018. "Congress Doesn't Seem to Know Its Own Strength." *New York Times*, June 21.

Christina G. Villegas is an assistant professor of political science at California State University, San Bernardino. She has a PhD from the Institute of Philosophical Studies, University of Dallas. She is author of two recent books: Alexander Hamilton: Documents Decoded *(2018) and* The Youth Unemployment Crisis: A Reference Handbook *(2018).*

Introduction

This chapter profiles the organizations and people involved in the politics of the American Congress. It begins with brief descriptions of thirty-one key stakeholder organizations that are active in the congressional political arena, presented here in alphabetical order. After describing the organizational actors in the arena of congressional politics, it profiles thirty-five individual actors involved. These stakeholders include congressional officials, several leaders of nongovernmental groups that actively lobby Congress, and a few scholars/analysts from major "think tanks" who study the American Congress. Their profiles are also presented in alphabetical order.

Organizations

America Leads

America Leads well exemplifies the "super political action committee (PAC)" approach of an organization—that is, an "independent-expenditure-only" PAC. It attempts to influence Congress by lobbying, most notably by its impact on congressional campaigns. It was established by Phil Cox, the former executive director of the Republican Governors Association (RGA),

Cory Booker (D-NJ) and Kamala Harris (D-CA) speak at the prayer breakfast for the 48th Annual Congressional Black Caucus Foundation on September 15, 2018, in Washington, D.C. (Earl Gibson III/Getty Images)

and Paige Hahn, the former director of finance of the RGA. It spent several millions of dollars in the 2016 election cycle.

American Federation of Labor and Congress of Industrial Organizations

The American Federation of Labor and Congress of Industrial Organizations is the largest and the premier labor union "umbrella" organization that represents 12.5 million members. It comprises a network of more than 14,000 unionized worksites around the nation and reaches out to nonunion members and their families and into communities. Its Workers' Voices PAC is among the more influential lobbying organizations active in American and congressional politics. It attempts to counter—although it hardly matches—the millions of dollars that the conservative political action committees (PACs) and super PACs raise and spend annually. Besides building a network of union and nonunion workers, it focuses on voter registration and voter protection. It is especially active in organizing workers of color and among seniors and student groups who have been impacted by voter suppression laws that have recently been passed in many states that have been pushed by corporate backers across the nation. In recent years it has become active in email and social network sites like Facebook and Twitter. Among its newer methods used to lobby Congress is its "click to call" technology to customize direct mail postcards to members of Congress. It uses relational voter data tools to merge online networks into phone banks and canvass persuasion efforts in congressional electoral districts. It publishes a congressional scorecard that ranks all members of the American Congress on their support or opposition to legislative proposals related to the interests of organized labor. An important leader in these efforts is its political director, Mike Podhorzer. Its president is Richard Trumka, elected in 2009.

Americans for Prosperity

Americans for Prosperity is a 501(c)(4) political action committee (PAC) founded in 2004 as one of the first and leading-
type political organizations. It is a very conservative political
advocacy group founded by David Koch and Charles Koch.
It notably raises what has been termed "dark money" to fund
largely negative TV ads against liberal opponents in key congressional campaigns. Its ads promote lower taxes, less government regulation, and economic prosperity. It established the
model for a host of similar right-wing-oriented 501(c)(4) organizations that, in the 2012 and 2016 election cycles, raised and
outspent all other types of PACs combined. It is headquartered
in Arlington, Virginia.

Brookings Institute

The Brookings Institute is one of the premier "think tanks"
based in Washington, D.C. It exemplifies a nonpartisan public policy think tank. It was founded in 1916 by philanthropist
Robert S. Brookings. As of writing this chapter its president is
former general John R. Allen. In 2008, the *Economist* described
Brookings as "perhaps America's most prestigious think tank."
Brookings is the most frequently cited think tank by the U.S.
media and politicians. A 1997 survey by congressional staff and
journalists ranked it first as the most influential of twenty-seven
think tanks considered, and first in credibility, and as the most
influential policy institute. It publishes an annual report, and
the Brookings Institution Press publishes numerous scholarly
books. It publishes several journals, such as the *Brookings Review*.
As of 2017, it had assets of more than $525 million, a revenue
of nearly $120 million, and expenditures of about $98 million.

CATO Institute

The CATO Institute is another prominent public policy "think
tank" located in Washington, D.C. It exemplifies a more

conservative-oriented perspective. It was founded in 1977 as a public policy research foundation. It is named for the *Cato Letters*, a series of libertarian pamphlets that helped lay the philosophical foundation of the American Revolution. It describes its mission as seeking to broaden the parameters of public policy debate to allow consideration of the traditional American principles of limited government, individual liberty, free markets, and peace. In pursuit of those lofty goals, it strives to involve the concerned lay public in questions of policy and the "proper role of government." It exemplifies the nonprofit, tax-exempt educational foundation or "think tank."

Club for Growth

The Club for Growth is a political advocacy group employing two political arms: Club for Growth Action and Club for Growth PAC, the latter exemplifying a 501(c)(4) super political action committee (PAC). It claims a national network of 100,000 progrowth and limited government Americans and is a leading progrowth advocacy group lobbying Congress for free market and limited government policies. Its founders are Stephen Moore, Richard Gilder, Harlan Crow, and Thomas Rhodes. Its president is David McIntosh. In the 2016 presidential election cycle, it ran anti-Trump ads. It issues what it terms KEY VOTE alerts and congressional scorecards that rank House and Senate members on the purity of their conservative votes on bills before Congress. It runs independent issue ads on television, particularly on Fox News, and on conservative talk radio. In 2016, it supported Senator Ted Cruz for the Republican presidential nomination.

Congressional Black Caucus

Since it was formed in 1971, the Congressional Black Caucus has been one of the more important and influential caucuses of the American Congress, pushing to help African Americans and other minority groups have an equal opportunity for attaining the American Dream. It seeks to empower them and to pursue the following policy agenda: reform the criminal justice system and eliminate barriers to reentry, combat voter suppression, expand access to quality education from pre-K to the postsecondary level, expand access to health care, expand access to twenty-first-century technologies like broadband, strengthen worker protection and fair wages and employment opportunities, expand access to capital for minority-owned businesses, and promote foreign policy initiatives in Africa and other countries consistent with the fundamental rights of human dignity. As of 2019, the caucus has fifty-five members in Congress (House and Senate). It represents eighty-two million Americans who comprise 25 percent of the population. Its members comprise 25 percent of the House Democratic Caucus and serve in the House leadership and committee and subcommittee ranking members, like James Clyburn (D-SC) who is the majority whip in the House, and five members who serve as ranking members of full House committees, and twenty-eight members as chairs of House subcommittees. In the 116th Congress, its chair is Representative Karen Bass (D-CA).

Congressional Budget Office

The Congressional Budget Office is a nonpartisan federal agency within the Congress that provides independent budget and economic analyses and information to the Congress to support its budget process. It was established by Title II of the Congressional Budget and Impoundment Control Act of 1974 (Pub. L. No. 93–344) and signed into law by President Nixon on July 12, 1974. It began operations in 1975, with Alice Rivlin as its first director. It was inspired by the California Legislative Analyst's Office. It has historically and consistently issued credible economic forecasts of the impact of both Democratic and Republican legislative bills without issuing any policy recommendations. Like the Joint Committee on Taxation, it estimates revenue for Congress and projects the fiscal effect on national debt and cost estimates for legislation. It is divided into eight divisions: (1) budget analysis; (2) financial analysis;

3) health, retirement, and long-term analysis; (4) macroeconomic analysis; (5) management, business, and information services; (6) microeconomic studies; (7) national security; and (8) tax analysis.

Congressional Hispanic Caucus

The Congressional Hispanic Caucus began in 1976 as a legislative service organization with the U.S. House of Representatives organized as a congressional member organization and governed by the rule of the U.S. House of Representatives. It addresses national and international issues before Congress and develops policies that impact the Hispanic American community. On civil rights and civil liberty issues and bills, its members routinely vote with the members of the Congressional Black Caucus. It serves as a forum for the Hispanic members of Congress to coalesce around a collective legislative agenda. It has been a strong advocate for enactment of a Dream Act and of comprehensive immigration reform. It voices and advances a policy agenda affecting Hispanics in the United States, Puerto Rico, and the Commonwealth of the Northern Mariana Islands. As of the 116th Congress (2019–2021), it has thirty-seven full members. It is currently chaired by Representative Joaquin Castro (D-TX) (https://congressionalhispaniccaucus-lujangrisham.house.gov/about).

Congressional Research Service

Sometimes known as the "think tank of the U.S. Congress," the Congressional Research Service began in 1914 at the insistence of then Senator Robert La Follette Sr. (R-WI) and Representative John Nelson (R-WI). The Service publishes an annual *Congressional Research Service Review*. It works exclusively for Congress, providing policy and legal analysis to committees and to members of both the U.S. House of Representatives and the Senate regardless of political party affiliation. It is a legislative branch agency within the Library of

Congress. It has been a valuable and respected resource for more than a century. Its analyses are authoritative, confidential, objective, and nonpartisan. It has recently issued research reports on a variety of public policy areas of proposed legislation. It employs a staff of six hundred analysts located in Washington, D.C.

Democratic Congressional Campaign Committee

The Democratic Congressional Campaign Committee (DCCC) is the official campaign arm of the Democratic Party in the U.S. House of Representatives. It recruits candidates to run for and supports their elections to Congress. It raises campaign funds, plans national strategies each election cycle for their expenditure by deciding which key district races have the best prospects for victory, and advises candidates on campaign strategies and position on issues before Congress. It supports television and other media ads. The DCCC chairman is Representative Ben Ray Lujan (D-NM) who was first elected to Congress in 2009. The DCCC is active on social media outlets like Facebook and Twitter, has four regional vice chairs, and about twenty to twenty-five chairs or cochairs who liaison with various outside groups and organizations.

Democratic National Committee

The Democratic National Committee (DNC) was founded in 1848 and is the official national organization of the Democratic Party. It is headed by a chairperson selected by the National Convention in presidential campaign years. In 2016, it selected the current chair, Tom Perez. The DNC drafts and supports policy positions, called planks in the party platform, that are adopted at the National Convention held each presidential election year. In 2016, the platform was notably prochoice, progay marriage, prodevelopment of alternative energy, health-care reform (e.g., health care for all with a public option or adoption of a single-payer system, sometimes referred to as Medicare for All), education reform, and comprehensive immigration reform.

Democratic Senatorial Campaign Committee

The Democratic Senatorial Campaign Committee, like its House counterpart, recruits and supports candidates for the U.S. Senate. It raises campaign funds, works to elect candidates to the U.S. Senate, offers campaign advice for strategy, and promotes common campaign themes and media ads. Its current chair is Chris Van Hollen, the junior senator from Maryland. Its executive director is Tom Lopach. In 2018, it was targeting more seats up for reelection than are Republican senators seeking reelection. There are more than a dozen seats considered close or "toss-up" seats. The Democratic Party hoped to "flip the Senate" in the midterm, 2018 elections.

EMILY's List

EMILY's List is a pro-Democratic, prochoice political action committee supporting candidates for office at all levels and is particularly active in recruiting and supporting women running for Congress. It was founded by Ellen Malcolm in 1985. Its name stands for "Early Money Is Like Yeast," which is meant to convey the power of early donations in a race. Currently, it is led by its president, Stephanie Schriock. It claims three million members and has claimed an 80 percent win record. It bundles money that it uses to independently support candidates for congress, notably women in 2018, running in what it assesses are key "swing" congressional districts. It is decidedly "anti-Trump" and has a goal to "flip" both chambers of Congress to serve as a "check and balance" to President Trump.

Federal Elections Commission

The Federal Elections Commission (FEC) is an independent regulatory agency established in 1975 by amendment to the

Federal Election Campaign Act (FECA) of 1974. Congress established the FEC to administer the FECA, the law that governs the financing of federal elections (congressional and presidential). Its duties are to disclose campaign finance information, enforce provisions of the FECA, and oversee the public funding of presidential elections (although that provision is now unused as presidential candidates of both major parties reject public funding). The commission is comprised of six members: three Democrats and three Republicans, appointed by the U.S. president with the advice and consent of the Senate. The commissioners serve six-year terms, staggered every two years. By law, no more than three members can be of the same political party. At least four votes are required for any official FEC action. The chair rotates among the members each year, with no commission member serving more than once during his or her term on the commission.

FreedomWorks for America

FreedomWorks is a libertarian advocacy group based in Washington, D.C. It trains volunteers, activists, and campaigners associated with the former Tea Party movement, and now with the Freedom Caucus in Congress. It was founded in 2004 by Matt Kibbe and Ryan Hecker. Kibbe is the president and CEO of FreedomWorks, Inc. FreedomWorks for America is a super political action committee (PAC) begun in 2011 with Ryan Hecker as its COO. It was notable for laying out the platform of the nascent Tea Party movement in his online *Contract with America*. It claims six million grassroots members in its volunteer database. It is a super PAC that backs conservative candidates for the American Congress. It employs extensively social media outlets like Twitter, Facebook, and YouTube. Its former chairman, Dick Armey, was a leading voice of the Tea Party movement and former House Republican majority leader who left FreedomWorks in 2012. FreedomWorks, Inc., is a 501 (c)(4) nonprofit that merged with Empower America and the Citizens for a Sound Economy in 2004. It is an industry-funded think tank and promotes deregulation. It is largely funded by Charles Koch and David Koch. It was a prominent supporter of Senator Ted Cruz (R-TX) in 2016, spending a half-million dollars to independently back his presidential nomination bid.

Government Accountability Office

The Government Accountability Office (GAO) is an independent, nonpartisan agency that works for Congress. Often referred to as the "congressional watchdog," the GAO investigates how the federal government spends taxpayer dollars. The GAO is headed by the comptroller general of the United States, who is appointed to a fifteen-year term by the president from a slate of candidates proposed by the Congress through a bipartisan, bicameral commission. The current comptroller general is Gene Dodaro, the eighth comptroller general, who assumed the office in 2010, nominated by President Obama and confirmed by the U.S. Senate. The GAO seeks to improve the performance and accountability of the federal government by providing Congress with timely information based on objective, fact-based, nonpartisan, nonideological, fair, and balanced studies. Its core values are accountability, integrity, and reliability. Its studies and analyses are carried out at the behest of congressional committees and subcommittees or are mandated by public laws or committee reports. The GAO supports congressional oversight by auditing agencies and operations, investigating allegations of illegal or improper activities, reporting on the effectiveness and efficiency of policies in meeting their objectives, performing policy analyses and outlining options for congressional consideration, and issuing legal decisions and opinions. The GAO advises Congress and heads of executive agencies about ways to make government more efficient, effective, ethical, equitable, and responsive. It is consistently rated as one of the best places to work in the federal government in the annual list of the Partnership for Public Service.

Heritage Foundation

The Heritage Foundation was begun in 1973 by Joseph Coors, Paul Weyrich, and Edwin Feulner. It is a conservative think tank and lobbying organization based in Washington, D.C. Its former CEO was Jim DeMint, the former representative (1999–2005, R-SC) and former U.S. senator (2005–2013, R-SC), who was a member and leading figure in the Tea Party movement. The Heritage Foundation was a leader of the neoconservative movement that rose to prominence during the Reagan administration. In 1980, it issued its "mandate for leadership," which became the blueprint for President Reagan's conservative policy agenda. The foundation has assets of more than $174 million, claims more than 500,000 members, and was a leading critic of the Obama administration's liberal policies. The board of the Heritage Foundation removed Jim DeMint as its CEO in 2017. He went on to become a senior advisor to Citizens for Self-Governance and was the founding chairman of the Conservative Partnership Institute, now a rival to the Heritage Foundation; it focuses on the professional development of congressional staffers and elected officials.

Majority Leader of the U.S. House and Senate

In Congress, the majority leader in the House and the Senate differ somewhat. In the House, the majority leader is elected by members of the American Congress in the caucus or conference of the party holding the largest number of seats in the House of Representatives. The power and influence of the majority leader in the House has varied over time depending on the political climate of the nation but typically sets the floor agenda and oversees the committee chairpersons. In the Senate, the majority leader (a.k.a. the majority floor leader) is the chief spokesperson for the majority party. According to Article I, Section 2 of the Constitution, the president of the Senate is the vice president of the United States, who officially presides over the Senate. In reality, however, he only rarely does so as it is a largely ceremonial role. Section 2 also specifies that they shall "chuse their other Officers"—over time as political parties developed and became more important in both the Congress and in American politics generally, the party leadership position formalized. Because of the sharply partisan division of the American Congress, the legislative process would likely not function without the efforts of the House and Senate majority party leaders and their whips. They are agents not only of contention but also, on occasion, of compromise. They impose adherence to party consensus.

Minority Leader of the U.S. House and Senate

The minority leaders in the two chambers of Congress are elected by the members of the minority party of the two chambers at the opening session of a new congress. The majority and minority leaders are assisted by whips, whose job is to enforce party discipline on votes considered to be crucial by the party leadership and to ensure that party members do not vote in a way not approved by the party caucus or conference. Some votes are viewed as so crucial that for a party member to vote against the party can lead to punitive measures being taken—such as demotion from choice committee assignments or by the national party organization backing primary opposition when the member seeks reelection or by denying financial support to the member.

National Archives and Records Administration

The National Archives and Records Administration (NARA) is the nation's record keeper. Of all documents and materials created in the course of business conducted by the U.S. federal government, only about 2–5 percent are considered so important for legal or historical purposes that they are kept by NARA forever. These include all the founding documents. NARA was established in 1934 by President Franklin D. Roosevelt, although its holdings date back to 1775. To give some sense of the scope and size of NARA's holdings, consider the following data: it holds ten billion pages of textual records, twelve million charts and architectural and engineering drawings, twenty-five million photographs and graphics, three hundred thousand reels of film, four hundred thousand videos and sound recordings, and 133 terabytes of electronic data. NARA's founding documents and major facility are located in Washington, D.C.; there is also a major center in College Park, Maryland. It has record centers in Atlanta, Boston, Chicago, Dayton, Denver, Fort Worth, Kansas City, Kingsridge (Ohio), Lee's Summit (Missouri), Lenexa (Kansas), New York City, Philadelphia, Pittsfield (Massachusetts), Riverside (California), San Bruno (California), San Francisco, Seattle, and St. Louis. NARA also runs various presidential libraries and museums: Herbert Hoover, Franklin D. Roosevelt, Harry S. Truman, Dwight D. Eisenhower, Lyndon Johnson, Richard Nixon, Gerald Ford, Jimmy Carter, George H. W. Bush, George W. Bush, William Clinton, and Barack Obama.

National Republican Congressional Committee

The National Republican Congressional Committee (NRCC) is the political committee devoted to recruiting and electing members to the American Congress in order to achieve and maintain a Republican majority in the House of Representatives. It began in 1866 when Republican caucuses of the House and Senate formed a "congressional committee." Today it is organized under Section 527 of the Internal Revenue Code. It supports election of Republicans to the House through direct financial contributions to candidates and Republican candidates and party organizations, voter registration, education, and voter turnout programs and other party-building activities. The NRCC relies heavily on individual contributions, many of whom are small donors ($25–50). The chairman of the NRCC is elected by members of the House Republican Conference after each congressional election. The Speaker of the House and seven other elected leaders of the conference serve as ex officio members of the NRCC's executive committee. Its day-to-day operations are overseen by an executive director, currently John Rodgers, who manages a staff of professionals with expertise in campaign strategy, development, planning, and management; digital research; communications; fundraising; administration; and legal compliance.

National Republican Senatorial Committee

Like its House counterpart, the National Republican Senatorial Committee is the only national organization solely devoted to strengthening the Republican majority in the Senate and electing Republicans to that chamber. It provides support and assistance to current members, helps recruit prospective members, and assists candidates in budget planning, election law compliance, fundraising, communication tools and messaging, research, and strategy. Its current chairman is Senator Cory Gardner (R-CO) and its vice chairman is Senator Thom Tillis (R-NC).

National Rifle Association

The National Rifle Association (NRA) is an American non-profit organization advocating for and lobbying for gun rights. It is unquestionably one of the three most powerful lobbying organizations in Washington, D.C. Its founders were William Conant Church and George Wood Wingate, and it was founded in 1871, in New York, to teach sharpshooting and firearm safety and competency. Its first president was Ambrose Burnside, the Union army general of the Civil War and former governor of Rhode Island. Since 1934, the NRA has informed its members about legislation; it has directly lobbied Congress since 1975. Its lobbying arm is the NRA Institute for Legislative Action. That arm manages its political action committee and its Political Victory Fund. It has lobbied legislatures at all levels of government, has initiated or participated in lawsuits, and endorses or opposes candidates for various offices at local, state, and federal levels. In 1991, its board named staff lobbyist Wayne LaPierre as its executive vice president and, in 1997, elected the movie star Charlton Heston as its president. In 2004, it successfully lobbied for expiration of the Federal Assault Weapons Ban. It has campaigned vigorously to deregulate guns at the state and local levels. During 1999–2001, it was rated by *Fortune* magazine as the most powerful lobbying organization. Internationally, the NRA opposes the Arms Trade Treaty, a Canadian gun registry, supported Brazilian gun rights, and criticized Australian gun laws. Its chief lobbyist is Chris W. Cox. In the 2016 election cycle, the NRA reported raising $366 million and spending $412 million on political activities. It claims six million members. Its current president is Carolyn Meadows and its chief executive and executive vice president is Wayne LaPierre.

Office of Congressional Ethics

The Office of Congressional Ethics (OCE) is an independent, nonpartisan office in the U.S. House of Representatives, which reviews allegations of misconduct by members and staff of the Congress and, when appropriate, refers matters to the House Committee on Ethics. It has a professional staff of attorneys and other professionals with expertise in ethics law and investigations. It is governed by an eight-person board of directors who are private citizens and cannot serve as members of Congress or work for the federal government. It was established in 2008 as the first-ever independent body overseeing the ethics of the House of Representatives to increase transparency and provide information to the public. It uses a two-stage investigative process; the first stage confidential, and if OCE cases are sent to the Ethics Committee, they must become public. It publishes a statistical summary of its actions on a quarterly basis. It held its first public hearings in 2009 and has met several times since then to address changes to its rules and to receive public comment.

Office of Management and Budget

The Office of Management and Budget (OMB) is a major office within the Executive Office of the President. It serves the president in overseeing the implementation of his agenda across the entire executive branch and gives important input to the American Congress over the president's proposed budgets, and its studies and reports assist the Congress in its oversight role. The OMB's mission is to assist the president in meeting his policy, budget, management, and regulatory objectives. It is integral to fulfilling the executive branch's statutory responsibilities. These include (1) budget development and execution; (2) management—including oversight of agency performance, human capital, federal procurement, financial management, and information technology; (3) regulatory policy coordination; (4) legislative clearance and coordination; and (5) executive orders and presidential memoranda. Its current director is Mike Mulvaney, nominated by President Trump in December 2016 and confirmed by the Senate in February 2017.

PEW Research Center

PEW is one of the most respected and influential public policy think tanks in Washington, D.C. It is nonpartisan. It began in 2004 and has assets of more than $37 million. PEW works to inform the public about issues, attitudes, and trends that shape America and the world. Its areas of research include U.S. politics and policy, journalism and the media, the internet, science and technology, religion and public life, Hispanic trends, global attitudes and trends, and social and demographic trends. Its published opinion and trend data are highly respected and influence congressional policy making and committees and caucuses (e.g., the Hispanic Caucus).

Republican National Committee

The Republican National Committee provides leadership for the Republican Party. It is responsible for organizing the National Convention, drafting the party platform, fundraising, and finalizing election strategy. It was founded in 1856. It is headquartered in Washington, D.C. It is the Republican Party counterpart to the Democratic National Committee. Its current chair is Ronna Romney McDaniel, the former chairwoman of the Michigan Republican Party and grand-daughter of former Michigan governor George Romney and niece of Mitt Romney. She replaced Reince Priebus (R-WI) as national chair of the party, when he was appointed President Trump's chief of staff.

Senate Majority PAC

The Senate Majority PAC was founded in 2011 to help win Senate races in response to the 2010 *Citizens United* decision, which allowed Karl Rove and a network of outside groups to raise and spend hundreds of millions of dollars on negative ads against Democratic candidates for the U.S. Senate. In 2016, those groups raised nearly $1 billion. The Senate Majority PAC raises and spends millions of dollars on electing Democratic senators pledged to provide opportunity and security for working-class families, to oppose cuts to Medicare and education, and to protect environmental protection laws.

Speaker of the House

The position of Speaker of the House is established in Article I, Section 2 of the U.S. Constitution, which simply states, "The House of Representatives shall chuse their Speaker and other Officers." The Speaker is the political and parliamentary leader of the House of Representatives. Since the early nineteenth century, various Speakers have continually redefined the office from a role of presiding over the House as its ceremonial head to aggressively pursuing a policy agenda, shaping the rules, and controlling the levers of power in the U.S. House of Representatives. The Speaker is the presiding officer, the party leader, and the institution's administrative head. The Speaker is elected at the beginning of each session of Congress by a majority of representatives from the majority party caucus or conference. The Speaker is third in line to succeed the president, and the Twenty-Fifth Amendment makes the Speaker a part of the process announcing presidential disability. As of 2019, the Speaker is Representative Nancy Pelosi (D-CA).

The Tea Party Movement

The Tea Party movement is a grassroots movement promoting conservative/libertarian positions on a host of issues before the Congress. It began in 2004. It considers the U.S. Constitution inherently conservative and advocates fifteen nonnegotiable core beliefs: (1) illegal aliens are here illegal and should be removed, (2) prodomestic employment is indispensable, (3) a strong military is essential, (4) special interests must be eliminated, (5) gun ownership is sacred, (6) government must be downsized, (7) the national budget must be balanced, (8) deficit spending must be ended, (9) bailout and stimulus plans are illegal, (10) reducing the personal income tax is a must, (11) reducing business income taxes is mandatory, (12) political offices must be available to average citizens, (13) intrusive government must be stopped, (14) English as our core language is required, and (15) traditional values are to be encouraged. It claims tens of millions of members. Its president is Attorney Steve Eichler. In 2016, the movement supported Dr. Ben Carson, Senator Ted Cruz, Senator Rand Paul, and finally Donald Trump as presidential nominee. It is closely aligned in the Congress with the Freedom Caucus.

People

Abramoff, Jack (1958–)

Jack Abramoff is a notorious Washington lobbyist who was embroiled in a lobbying scandal in 2006 that led to his name being synonymous with Washington political corruption. He was convicted of conspiracy, fraud, and tax evasion, all felonies, for which he served three years in prison. In all, twenty-one people were convicted in the scandal, including a couple of representatives and several staff aides, including an aide to the then powerful representative Tom Delay (R-TX). The scandal tarnished Ralph Reed and Grover Norquist as well and exposed the corruption associated with the K Street Project. Abramoff was the son of a wealthy father and attended Brandeis University. When the Republican Party won control of the Congress in 1994, Abramoff launched a lobbying scheme that defrauded a coalition of Indian tribes over casino gaming interests that was estimated at $85 million in fees. After his prison term, he authored a 2011 book, *Capitol Punishment: The Hard Truth about Washington Corruption from America's Most Notorious Lobbyist*. It was also made into a film. During 2016–2017, Abramoff returned as an official lobbyist again, this time lobbying for the Republic of the Congo, attempting to schedule a meeting between President Trump and the controversial president of the Republic of the Congo, Denis Sassou Nguesso. He retroactively filed and was registered as a lobbyist under the Foreign Agent Registration Act. The Department of Justice terminated his association with the Italian national Costel Iancu and the firm Global Structures Group in Bucharest, Romania, as well as with the Congolese government.

Armey, Richard "Dick" (1940–)

Dick Armey is a noted American politician and lobbyist. From 1985 to 2003, he served in the U.S. House of Representatives from Texas (R-TX-26). He was the Republican whip, then Republican Conference chair (1993–1995), and then its majority leader from 1995 to 2003. He left the House where he was succeeded as majority leader by John Boehner in 2003. He went on to serve as the executive director of FreedomWorks from 2003 to 2012. Along with Newt Gingrich, he was notable as one of the leaders of the 1990s "Republican Revolution" and its *Contract with America*. He is a former professor of economics. Since leaving FreedomWorks, he is a political consultant, advisor, and congressional lobbyist.

Boehner, John (1949–)

John Boehner served as the fifty-third Speaker of the House of Representatives from 2011 to 2015. He served as the representative of Ohio's Eighth Congressional District for just a few months less than twenty-five years (1991–2015, R-OH). As Speaker, he led the drive for a smaller, less costly, and more accountable federal government. As Speaker, he had to deal with an often contentious Republican Conference. He is the second oldest of twelve brothers and sisters. He attended Xavier University where he met his spouse, Debra Gunlack. They were wed in 1973 and have two daughters. He started a small business and became involved in state and local government. He was elected to the House in 1990, campaigning on an agenda of anti-pork-barrel spending and reform. He was part of the Gang of Seven, reform-minded representatives who forced the close of the scandal-ridden House Bank and House Post Office. He worked with Newt Gingrich to craft the historic 1994 *Contract with America* and helped enact the first balanced federal budget in a generation. He chaired the House Committee on Education and the Workforce and authored legislation to expand school choice, strengthen the nation's pension system, and reform the federal education bureaucracy. He was elected House majority leader in 2006. He led the opposition to President Obama's "cap and trade" initiative and the Affordable Care Act (a.k.a. Obamacare). He became Speaker in 2011, when Republicans took the House after winning sixty-three seats, replacing Democratic Speaker Nancy Pelosi. He focused on the Republican "Pledge to America"—a new version of the *Contract with America* that advocated removing government barriers to private-sector job creation and economic growth, eliminating "pork-barrel earmarks" and other congressional reforms. After leaving Congress, Boehner joined Squire Patton Boggs LLP, as senior strategic advisor, a leading law and public policy firm with clients in the United States and abroad, and focusing on global business development.

Calhoun, John C. (1782–1850)

John Calhoun was a prominent U.S. diplomat and noted defender of the slave-plantation system of the antebellum

South. He represented South Carolina (D-SC) in the House of Representatives, and as a leading "War Hawk," Calhoun helped steer the nation into war with Great Britain in 1812. After the Treaty of Ghent ended the war, Calhoun helped to establish the Second Bank of the United States. He wrote the bonus bill that would have established a nationwide network of roads and canals had not President James Madison vetoed the bill. He served as the U.S. secretary of war and briefly as secretary of state. He opposed the Mexican-American War and the admission to the union of California as a free state. He ran for president in 1824 but settled for the vice presidency, being twice elected to that office. Initially, he supported the Tariff of 1828 (a.k.a. the Tariff of Abominations) but later opposed it, responding to intense opposition to it by his constituents as it being unfair to the agrarian South and favoring the industrializing North. He wrote the essay "South Carolina Exposition and Protest," claiming original sovereignty for the people and advocating state veto (or nullification) of any national law held to impinge on states' rights. Another of his essays, "Disquisition on Government and Discourse on the Constitution," argued the classic case for minority rights within the framework of majority rule. Along with Henry Clay, he worked out the Compromise Tariff of 1832–1833. He resigned from the vice presidency to be reelected to the U.S. Senate from Carolina where for the remainder of his life, he defended the slave-plantation system against the growing antislavery movement. He joined the Tyler administration as secretary of state, laying the groundwork for the annexation of Texas and the settlement of the boundary of Oregon with Great Britain. He was reelected to the Senate in 1845 and opposed the Mexican-American War. A gifted debater and original thinker in political theory, he, along with Daniel Webster, Henry Clay, and Andrew Jackson, dominated American political life from 1815 to 1850. His reputation in public life as the "Cast Iron Man" on economic and social issues contrasted with his personal warmth and affectionate nature in his private life.

Cannon, Joseph Gurney (1836–1926)

Arguably the most powerful Speaker of the House of Representatives, "Uncle Joe" Cannon was a representative to the House from Illinois and the leader of the Republican Party. He served as Speaker from 1903 to 1911, the second-longest serving Republican Speaker in U.S. history. At forty-six cumulative years of service, he was the longest serving Republican representative ever and the first ever from either party to serve longer than forty years. Born in North Carolina in 1836, his family moved to Indiana. At age nineteen, he went to Cincinnati, Ohio, to study at the University of Cincinnati law school and was admitted to the bar in 1858. He moved to Illinois, serving as state's attorney from 1861 to 1868. He married Mary Reed, with whom he had two daughters. He became a follower of Abraham Lincoln during the Lincoln-Douglas debates in 1858. He was elected to the House and served from 1873 to 1891. He went on to chair several important committees (Committee on Expenditures in the Post Office Department, Committee on Appropriations, and Committee on Rules). He ran for the Speaker's office four times before succeeding. He often clashed with Republican president Theodore Roosevelt. He wielded the Speakership with unprecedented power as concurrent chair of the powerful Rules Committee, which enabled him to control every aspect of the House's agenda and reserve to himself the right to appoint not only the chairs of the various House committees but also all of the committees' members, thereby appointing allies and protégés to leadership position and punishing those who opposed his legislation. In 1910, after two earlier attempts to curb his power failed, Nebraska representative George Norris led a coalition of 42 progressives and the entire delegation of 149 Democrats to revolt that passed a resolution stripping the Speaker from the Rules Committee and his power to assign committees. He was defeated in his reelection bid in 1912 but returned in 1914 and served until 1920. He opposed Woodrow Wilson and entry of the United States into

World War I and its joining the League of Nations. He retired in 1923. He died in 1926, during a deep sleep.

Clay, Henry (1777–1852)

Henry Clay was born in Virginia in 1777 to a moderately wealthy family, the seventh of nine children. In 1797, he was admitted to the Virginia bar but soon moved to Lexington, Kentucky, then a hotbed of land-title disputes. He married Lucretia Hart, the daughter of a wealthy businessperson in 1799, with whom he had eleven children. He began his political career in 1803, with his election to the Kentucky General Assembly as a Jeffersonian Democratic-Republican who opposed the Alien and Sedition Acts of 1798. As a lawyer, he represented Aaron Burr in 1806, but later, when it was revealed that Burr was guilty, Clay spurned him. In 1806, Clay was appointed to the U.S. Senate to fill an unexpired term. He was elected to the U.S. House of Representatives in 1811, serving multiple terms in the House (1811–1814, 1815–1821, and 1823–1825) and in the U.S. Senate (1806–1807, 1810–1811, 1831–1842, and 1849–1852). He went on to serve as Speaker of the House, being the youngest to serve up to that time (1811–1814) and served as secretary of state under President John Quincy Adams (1825–1829). He came to the House as a War Hawk pushing for the War of 1812. President James Madison appointed Clay as one of five delegates to negotiate a peace treaty with Britain, at Ghent, Belgium. He advocated for a national bank and negotiated the Missouri Compromise of 1820, for a time a settlement of the free-state, slave-state conflict. In 1833, he walked South Carolina back from secession with the Compromise Tariff Act of 1833. In 1850, Clay negotiated the Compromise of 1850 that enabled California to enter the union as a free state and settled the Texas boundary line, the fugitive slave law, and the abolition of the slave trade in the District of Columbia. His negotiating skills earned him the nicknames "The Great Compromiser" and "The Great Pacificator." Clay ran for the presidency twice, thwarted by John Quincy Adams and Andrew Jackson. Clay led the National Republican Party in 1828, which was eventually absorbed into the Whig Party. In 1831, Clay was elected to the Senate and led the Whig Party. He sought the Whig Party nomination for president in 1840, losing to General William Henry Harrison, who ran with John Tyler as his vice president. After Harrison's death just a month in office, Tyler became president. Clay retired from the Senate and returned to Kentucky, but in 1844, the Whig Party selected Clay. Clay opposed the annexation of Texas. He lost to James K. Polk, who supported annexation and the idea of Manifest Destiny. Clay died of tuberculosis in 1852.

Collins, Susan (1952–)

Susan Collins is the senior senator from Maine. First elected to the Senate in 1996, she earned a national reputation as one who works effectively across party lines and seeks consensus on a host of important national issues. She has been ranked for five years as the most bipartisan member of the U.S. Senate by the Lugar Center and by Georgetown University. Collins ranks thirteenth in Senate seniority and is the Republican Party's most senior woman. She chairs the Senate Aging Committee and the Transportation, Housing, and Urban Development Appropriations Subcommittee. She serves on the Intelligence Committee and the Health, Education, Labor, and Pensions Committee. She has never missed a vote in her twenty-one years in office, casting more than sixty-seven hundred votes. *Elite Magazine* named her one of the most powerful women in Washington. She has coauthored critical legislation in homeland security, national defense, education, business development, and health care. Along with Senator Joseph Lieberman (D-CT), she authored a major overhaul of the nation's intelligence after the 9/11 attacks and was important to the successful effort to repeal the "Don't Ask, Don't Tell" law that prohibited gay and lesbian Americans from serving openly in the U.S. military. She is cofounder of the Common Sense

Coalition, a bipartisan group of senators who wrote the framework for plans that ended the government shutdowns in 2015 and 2018. In 1997, she founded the Senate Diabetes Caucus that led to more than triple the funding for diabetes research. She is a founder and cochair of the Congressional Task Force on Alzheimer's Disease. She has received a 100 percent rating from the National Federation of Independent Businesses. She was born in Caribou, Maine, where her family runs a fifth-generation lumber business, founded in 1844. She is a Phi Beta Kappa graduate of St. Lawrence University. She is married to Thomas Daffron, and they reside in Bangor, Maine.

Cruz, Rafael Edward "Ted" (1970–)

Ted Cruz is a Republican U.S. senator from Texas who first rose to national attention in 2013 for leading the effort to shut down the federal government over Obamacare and led another shutdown in 2018. He is one of the least popular U.S. senators but holds considerable sway over members of the Freedom Caucus in the U.S. House of Representatives. In the Senate, Cruz chairs the Senate Judiciary's Subcommittee on Oversight, Federal Rights, and Agency and the Commerce Committee's Subcommittee on Space, Science, and Competitiveness. He was the top contender against front-runner Donald Trump for the GOP presidential nomination in 2016 and, when speaking at the 2016 Republican Convention, was notable for refusing to endorse Trump. A divisive voice in U.S. politics and in the Senate, he is an ideological purist who is popular among Tea Party Republicans, and he supports their core beliefs and positions. He graduated from Princeton University in 1992 and from Harvard Law School in 1995. He served as a law clerk to Chief Justice William Rehnquist on the U.S. Supreme Court. He was first elected to the U.S. Senate in 2012. Prior to 2012, he was the solicitor general of Texas (2003–2008), the first Hispanic to hold that office. He taught U.S. Supreme Court litigation as an adjunct law professor at the Law School, University of Texas. From 2001 to 2003, he was director of the Office of Policy Planning at the Federal Trade Commission and was associate deputy attorney general at the Department of Justice. In the 2000 presidential campaign, Cruz was a domestic policy advisor to the George W. Bush campaign. Cruz was born in Canada. His mother was a U.S. citizen working in Canada as a computer programmer, and Cruz therefore claims he was a U.S. citizen by birth. His father was a Cuban American who had fought in the Cuban Revolution but was later imprisoned and tortured. His father fled to Texas and started an oil and gas business and later became a pastor. Cruz lives in Houston with his wife, Heidi, and their two children.

Dingell, John (1926–2019)

John Dingell, Jr., was the longest-serving member of Congress in American history. He represented Michigan's Twelfth Congressional District (Detroit area) for fifty-nine years. In 2009 he broke the record of Senator Robert Byrd (D-WV), who died in office. John Dingell was one of the most powerful House Committee chairs and used his position to protect the automobile industry, an important hometown interest. Chairman Dingell was a noted champion of civil rights and environmental policy. He was first elected to the U.S. House of Representatives in 1955, filling the seat of his father, who died in office after serving for twenty-two years. He was replaced, upon his retirement in 2014, by his wife, Debbie Dingell. Thus, someone from the Dingell family has represented Michigan's Twelfth Congressional District for ninety years. John Dingell was chairman of the House Energy and Commerce Committee (1981–1995), which has a vast portfolio. He was notably instrumental in the passage of Medicare, Medicaid, the Endangered Species Act, the Wilderness Act, the Environmental Policy Act, the Clean Air and the Clean Water acts, and the Superfund law. Dingell also chaired the Oversight and Investigations Subcommittee where its inquiries led to the resignation of Michael Deaver, one of President Ronald Reagan's top advisors, for lying to Congress about his lobbying activities. John Dingell was born in 1926. He was a House page when Congress declared war on Japan in December 1941, and he served in the US Army in World War II. He earned a BS degree from Georgetown University, and his law degree from Georgetown Law school.

Feinstein, Dianne (1933–)

Dianne Feinstein is the senior senator from California. She was elected in 1992, the first "Year of the Woman." She was reelected in 2000, 2006, and 2012. She received her BA from Stanford University in 1955. Prior to her election to the U.S. Senate, she served on California's Women's Parole Board (1960–1966), on the San Francisco Board of Supervisors (1970–1978) and as mayor of San Francisco (1978–1988). Senator Feinstein serves on several committees: notably she is the ranking member of the Senate Judiciary Committee and is a member of its Subcommittee on Security and Immigration and of its Subcommittee on Terrorism. She also serves on the Senate Committee on Appropriations and is the ranking member of its Subcommittee on Energy and Water Development. She has notably worked across the aisle on some issues but has compiled a strongly liberal voting record. For example, she has received the following ratings from various advocacy organizations: Human Rights Campaign = 100 percent; Planned Parenthood Action Fund = 100 percent; League of Conservation Voters = 89 percent; American Civil Liberties Union = 70 percent; U.S. Chamber of Commerce = 49 percent; Numbers USA = 32 percent; Club for Growth = 9 percent; Americans for Prosperity = 3 percent; and FreedomWorks = 0 percent. On the recent Judiciary Committee hearings on the confirmation of Judge Brett Kavanaugh to the U.S. Supreme Court, Feinstein was a leading voice against the nomination. She has been married three times: to Richard Blum (1980 to present), Bertram Feinstein (1962–1978), and Jack Berman (1956–1959).

Gingrich, Newt (1943–)

Newt Gingrich is an American politician and author. He was born in Pennsylvania but his family moved to Georgia, and he was later elected as a representative from Georgia in the

American Congress. He earned a BA in history from Emory University and a MA and PhD in history from Tulane University and went on to teach at West Georgia College. He was elected to the U.S. House of Representatives, representing Georgia's Sixth Congressional District from 1979 to 1999. He served as Republican whip from 1989 to 1995 and as the fiftieth Speaker of the House from 1995 to 1999. He is the coauthor of the *Contract with America* and a leader of the "Republican Revolution" of 1994. In 1995, *Time* magazine named him its "Man of the Year" for his role in ending the four-decade-long Democratic majority in the U.S. House of Representatives. As Speaker, he oversaw passage of welfare reform bills and a capital gains tax cut in 1997. He was reprimanded for ethics violations, and revelations of an extramarital affair with a congressional employee twenty-three years his junior, while leading efforts to impeach President Clinton for his sexual scandal, resulted in Gingrich's resignation from the Speakership in 1998 and from the House in 1999. Since leaving the House, he has remained active in public policy, working as a political consultant. He chaired two policy think tanks: American Solution for Winning the Future and the Center for Health Transformation. He has authored twenty-seven books, including several historical fiction novels and *Lessons Learned the Hard Way* (1998), *To Save America* (2010), and *A Nation like No Other* (2011). He ran for the Republican presidential nomination in 2012, losing to Mitt Romney. He was one of the earliest endorsers of Donald Trump for president in 2016 and was briefly on the short list for Trump's vice president. Married three times, he married his current spouse, Callista, in 2000. They have two children.

Johnson, Lyndon B. (1908–1973)

Lyndon B. Johnson, known as LBJ, was the thirty-sixth president of the United States, sworn into office after the assassination of John F. Kennedy in November 1963. During his presidency (1963–1968), he notably crafted the ambitious policy program of progressive reforms known as "The Great

Society," arguably passing the most legislation in his first term since FDR's "New Deal." He championed Medicare, Medicaid, Head Start, the Civil Rights Act of 1964, the Voting Rights Act of 1965, and the Civil Rights Act of 1968. His legacy is marred by the political quagmire of the Vietnam War. He declined to run for a second term, retiring to his Texas ranch in 1969. Johnson was born in the central Texas community of Johnson City, the first of five children of Sam Johnson Jr., a farmer, businessperson, and state legislator. Johnson graduated from the Southwest State Teachers College (now Texas State University) in 1930. He taught school for disadvantaged Mexican American students in south Texas. In 1934, he married Claudia "Lady Bird" Taylor with whom he had two daughters. In 1935, Johnson became the Texas director of the National Youth Administration, a New Deal program. He began his political career in earnest in 1937 when he was elected to the U.S. House of Representatives (D-TX). He was the first member of Congress to volunteer for active duty in the U.S. military (Navy) when the United States entered World War II, serving as a lieutenant commander until all members of Congress in the military were recalled to Washington in the summer of 1942. In 1948, he was elected to the U.S. Senate, winning the Democratic primary by eighty-seven votes. In 1953, at age forty-four, he became the youngest member to serve as minority leader of the Senate, and in 1955, when the Democrats won control of Congress, he became the Senate majority leader, serving until 1960. LBJ worked productively with Republican president Dwight D. Eisenhower and his unifying his party on important legislation made LBJ a powerful figure in Washington. In 1960, Kennedy won the party's presidential nomination after a close contest with LBJ and selected Johnson as his running mate, and the ticket went on to win over Republican Richard Nixon. Nixon won the presidency in 1968, after the Vietnam War escalation resulted in Johnson's decision not to seek a second term. Johnson retired to his Texas ranch, working on his memoirs and on establishing his presidential library at the University of Texas at

Austin. He died of a heart attack at his ranch at age sixty-four, on January 22, 1973.

Kennedy, Edward Moore "Ted" (1932–2009)

Known as the "Lion of the Senate," Ted Kennedy was the youngest brother of John F. Kennedy (JFK) and Robert Kennedy. He was elected to the Senate in 1962, when he was thirty, and served until his death in 2009. He was an icon of political progressivism and liberal thought. Ted's grandfather was John "Honey Fitz" Fitzgerald, mayor of Boston. His father was millionaire businessperson, Joseph Kennedy, who held many important posts in and out of government. Ted attended Harvard University, the International Law School at The Hague, and then Virginia Law School, receiving his law degree in 1959. He campaigned for JFK in his 1960 presidential race.

In 1962, he was elected to JFK's Senate seat. After Robert Kennedy's assassination in 1968, Ted became the standard-bearer of the Kennedy clan. He became the majority whip of the Senate in 1969. A deadly auto accident in 1969, off an unmarked bridge in Chappaquiddick Island, which killed his twenty-eight-year-old companion, ended his presidential ambitions. He returned to the Senate. In 1980, he briefly ran for the presidential nomination, losing to Jimmy Carter. He gave a hallmark convention speech that year. In 1982, he was divorced from his wife, Joan. He was reelected to the Senate in 1982 and 1988. In 1992, he remarried, to Victoria Reggie, with whom he had two more children. During Bill Clinton's presidency, Ted Kennedy led the effort for health-care reform and authored the 1997 Children's Health Act. By the 1990s, Ted became the Senate's most prominent member, amassing an impressive record of bills sponsored and enacted on immigration reform, criminal code reform, fair housing, public education, health care, AIDS research, and various programs for aid to the poor. He served on the Senate Judiciary Committee, advocating liberal positions on abortion, capital punishment, and busing. He maintained notable bipartisan friendships with such conservative stalwarts as Senators Nancy Kassebaum, John McCain, and Orrin Hatch and worked to enact President Bush's signature No Child Left behind Act. After the 9/11 attacks in 2001, Ted sponsored the bipartisan Bioterrorism Preparedness and Response Act. He suffered a seizure in 2008 and was diagnosed with a brain tumor, which was surgically removed. He suffered another seizure in 2009 and passed away in August 2009 on Cape Cod, Massachusetts.

Koch, David (1940–)

David Koch is the executive vice president of Koch Industries. He was born in Wichita, Kansas. He earned his BS degree from the Massachusetts Institute of Technology. He joined the family oil business in 1970, which he and his brother, Charles, built into Koch Industries, a diversified corporation of pipelines, refineries, building materials, paper towels, and Dixie Cups, valued at $115 billion. David Koch's 2017 estimated worth was $48 billion. He resides in New York City. In 1984, David founded Americans for Prosperity and Citizens for a Sound Economy. In 1980, he ran for vice president on the Libertarian ticket with Ed Clark for president. He is a noted philanthropist: in 2006, he gave $20 million to the Johns Hopkins University School of Medicine for cancer research; in 2008, he pledged $100 million over ten years to renovate New York State Theatre in the Lincoln Center for the Performing Arts; and $10 million to renovate the fountain outside the Metropolitan Museum of Art. David and Charles pledged to spend $900 million on political activity, education, and criminal justice reform in 2016. They normally are big donors to the Republican Party and its presidential candidate, but with Donald Trump as the nominee, they spent their money on congressional "down-ticket" races. According to *Forbes* magazine, David ranks ninth among billionaires and seventh in the United States and was ranked sixth in 2005.

Lieberman, Joseph (1942–)

Joseph Lieberman was a U.S. senator from Connecticut (serving as Democrat from 1989 to 2006 and as an Independent from 2007 to 2012). He served in the Senate from 1989 to 2012. He was moderately conservative and an effective legislator, being the primary sponsor of twenty-eight enacted bills. Lieberman was elected Connecticut attorney general, serving from 1983 to 1988. He was elected to the Connecticut state senate (1970–1980). He received his bachelor's degree from Yale in 1964 and his law degree from Yale Law School in 1967. After gaining popularity for his consumer and environmental advocacy, he won his first election to the U.S. Senate in 1988. He was the Senate's first Orthodox Jew. He achieved a reputation for pragmatic independence, personal integrity, and moral rectitude. In the Senate he formed a close friendship with Republican senator John McCain, who briefly considered asking him to run as his vice president running mate. In 2000, Lieberman was the Democratic vice presidential running mate of Al Gore, the first Jew on an American national ticket. In 2004, Lieberman announced his candidacy for the Democratic presidential nomination but soon dropped out of the race. In 2006, he won reelection to the U.S. Senate as an Independent after losing the Democratic primary race. He caucused with the Democrats in the Senate. He lives in New Haven, CT, with his wife, Hadassah. They have four children. Lieberman is author of five books, including *In Praise of Public Life* (2000) and *An Amazing Adventure* (2003).

Limbaugh, Rush (1951–)

Rush Limbaugh is an American entertainer, radio talk show host, writer, and conservative political commentator. He was born in Cape Girardeau, Missouri. He attended but did not graduate from Southeast Missouri State University. He worked for several years in various radio capacities, as a disc jockey and sports newscaster, until he began a radio talk show in California in 1984. In 1988, he began broadcasting his own radio show from WABC in New York City. He is oft married, four times with three divorces, which is ironic given the party's emphasis on family values. His current spouse is Kathryn Rogers, whom he married in 2010. He has received numerous awards: the Marconi Award for Syndicated Radio Personality of the Year, in 1992, 1995, 2000, and 2004, and the William F. Buckley Jr. Award for Media Excellence in 2007. From 1992 to 1996, he broadcast a one-half-hour syndicated television show produced by Roger Ailes. He launched a line of neckties designed by his then wife, Marta. Ronald Reagan called him the number one voice for conservatism in America. His talk shows are enormously successful: his weekly cumulative audience is estimated at 13.25 million listeners, the most listened-to talk show program in America. His *Rush Limbaugh* television show airs for three hours on weekdays. In 2008, he signed a $400 million contract to run until 2016. In 2015, *Forbes* magazine listed his earnings at $79 million for 2014. He was ranked by *Forbes* as the eleventh highest-earning celebrity in the world. In 2003, his career survived a prescription-drug addiction scandal. He has authored numerous books, including *The Way Things Ought to Be* (1993) and *See: I Told You So* (1993), both *New York Times* bestsellers. His other books are a series: *Rush Revere and the Brave Pilgrims* (2013), *Rush Revere and the First Patriots* (2014), *Rush Revere and the American Revolution* (2014), and *Rush Revere and the Star-Spangled Banner* (2015). He is widely considered *the* voice of the conservative movement, a powerful voice in the Tea Party movement, and the most influential commentator in Republican politics.

Lujan, Ben Ray (1972–)

Ben Ray Lujan (D-NM) is a representative in Congress and serving as chair of the Democratic Congressional Campaign Committee. Born and raised in New Mexico, he earned his BA degree in business administration from New Mexico Highlands University. He served as New Mexico Cultural Affairs

Department's director of administrative services and chief financial officer. Lujan then served as chairman of the New Mexico Public Regulation Commission and worked to increase renewable energy portfolios to include solar energy, and when New Mexico, California, Oregon, and Washington formed the Joint Action Framework on Climate change, he helped craft its regional solutions to climate change. He worked to overhaul the New Mexico Fire Fund to improve fire services in New Mexico and to improve health care by investigating denial practices of the health insurance industry. Lujan sits on the Energy and Commerce Committee and the Health Subcommittee. He participates in a variety of caucus in the U.S. House of Representatives that reflect the diversity of his congressional district: Congressional Hispanic Caucus, Native-American Caucus, and the Natural Gas Caucus. Along with Representative Frank Wolf (R-VA), Lujan founded the bipartisan Technology Transfer Caucus to help move technology innovations. He serves as cochair to two bipartisan caucuses: the National Labs Caucus and the Congressional Cleanup Caucus. He was assigned to the House Democratic leadership as chief deputy whip in 2013.

Madison, James (1751–1836)

James Madison was a founding father and the fourth American president (1809–1817). The Virginia-born Madison composed the first drafts of the Constitution and the Bill of Rights, earning the nickname "Father of the Constitution." Along with Thomas Jefferson, in 1792, he founded the Democratic-Republican Party, America's first opposition political party (to the Federalists). Madison served President Thomas Jefferson as secretary of state, negotiating the Louisiana Purchase from France in 1803. While president, Madison convinced the Congress to declare war against Great Britain in 1812. He was born in Virginia in 1751, the oldest of twelve children and raised on the family plantation, Montpelier. In 1769, he attended the College of New Jersey (now Princeton University). In 1776, he represented Orange County at the Virginia Constitution Convention to organize a new government independent of British rule. While in the Virginia legislature, he met his lifelong friend, Thomas Jefferson. Madison, with Jefferson, fought for religious freedom. In 1780, he became a Virginia delegate to the Continental Congress in Philadelphia and left Congress in 1783 to return to the Virginia Assembly to craft its religious freedom statute. Called back to Congress to help draft a new Constitution to amend the Articles of Confederation, Madison studied other world governments. In 1787, at the Constitutional Convention in Philadelphia, Madison presented his "Virginia Plan," which detailed the separation of powers or checks and balances system with three parts: legislative, executive, and judicial branches. Madison led efforts to get the new Constitution ratified, writing a number of essays anonymously under the title "The Federalist Papers"; in all, eighty-five essays were produced between 1787 and 1788 by Madison, Alexander Hamilton, and John Jay. The new Constitution was ratified in 1788, and Madison was elected to the newly formed U.S. House of Representatives, serving from 1789 to 1797. He drafted the Bill of Rights, ratified by the states in 1791. After he and Jefferson founded the Democratic-Republican Party in 1792, he, along with Jefferson and James Monroe, became the only Democratic-Republicans elected as U.S. presidents. In 1794, Madison, at age forty-three, married twenty-six-year-old Dolley Todd, a Quaker widow with one son. During their forty-one years of marriage, they were rarely apart. When Jefferson became the third president, he appointed Madison as his secretary of state (1801–1809). In the presidential election of 1808, Madison defeated Federalist Charles Pinckney to win the office. In 1812, in response to British attacks on American ships and an embargo, Madison urged Congress to declare war, which soon became known as "Mr. Madison's War." In 1816, Madison ran for reelection against Federalist DeWitt Clinton. In 1814, British troops invaded and burned down the White House, the Capitol, and the Library of Congress. Weary of battle, Britain and the United States negotiated an end to the war, with the Treaty of Ghent signed in December 1814. Madison left Washington in 1817, returning to Montpelier much respected as a great thinker, communicator, and diplomat. In 1826, he became rector of the University of Virginia, founded by Jefferson. Madison died at Montpelier at age eighty-five, in June 1836.

Mansfield, Mike (1903–2001)

Mike Mansfield was born in New York City in 1903, but the family moved to Great Falls, Montana, in 1910, after his mother's death. Mike was raised by an aunt and uncle there. At fourteen, lying about his age, he joined the U.S. Navy for World War I, later serving in the army and the marines in the Philippines and China, beginning his lifelong interest in Asia. In 1922, he returned to Montana to work in the copper mines and attend the Montana School of Mines. While in Butte, he married Maureen Hayes, in 1932, and began a lifelong partnership lasting until her death in 2000. He graduated from the Montana State University (now the University of Montana) in 1933 and earned a master's degree in 1934. He taught Latin American and east Asian history at the University of Montana until 1942. He began his political career then, being elected to the U.S. House of Representatives, where he served five terms from Montana's first district. He was elected to the U.S. Senate in 1952 and reelected in 1958, 1964, and 1970. He was selected as Democratic assistant majority leader in 1957, and in 1961, Senate majority leader, in which office he served until 1977, longer than any other majority leader in U.S. history. He worked with leaders across the aisle and was respected by both sides. He led the passage in the Senate of the "Great Society" legislation. Presidents Truman and Eisenhower appointed him delegate to the United Nations (in 1951 and 1958, respectively). He became an authority on U.S.-Asia relations and undertook foreign policy assignments for Presidents Roosevelt, Kennedy, Johnson, Nixon, and Ford and paved the way for Nixon's visit to China in 1972. In 1977, President Carter appointed Mansfield ambassador to Japan. He was reappointed by President Reagan, serving until 1989, the longest-serving ambassador to Japan. Following his retirement in 1989, he served as senior advisor to the international financial firm of Goldman Sachs in Washington, D.C. He died there in October 2001.

McCain, John (1936–2018)

Senator John McCain (R-AZ) was born at the Coco Solo Naval Station, Panama Canal, a son of Admiral John S. McCain Jr. Both his father and grandfather were four-star admirals. McCain graduated from the Naval Academy in 1958 and the Naval Flight School in 1960. He volunteered for Vietnam and, in 1967, was shot down on his twenty-third mission. He was moved to the "Hanoi Hilton" in 1969 and spent five and a half years in prison there. A true war hero, he was awarded the Silver Star, the Bronze Star, a Purple Heart, the Legion of Merit, a Distinguished Flying Cross, and a Naval Commendation Medal. In 1981, he retired as a captain and moved to Arizona. He was first elected to the U.S. House of Representatives in 1982, representing Arizona's first district, and reelected in 1984 and 1986. He became embroiled in a campaign finance scandal, known as the Keating Affair, but survived the controversy and went on to sponsor campaign finance reform, the McCain-Feingold Act of 2002. In 1987, he ran for the U.S. Senate, serving until his death in 2018. A consummate "establishment Republican," while in the Senate, McCain served on various committees, including terms as chair of the Armed Services Committee, chair of the Senate Commerce Committee, and chair of the Indian Affairs Committee, and on the Committee on Homeland Security. He was an ex officio member of the Committee on Intelligence and cochaired the Senate National Security Caucus. McCain ran unsuccessfully for the Republican presidential nomination in 2000, losing to George W. Bush, and ran and won the nomination in 2008 but lost to then Senator Barack Obama. McCain enjoyed a reputation for being a "maverick" in the Senate, often crossing party lines and voting in a bipartisan manner on some key bills but compiling overall a solidly conservative record. He was the primary sponsor of fifty-three bills that became law. His voting record is captured well by his ratings from numerous outside organizations: Americans for Prosperity = 89 percent; U.S. Chamber of Commerce = 83 percent; Club for Growth = 78 percent; FreedomWorks = 45 percent; ACLU = 35 percent; Numbers USA = 27 percent; League of Conservation Voters = 20 percent; Human Rights Campaign = 0 percent; and Planned Parenthood Action Fund = 0 percent. His most controversial vote in 2017 was his deciding vote that kept in place the Affordable Care Act (Obamacare), chiding his fellow Republicans for failing to consider the law under regular order. McCain was married twice, to Carol Shepp (1965–1980) and to Cindy Hensley (1980–2018) and had seven children. He was diagnosed with a fatal brain cancer condition and died on August 25, 2018, in Arizona.

McConnell, Mitch (1942–)

Senator Mitch McConnell (R-KY) became the Senate majority leader after the 2014 Senate elections, only the second senator from Kentucky (after Henry Clay) to serve as majority leader. As such, McConnell plays a key role in all Senate legislative proceedings. He led their efforts in strident opposition to comprehensive immigration reform and to the vigorous border control and other conservative policy positions of the majority on a broad array of policy issue matters. He previously served as Senate minority leader in the 110th and 113th Congresses and as majority whip in the 108th and 109th Congresses. He served as chairman of the National Republican Senatorial Committee (1998–2000). He was first elected to the U.S. Senate in 1984. He graduated cum laude from the University of Louisville College of Arts and Sciences and took his JD from the College of Law, University of Kentucky, where he served as president of the Student Bar Association. Prior to his election to the U.S. Senate, he served as deputy assistant attorney general to President Gerald Ford and as judge-executive of Jefferson County, Kentucky, from 1978 to 1985. He served as a senior member of the Appropriations, Agriculture, and Rules Committees in the Senate.

Murdoch, Rupert (1931–)

Rupert Murdoch is the Australian-born American media mogul and multibillionaire (his 2018 net worth was estimated at $17.5 billion). He was born in Melbourne, Australia, the son of the owner of several local and regional newspapers. In 1982, his father died and he took over the Adelaide newspapers *News* and *Sunday Mail*. By 1956, he expanded to Perth and then to Sydney in 1960. In 1965, he founded the country's first daily paper. He moved to London in 1968, buying the *News of the World*, a Sunday tabloid. He expanded to the United States in 1973, buying the *San Antonia News*, and founded *Star*, in 1974. In 1976, he bought the *New York Post* and, in 1979, founded and headed News Corp, a global conglomerate. In the 1980s and 1990s, he expanded his media empire buying *Chicago Sun-Times*, *Village Voice*, *New York Magazine*, and the *Times* and *Sunday Times* in London. In 1985, he acquired 20th Century Fox and Fox Film, which he consolidated into Fox, Inc. In 1990, he set up STAR TV in Hong Kong. He is also part owner of the Los Angeles Kings, NHL franchise, the Los Angeles Lakers, Staple Center, Fox Sports Radio, and Fox Sports.com. In 2007, he purchased Dow Jones and the *Wall Street Journal*. Always involved in conservative politics, in 2010, he donated $1 million each to the RGA, the U.S. Chamber of Commerce, and various Republican candidates. In 2015, he handed leadership of 21st Century Fox to his son, James. Fox News has developed into the dominant voice of conservative politics in the United States and has played a particularly important role in Republican presidential politics, on occasion backing primary election challengers to establishment Republicans.

Murkowski, Lisa (1957–)

Senator Lisa Murkowski is the first Alaska-born senator and only the sixth senator to serve the state. As the state's senior senator, she is a third-generation Alaskan, born in Ketchikan. She joined the Senate in 2002, focusing on energy, health care, education, military or veterans affairs, and infrastructure development. Murkowski is only the thirty-second woman to serve in the U.S. Senate since its founding in 1789. She rose to leadership roles quickly, chairing the Senate Energy and Natural Research Committee and on the Senate Appropriations Committee, where she chairs its Interior and Environmental Subcommittee. She is a member of the Senate Health, Education, Labor and Pensions Committee, the first Alaskan to serve on that panel, and is a senior member of the Senate Indian Affairs Committee. Murkowski earned a BA in economics from Georgetown University in 1980 and her law degree from Willamette University in 1985. She practiced commercial law in Anchorage before being elected to the Alaska House of Representatives (1999–2002). She was appointed to the U.S. Senate in 2002, by her father, who resigned the seat to become governor of Alaska. She won her first full term in 2004 and was reelected in 2010 in a historic write-in campaign, the first successful write-in effort to the Senate since 1954. She became Alaska's senior senator after her reelection in 2016. She was elected vice chair of the Senate Republican Conference (2009–2010). She is married to Verne Martell, and they have two children.

Norquist, Grover (1956–)

Grover Norquist grew up in Weston, Massachusetts, and is of Swedish ancestry. He became involved in politics in 1968 as a volunteer for the Nixon campaign. He enrolled in Harvard University in 1974, earning an AB and MBA degree. He was editor at the *Harvard Crimson* and helped publish libertarian-leaning *Harvard Chronicle* and was a member of the Hasty Pudding

Theatricals. Norquist was the executive director of both the National Taxpayers Union and the National College Republicans and served as the economist and chief speechwriter at the U.S. Chamber of Commerce (1983–1984). He is best known for founding the Americans for Tax Reform (ATR), in 1985, at the request of President Ronald Reagan. ATR advocated the Taxpayer Protection Pledge, which in 2012 was signed on by 95 percent of all Republicans in Congress. ATR lobbies in Congress to reduce government revenues by a percentage of the gross domestic product (GDP), opposes all tax increases, and supports the Taxpayer Bill of Rights (TABOR) and transparency initiatives. Norquist and ATR oppose cap and trade and efforts to regulate health care. He vigorously opposed President Bill Clinton's health-care plan. Their annual meetings went on to become the most-attended event for Republican operatives and "Grand Central Station" for the conservative movement. In 2011, Senate Majority Leader Harry Reid (D-NV) blamed Norquist for the lack of progress of the Joint Select Committee on Deficit Reduction as the Norquist Pledge binds signatories to oppose deficit reduction that include any element of increased tax revenue. He is listed as one of the five primary leaders of the post-Goldwater conservative movement. He is considered one of the coauthors of the 1994 *Contract with America* and helped rally the grassroots efforts to win the Republican majority in the U.S. House of Representatives. He chronicled the campaign in his book *Rock the House*. In 1988, 1992, and 1996, Norquist was a member of the Republican Platform Committee. It was an early supporter of George W. Bush's presidential campaigns, serving as its unofficial liaison to the conservative movement. He is involved with various ethnic and religious minorities and the free-market community with such groups as the Action Institute, the Christian Coalition, and Toward Tradition. He is active in the Tea Party movement. Jack Abramoff claims Norquist and the ATR were involved in his Indian lobbying scandal, which Norquist denies; he has not been charged with any crime. In 2004, he helped California governor Arnold Schwarzenegger with plans to privatize the CalPERS system. Norquist favors statehood for Puerto Rico. He serves on various boards of directors, including the National Rifle Association, the American Conservative Union, the Hispanic Leadership Fund, the Indian-American Republican Caucus, and ParentalRights.org, which advocates a parental rights constitutional amendment. In 2010, he joined the advisory board of GOProud, a lesbian, gay, bisexual, and transgender conservatives' organization. He is cofounder of the Merritt Group and is a member of the Council on Foreign Relations. In 2004, at age forty-eight, he married a Palestinian Muslim, Samah Alrayyes, a Kuwait PR specialist, and they adopted two children.

O'Neill, Thomas Philip, Jr. "Tip" (1912–1994)

Representative Tip O'Neill was a representative from Massachusetts to the U.S. House of Representatives from 1953 to 1987, from JFK's district, and the third-longest serving Speaker of the House (1977–1987) in U.S. history. He was born in Cambridge, Massachusetts, in 1912; graduated from Boston College in 1936; and was an insurance agent and realtor before being elected to the Massachusetts State House of Representatives, serving from 1936 to 1953, including as its Speaker from 1949 to 1952. He was elected to the U.S. House of Representatives in 1953. He served as chair of the Select Committee on Campaign Expenditures, was the House majority whip (1971–1973), and then Speaker of the House of Representatives. Tip married Millie Miller, with whom he had five children. He authored, with William Novak, *Man of the House: The Life and Political Memoirs of Speaker Tip O'Neill* (1987). He decided not to run for reelection in 1986. He died on January 5, 1994, in Boston.

Pelosi, Nancy (1940–)

Nancy Pelosi was first elected to the U.S. House of Representatives in 1987. She was born in Baltimore, Maryland, and now resides in San Francisco. She took her BA from Trinity College in 1962. She also studied at the Institute of Notre Dame and at Washington University. She was a PR executive from 1986 to 1987 and served as the California Democratic Party northern chair from 1977 to 1981. She was state chair of the party from 1981 to 1963 and served as the Democratic Senatorial Campaign Committee finance chair from 1986 to 1987. She once again served as the minority leader in the U.S. House of Representatives, after a distinguished term as Speaker of the House (2001–2014). She has an almost perfect liberal voting record. She has been elected and reelected by huge margins. She joined with Senator Dianne Feinstein on sponsoring bills to increase border security along the California-Mexico border and for the House comprehensive immigration reform bill in 2013. In 2019, she once again became Speaker of the House and leads the party in opposition to President Trump's and the Republican Party's policy agenda.

Rankin, Jeannette (1880–1973)

Jeannette Ranking was the first woman elected to Congress (R-WY), one of the few suffragists elected to Congress, and the only member of Congress to vote against the U.S. entry into both World War I and World War II. She was the daughter of a rancher and a schoolteacher, born near Missoula, Montana. She graduated from Montana State University (now the University of Montana) in 1902 and went on to attend the New York School of Philanthropy (now the Columbia University School of Social Work). She briefly was a social worker in Spokane, Washington, attended the University of Washington in Seattle, and there joined the woman suffrage movement and achieved the goal of woman's suffrage in Washington State in 1910—a full decade before enactment of the Nineteenth Amendment to the U.S. Constitution. She became a professional lobbyist for the National American Woman Suffrage Association (NAWSA) and organized efforts to gain the vote for women in 1914. She ran for the U.S. House of Representatives from

Montana in 1916, winning the GOP's nomination for one of two at-large House seats, on a progressive platform pledging to work for a constitutional women's suffrage amendment. A lifelong pacifist, she voted against going to war, which won in the House 373–50. As the first woman member of the House, she was on the front lines of the suffrage fight, advocating creation of the Committee on Woman Suffrage, and was appointed to it when it was created in 1918. She opened the first floor debate on the amendment in 1918. She served in the House (1917–1919) and was a member of the Committee on Public Lands, crucial to Montana, and focused on western issues. She advocated on behalf of miners after a mine disaster in Butte, earning the opposition of mine owners. She ran on a third-party ticket in 1919 and lost. After her first service in Congress, she campaigned for pacifism and social welfare, attending the Women's International Conference for Permanent Peace in Switzerland in 1919, joined the Woman's International League for Peace and Freedom, and founded in 1938 the Georgia Peace Society. She was the leading lobbyist for the National Council for the Prevention of War from 1929 to 1939 and was the field secretary for the National Consumers League. She won a seat in Congress in 1940, serving from 1941 to 1943. She was supported by eminent progressives like Senator Robert La Follette Jr. (R-WI) and Mayor Fiorello La Guardia of New York City. She won by 54 percent of the vote. She again served on the Committee on Public Lands and the Committee on Insular Affairs, both useful to her western constituency. She opposed the Lend-Lease Bill, and when, after the Pearl Harbor attack, the House voted for a war resolution, she was the sole vote against it as it passed 388–1. She decided not to run for reelection in 1942, and her district seat went to the internationalist Democrat, Mike Mansfield. After her second term in Congress, Rankin divided her time between Montana and Georgia, and she traveled to India to support the nonviolent protest tactics of Mohandas Karamchand Gandhi. On her ninetieth birthday, in 1970, she was celebrated in the Rayburn House Office

Building with a reception and dinner. She died in Carmel, California, in 1973 while considering another run for Congress to oppose the Vietnam War.

Rayburn, Samuel Taliaferro (1882–1961)

Sam Rayburn was a representative from Texas (D-TX, fourth) who served in the U.S. House of Representatives from 1913 to 1961. He was born near Kingston, Texas, in 1882. He graduated from East Texas Normal College in 1903, then studied law at the University of Texas at Austin, and was admitted to the bar in 1908. He practiced law in Bonham, Texas. He was elected to the Texas House of Representatives (1907–1913), including as its forty-second Speaker (1911–1913). Rayburn was elected to the U.S. House of Representatives in 1913 and chaired the Committee on Interstate and Foreign Commerce (1933–1937), was majority leader (1937–1941) and minority leader (1947–1951, 1953–1955), and was elected Speaker of the House in 1940 to fill the vacancy caused by the death of Speaker William Bankhead. Rayburn was then reelected Speaker in 1941 and served in that office from 1941 to 1947, again from 1949 to 1953, and in 1955 until his death in 1961 at age seventy-nine of cancer. He held the longest tenure as Speaker, over seventeen years in all. He was noted for fairness and integrity. For example of the latter, he paid for his own travel on an inspection trip to the Panama Canal. He was a mentor to Lyndon Johnson. He was influential in the construction of the famous U.S. Route 66, about which he coined the phrase "sun belt." He was married briefly to Matze Jones (divorcing only a few months later) and had no children. Texas honored him by dedicating his home as the Sam Rayburn House Museum.

Reid, Harry (1939–)

Harry Reid was a five-term Democratic senator from Nevada and Senate majority leader from 2007 through 2014. He was born in Searchlight, Nevada, in 1939. He was the third of four sons. His father was a miner who committed suicide in 1972.

He attended the College of Southern Utah and Utah State University, earning a degree in political science and history. He went on to earn a JD from George Washington University School of Law. He entered public service after law school, serving as Henderson city attorney and member of the Nevada Assembly. He was elected Nevada lieutenant governor in 1970 and served until 1974, when he ran for a seat in the U.S. Senate, losing to his Republican opponent, former Nevada Governor Paul Laxalt. He served five years as chairman of the Nevada Gaming Commission and then ran for and won election to the U.S. House of Representatives in 1982. He was elected to the U.S. Senate in 1986. In the Senate he quickly rose to leadership positions. He was the Senate Democratic whip from 1999 to 2005 while also serving as chair of the Senate Ethics Committee (2001–2003). In 2005, he succeeded South Dakota's Tom Daschle as Senate minority leader and became majority leader in 2006, after the midterm elections saw the Democrats taking control of the Senate. He spearheaded ethics reform bills, and when Barack Obama became president, Reid pushed through his legislative agenda, most notably the American Recovery and Reinvestment Act of 2009 and the Patient Protection and Affordable Care Act (a.k.a. Obamacare) of 2010. In 2012, he reversed his position on same-sex marriage along with a majority of his party. He survived alleged involvement with the Jack Abramoff scandal. He saved construction of the Las Vegas CityCenter casino and shopping complex, secured funding for alternative-energy projects, and promoted tourism overseas. He fought designation of Nevada's Yucca Mountain as a site for spent nuclear waste. He was central to Republican and Democratic negotiations over spending cuts and tax increases, criticizing House Speaker John Boehner, and he helped draft a version of the so-called fiscal cliff legislation, passed in 2013. Republican wins in the 2014 midterms pushed him back into the role of minority leader. In 2016, he opted not to run for reelection. Harry Reid was married to Landra Gould in 1959, and they have a daughter and four sons. He and his wife converted to

Mormonism while attending college and addressed issues of his "conflict between Mormonism and his Democratic political possessions" at a speech at Brigham Young University in Utah in 2007. He suffered a stroke in 2005 and was involved in a car crash in 2012 that left him blind in his right eye.

Ryan, Paul (1970–)

Representative Paul Ryan (R-WI) was the Speaker of the House between October 2015 and January 2019. He was born in Janesville, Wisconsin. In 2000, he married Janna Little. He was educated at Miami University of Ohio, earning his degree in economics and political science, and at American University. In his early career, he worked for a media consulting firm and was legislative aide to Senator Bob Kasten, Senator Sam Brownback, and Representative Jack Kemp. In 1998, at age twenty-eight, he was elected to the House of Representatives from Wisconsin's First District. He served on and chaired the House Budget Committee (2011–2015), where he notably issued the Republican budget plan, *The Path to Prosperity*. He chaired the House Ways and Means Committee in 2015. He was the Republican Party's nominee for vice president in 2012, with Mitt Romney for president. In 2013, he sponsored, with Democratic senator Patty Murphy, the Bipartisan Budget Act of 2013. When Representative John Boehner suddenly resigned as Speaker, and from Congress, in October 2015, Paul Ryan was elected to that position.

Sanders, Bernie (1941–)

Bernie Sanders (I-VT) is in his second term in the U.S. Senate, one of two officially "independent" senators who caucus with the Democrats (the other is Angus King, I-ME). Former Senator Joseph Lieberman (I-CT) was also an Independent who caucused with the Democrats, but he retired from the Senate in 2006. Bernie is the longest-serving Independent in congressional history. Bernie Sanders was first elected to the Senate in 2006, reelected in 2012, and is running for reelection in 2018.

He was born in Brooklyn, New York, and attended Brooklyn College and the University of Chicago, where he earned his degree in political science. After graduating in 1964, he moved to Vermont. In 1981, he ran for and won (by only twelve votes) the office of mayor of Burlington, serving four terms—until 1989. He was married to Deborah Shiling (1964–1966), met and had a son with Susan Mott (in 1969), and married his second wife, Jane O'Meara, in 1988. She was president of Burlington College and has three children from a previous marriage. He lectured at the John F. Kennedy School of Government at Harvard and at Hamilton College in upstate New York. Sanders served in the U.S. House of Representatives (1991–2007). In the Senate, he focuses on single-payer health care; more affordable higher education; tuition-free colleges and universities; expansion of Social Security, Medicare, and Medicaid; and same-sex marriage and is prochoice. Bernie has served on the Senate Committee on Budget; Committee on Health, Education, Labor and Pensions; Committee on Veterans Affairs; Committee on Environment and Public Works; and Committee on Energy and Natural Resources. He has championed for an amendment to overturn the Supreme Court case of *Citizens United*. During 2015–2016, he registered as a Democrat to run for the Democratic Party nomination against Hillary Clinton, the only Jewish candidate for the office from a major political party who stayed in the race throughout the primary election season. He lost only after a long-fought battle and winning 43 percent of the primary votes.

Schumer, Charles "Chuck" (1950–)

Charles "Chuck" Ellis Schumer is the senior U.S. senator from New York. He was born in Brooklyn. He and his wife, Iris Weinshall, reside in Brooklyn with two daughters. In 1980, he ran for and won a seat in the Ninth Congressional District and served the district for eighteen years. In 1998, he was elected to the U.S. Senate and became senior senator when Daniel Patrick Moynihan retired in 2000. Reelected in 2004, Schumer served on the Senate Finance Committee and as chair of the Democratic Senatorial Campaign Committee for two cycles, stepping down in 2008. In 2006, he was selected to serve as vice chair of the Democratic Conference and, in 2010, as chair of the Democratic Policy and Communications Center. He is the ranking member on the Senate Rules Committee, which oversees federal elections, voting rights, campaign finance, and the operation of the Senate complex. He sits on the Banking, Housing, and Urban Affairs Committee; is the ranking member of the Judiciary Committee and its Subcommittee on Immigration, Refugees, and Border Security; and serves on the Joint Committee on the Library of Congress. In 2017, he replaced Senator Harry Reid as his party's leader in the U.S. Senate.

Soros, George (1930–)

George Soros is the founder and chair of the Soros Fund Management and the Open Society Foundation. He was born in Budapest, survived the Nazi occupation, and fled communist Hungary for England in 1947. He graduated from the London School of Economics. He moved to the United States, becoming a billionaire through the international investment fund he founded and managed. He is a renowned philanthropist, whose Open Society supports efforts in more than one hundred countries, and in 2011, Soros spent $835 million to promote human rights and transparency. He has authored more than a dozen books, including *The Tragedy of the European Union* (2014). He is a leading financial supporter of the liberal Democratic Party's electoral efforts and Democratic-related super political action committees. He is the Democratic Party's equivalent to the Republican's Koch brothers.

Trumka, Richard (1949–)

Richard Trumka is president of the American Federation of Labor and Congress of Industrial Organizations (AFL-CIO), which, at an estimated 12.5 million members, is the largest labor union organization in the United States. He was elected president of the AFL-CIO in 2009, after serving as its secretary-treasurer, from 1995 to 2009. He spearheaded union organizing and collective bargaining, affiliating with other labor and worker alliances. In 2014, the union fulfilled a $10 billion pledge to the Clinton Global Initiative to invest in the nation's crumbling infrastructure while boosting the sagging job market. He led the AFL-CIO in revamping its political campaign, expanded its political outreach beyond union members and their families, and created a capacity for year-round mobilization. He was instrumental in President Obama's 2008 and 2012 elections, as well of the election of progressives like Senators Elizabeth Warren (D-MA) and Sherrod Brown (D-PA).

Van Buren, Martin (1782–1862)

Martin Van Buren was the first president to be born a citizen of the United States. He rose quickly in New York politics, winning a U.S. Senate seat in 1821 and presiding over a sophisticated state political organization known as the Albany Regency. He helped form a new Democratic Party from a coalition of Jeffersonian Republican-Democrats in order to back the military hero, Andrew Jackson, for president. He was born six years after the colonists declared independence from Britain, of Dutch descent. His father was a local farmer and tavern keeper. Van Buren apprenticed with a lawyer in 1796 and opened his own practice in 1803. In 1807, he married his cousin and childhood sweetheart, Hannah Hoes, and they had four sons. Hannah died in 1819 of tuberculosis, and Martin never remarried. Van Buren served two terms in the New York state senate and was the state attorney general. He was elected to the U.S. Senate in 1821. After John Quincy Adams won the presidency in 1824, Van Buren led the opposition to back Andrew Jackson, who won the office in 1828. Martin left the Senate in 1828 to run for governor of New York. When Jackson won the presidency, Van Buren resigned as governor to become minister to Great Britain and, in 1832, earned the Democratic nomination for vice president with Jackson, opposing the rechartering of the Bank of the United States. The Jackson-Van Buren ticket easily defeated Henry Clay and the Whig Party. Jackson handpicked Van Buren as his successor in 1836, and Van Buren defeated William Henry Harrison, also a Whig. A financial panic—a depression in today's terms—hit in 1837, and Van Buren's administration never recovered from it, and his popularity also declined during a long and costly war with the Seminole Indians of Florida. He lost his reelection bid to Harrison in 1840. He tried and failed again to get the Democratic nomination in 1844, refusing to endorse annexation of Texas, which led to James Polk being elected. Van Buren then ran as the Free Soil candidate against Zachary Taylor, who won in 1848. He returned to his Kinderhook estate, watching the slavery issue tear the county apart in the 1850s. He returned to the Democratic Party in 1852 supporting the moderate Democrats led by Stephen Douglas. He wrote his autobiography and died in 1862, less than a year after the Civil War broke out.

Webster, Daniel (1782–1852)

Daniel Webster was a Whig Party leader, member of Congress, and secretary of state. He was born in 1782 in Salisbury, New Hampshire. He graduated from Dartmouth College in 1801 and became a successful Boston lawyer. He was elected to the U.S. House of Representatives in 1812 and, in 1827, to the U.S. Senate. He led the Whig Party in opposition to Andrew Jackson and the Democrats. He ran for the presidency but lost in 1836. In 1840, when William Henry Harrison won the office, Harrison named Webster secretary of state. Harrison died in office in 1841; when John Tyler assumed the office, all the Whig cabinet members resigned except Daniel Webster. In 1842, he successfully negotiated the Webster-Ashburton Treaty with Great Britain, resolving a dispute over the Maine-Canada border. He returned as secretary of state in 1850, appointed by President Millard Fillmore. He oversaw enforcement of the Fugitive Slave Act. He died in 1852 in Marshfield, Massachusetts.

This chapter presents in full or in synopsis several data and documents related to Congress. In its first section, it presents eleven tables and figures that graphically illustrate data about Congress. The final section presents excerpts of key documents that span the history of the American Congress. They synthesize laws, treaties, declarations, resolutions, and Supreme Court decisions that shaped the evolution of the functions and power of Congress, as discussed throughout this volume.

Data

The following table depicts which party held the majority in each chamber of Congress since 1955. The last twenty years, in particular, have seen frequent shifts in partisan control in Congress.

Table 5.1   Partisan Control of Congress

Session	Years	Senate Control	House Control
84th–96th	1955–1981	Democrat	Democrat
97th–99th	1981–1987	Republican	Democrat
100th–103rd	1987–1995	Democrat	Democrat
104th–106th	1995–2001	Republican	Republican

(Continued)

Lawmakers watch as President Donald Trump delivers the State of the Union address in the chamber of the U.S. House of Representatives at the U.S. Capitol Building on February 5, 2019, in Washington, D.C. A group of female Democratic lawmakers chose to wear white to the speech in solidarity with women and a nod to the suffragette movement. (Alex Wong/Getty Images)

Table 5.1 (Continued)

Session	Years	Senate Control	House Control
107th	2001–2002	Republican, then Democrat	Republican
108th	2003–2005	Republican	Republican
109th	2005–2007	Republican	Republican
110th	2007–2009	Democrat	Democrat
111th	2009–2011	Democrat	Democrat
112th	2011–2013	Democrat	Republican
113th	2013–2015	Democrat	Republican
114th	2015–2017	Republican	Republican
115th	2017–2019	Republican	Republican
116th	2019–2012	Republican	Democrat

The Constitution first mandated that there be one member of the House of Representatives for every thirty thousand citizens and every state must have at least one representative (Article I, Section 2). The House of Representatives continued to grow after each census and with new states being added to the Union until the Permanent Apportionment Act of 1929 set the number at 435. Today, the average district contains seven hundred thousand people, and that number is expected to grow substantially if the number of members is not increased.

Both House and Senate incumbents who run for reelection are reelected at high rates. While House members enjoy a slightly higher reelection rate, Senate incumbents also enjoy a significant incumbency advantage.

Reapportionment occurs after each census. This means states can gain or lose members of Congress, thus representation. The following figure shows which states gained or lost seats, or remained the same after the 2010 census, and how many representatives each state has had since 2012. The upper Midwest continues to lose seats, while the South and West gain seats. The next census will take place in 2020; thus, the 2022 election will reflect the new numbers.

The following figure shows how much the average winner spends in each type of election. To win a House seat costs about $1.6 million, while winning a Senate seat will cost on average $12 million. Both of these amounts have risen considerably over the past thirty years.

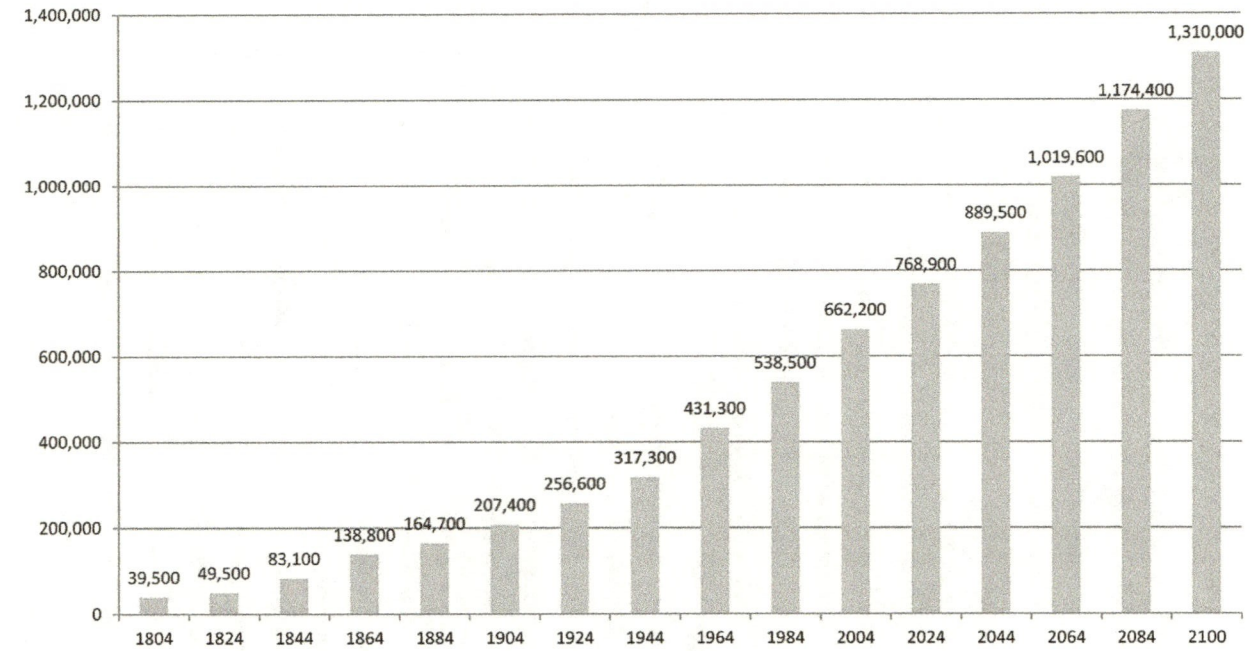

Figure 5.1 Population per U.S. House District

Source: thirty-thousand.org

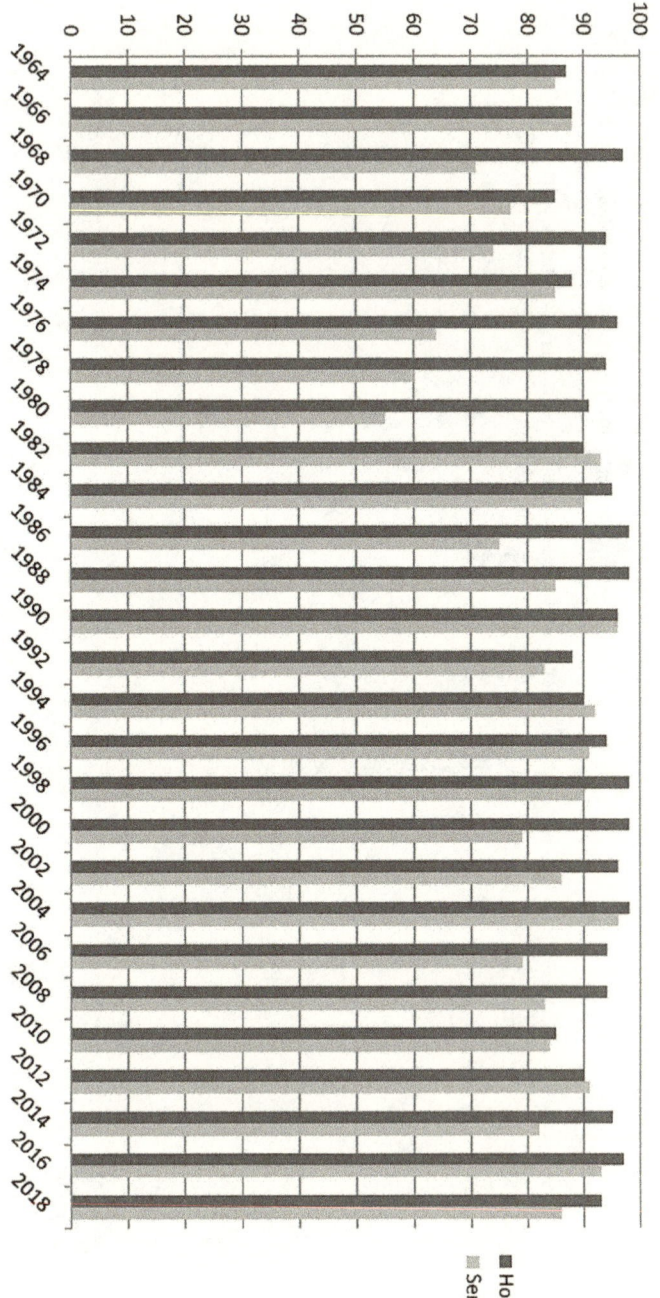

Figure 5.2   U.S House and Senate Reelection Rates, 1964–2018

Source: OpenSecrets. https://www.opensecrets.org/overview/reelect.php

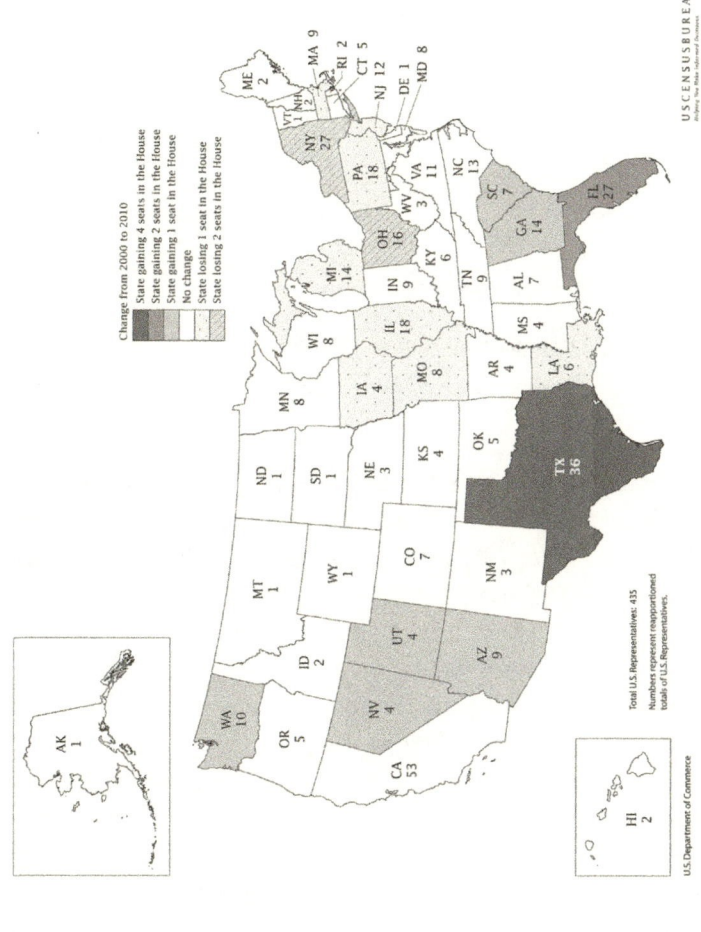

Figure 5.3 Changes in Seats after the 2010 Census

Source: U.S. Census

225

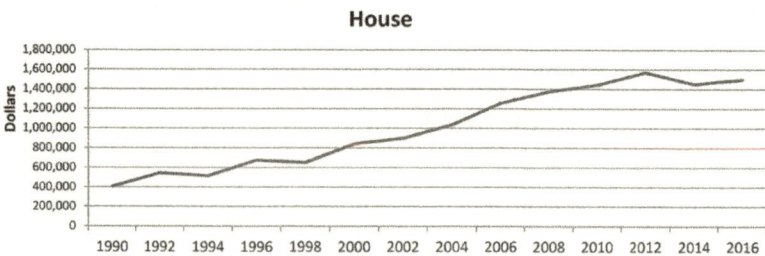

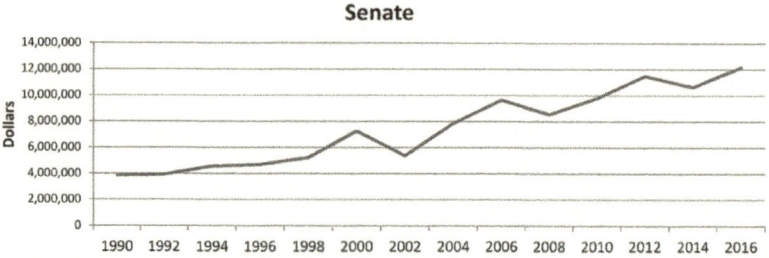

Figure 5.4   Average Spending by Winner, 1990–2016

Source: https://www.opensecrets.org/overview/election-trends.php?cycle=2016

The following figure shows the number of nonwhite members of both the House and Senate. While the numbers of minorities are growing, they are still slightly below parity with where they are in the actual U.S. population.

This figure depicts the number of women in the House and Senate since 1917. While the numbers are growing, with the House numbers more significant than the Senate, women are a long way from composing 50 percent of either body.

The presidential veto is one of the president's most important constitutionally given legislative powers. This figure shows the number of vetoes issued by the president since the first session of Congress. There were noticeable spikes during the Cleveland and Roosevelt presidencies.

Congress, using its constitutional war powers, has only declared war eleven times, while the United States has been involved in numerous other military engagements. The following table shows those declarations as well as the significant military engagements (but is not an exhaustive list of all military engagements).

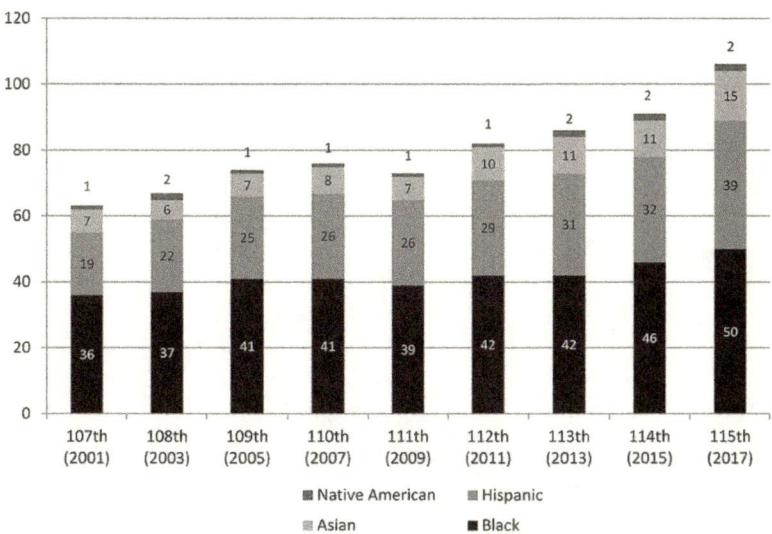

Figure 5.5   Racial and Ethnic Diversity in Congress

Source: Bialik, Kristen, and Jens Manuel Krogstad. 2017. "115th Congress Sets New High for Racial, Ethnic Diversity." Pew Research Center, January 24. http://www.pewresearch.org/fact-tank/2017/01/24/115th-congress-sets-new-high-for-racial-ethnic-diversity/ft_17-01-23_congressdiversity/

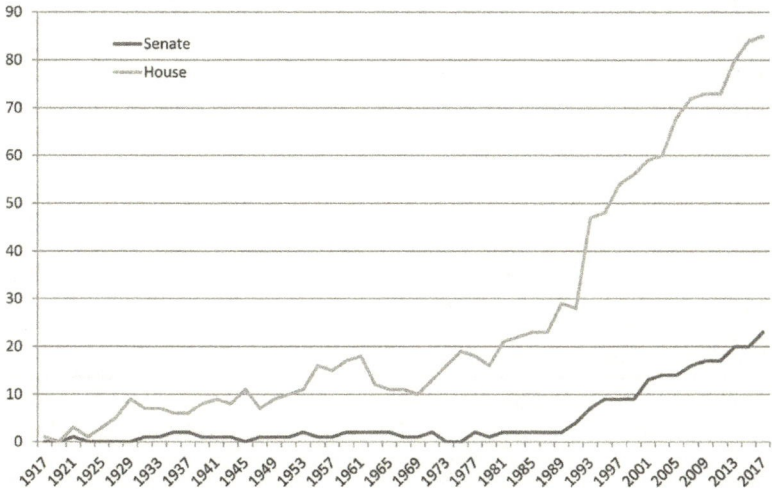

Figure 5.6   Number of Women in the House and Senate

Source: Center for American Women and Politics. http://www.cawp.rutgers.edu/history-women-us-congress

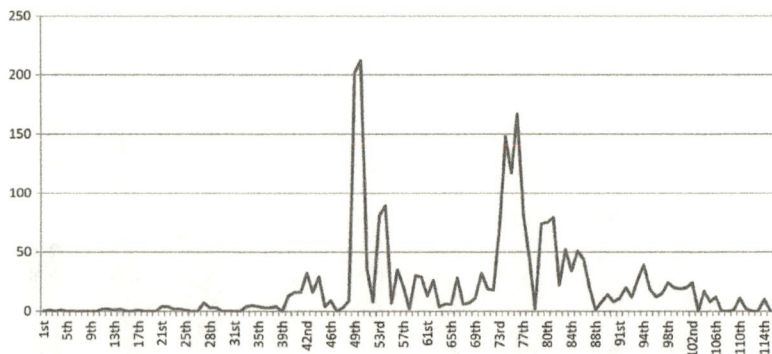

Figure 5.7   Number of Presidential Vetoes per Congress

Source: American Presidency Project. https://www.presidency.ucsb.edu/
statistics/data/presidential-vetoes

Table 5.2   Declarations of War and Military Engagement by Congress

Official Declarations of War	
1812	Great Britain
1846	Mexico
1898	Spain
1917	Germany
1917	Austria-Hungary
1941	Japan
1941	Germany
1941	Italy
1942	Bulgaria
1942	Hungary
1942	Rumania

Unofficial Military Engagements	
1798	France
1802	Tripoli
1815	Algeria
1819	Pirates
1950	Korea
1955	Formosa

Unofficial Military Engagements

1957	Middle East
1960	Vietnam
1964	Southeast Asia
1974	Evacuations from Cyprus, Southeast Asia, and Lebanon
1975	Cambodia
1980	Iran
1981	El Salvador
1982	Honduras
1982	Lebanon
1983	Grenada
1986	Libya
1987	Persian Gulf
1989	Colombia, Bolivia, and Peru
1989	Panama
1991	Iraq and Kuwait
1991	Zaire
1992	Somalia
1992	Bosnia
1993	Iraq
1999	Kosovo
1993	Haiti
2001	Afghanistan
2002	Iraq

Source: "Official Declarations of War by Congress." https://www.senate.gov/pagelayout/history/h_multi_sections_and_teasers/WarDeclarationsbyCongress.htm; National War Powers Commission Report, Appendix 3. https://millercenter.org/issues-policy/foreign-policy/national-war-powers-commission; Franke-Ruta, Garance. 2013. "All the Previous Declarations of War." *Atlantic*, August 31. https://www.theatlantic.com/politics/archive/2013/08/all-the-previous-declarations-of-war/279246/

As the president of the Senate, the vice president's official duty is to break any tied votes in that body. The following table shows those tie-breaking votes by the vice president. If they are not listed (like Vice President Biden), they did not cast any such votes. The most were cast by the first vice president, John Adams.

Table 5.3   Tie-Breaking Votes by the Vice President

John Adams	1789–1797	29
Thomas Jefferson	1979–1801	3
Aaron Burr	1801–1805	3
George Clinton	1805–1812	14
Elbridge Gerry	1813–1814	9
Daniel D. Tompkins	1817–1825	6
John C. Calhoun	1825–1832	31
Martin Van Buren	1833–1837	4
Richard M. Johnson	1837–1841	14
George M. Dallas	1845–1849	19
Millard Fillmore	1849–1850	3
John C. Breckinridge	1857–1861	10
Hannibal Hamlin	1861–1865	7
Schuyler Colfax	1869–1873	18
Henry Wilson	1873–1875	1
William A. Wheeler	1877–1881	6
Chester A. Arthur	1881	3
Levi P. Morton	1889–1893	4
Adlai Stevenson	1893–1897	2
Garret A. Hobart	1897–1899	1
James S. Sherman	1909–1912	4
Thomas R. Marshall	1913–1921	9
Charles G. Dawes	1925–1929	2
Charles Curtis	1929–1933	3
John N. Garner	1933–1941	3
Henry A. Wallace	1941–1945	4
Harry S. Truman	1945	1
Alben W. Barkley	1949–1953	8
Richard M. Nixon	1953–1961	8
Hubert H. Humphrey	1965–1969	4
Spiro T. Agnew	1969–1973	2
Walter Mondale	1977–1981	1
George H. W. Bush	1981–1989	7
Albert Gore Jr.	1993–2001	4
Richard Cheney	2001–2009	8
Michael Pence	2017–present	11

Note: Vice presidents not listed did not cast a tie-breaking vote.

Source: "Occasions When Vice Presidents Have Voted to Break Tie Votes in the Senate." Senate Historical Office. November 29, 2018. https://www.senate.gov/artandhistory/history/resources/pdf/VPTies.pdf

Recently, Americans have been increasingly distrustful of their government, specifically Congress. Trust hit a high point directly after September 11, 2001, and has been declining since then. However, incumbents are still reelected and Americans tend to approve of their own members of Congress.

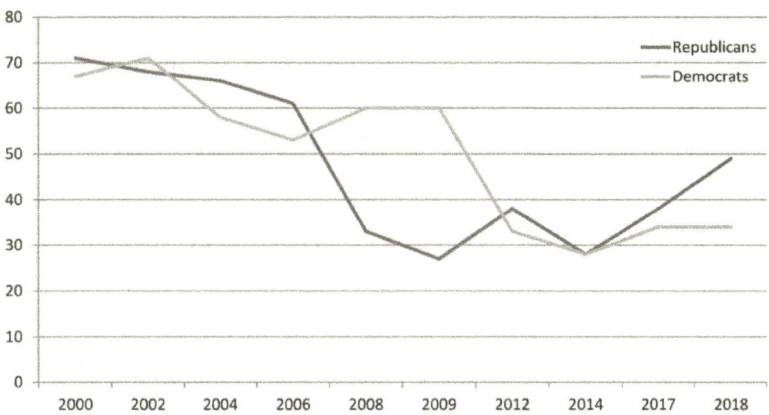

Figure 5.8 Trust in the Legislative Branch

Source: Brenan, Megan. 2018. "Trust in U.S. Legislative Branch 40%, Highest in Nine Years." Gallup, October 1. https://news.gallup.com/poll/243293/trust-legislative-branch-highest-nine-years.aspx

Percentage of respondents with "great deal" or "fair amount" of trust.

Documents

The Constitution of the United States

The Constitution set up the structure and detailed the powers of the Congress in Article I. This document presents Article I, Section 8, which establishes the enumerated powers of Congress, plus two of the amendments that provided for the direct (popular) election of senators and addressed compensation for members of Congress. Interestingly, the Twenty-Seventh Amendment, which addresses congressional pay, was first proposed and passed by both houses of Congress in 1789 along with the first ten amendments, which became the Bill of Rights. It was not ratified until 1992.

Article 1, Section 8 (1787)

The Congress shall have Power To lay and collect Taxes, Duties, Imposts and Excises, to pay the Debts and provide for the common Defence and general Welfare of the United States; but all Duties, Imposts and Excises shall be uniform throughout the United States;

To borrow Money on the credit of the United States;

To regulate Commerce with foreign Nations, and among the several States, and with the Indian Tribes;

To establish an uniform Rule of Naturalization, and uniform Laws on the subject of Bankruptcies throughout the United States;

To coin Money, regulate the Value thereof, and of foreign Coin, and fix the Standard of Weights and Measures;

To provide for the Punishment of counterfeiting the Securities and current Coin of the United States;

To establish Post Offices and post Roads;

To promote the Progress of Science and useful Arts, by securing for limited Times to Authors and Inventors the exclusive Right to their respective Writings and Discoveries;

To constitute Tribunals inferior to the supreme Court;

To define and punish Piracies and Felonies committed on the high Seas, and Offences against the Law of Nations;

To declare War, grant Letters of Marque and Reprisal, and make Rules concerning Captures on Land and Water;

To raise and support Armies, but no Appropriation of Money to that Use shall be for a longer Term than two Years;

To provide and maintain a Navy;

To make Rules for the Government and Regulation of the land and naval Forces;

To provide for calling forth the Militia to execute the Laws of the Union, suppress Insurrections and repel Invasions;

To provide for organizing, arming, and disciplining, the Militia, and for governing such Part of them as may be employed in the Service of the United States, reserving to the States respectively, the Appointment of the Officers, and the Authority of training the Militia according to the discipline prescribed by Congress;

To exercise exclusive Legislation in all Cases whatsoever, over such District (not exceeding ten Miles square) as may, by Cession of particular States, and the Acceptance of Congress, become the Seat of the Government of the United States, and to exercise like Authority over all Places purchased by the Consent of the Legislature of the State in which the Same shall be, for the Erection of Forts, Magazines, Arsenals, dock-Yards, and other needful Buildings;—And

To make all Laws which shall be necessary and proper for carrying into Execution the foregoing Powers, and all other Powers vested by this Constitution in the Government of the United States, or in any Department or Officer thereof.

AMENDMENT XVII, Direct Election of Senators (passed 1912; ratified 1913)

The Senate of the United States shall be composed of two Senators from each State, elected by the people thereof, for six years; and each Senator shall have one vote. The electors in each State shall have the qualifications requisite for electors of the most numerous branch of the State legislatures.

When vacancies happen in the representation of any State in the Senate, the executive authority of each such State shall issue a writ of election to fill such vacancies; *Provided*, That the legislature of any State may empower the executive thereof to make temporary appointments until the people fill the vacancies by election as the legislature may direct.

This amendment shall not be so construed as to affect the election or term of any Senator chose before it becomes valid as part of the Constitution.

AMENDMENT XXVII, Congressional Compensation (proposed 1789; ratified 1992)

No law varying the compensation for the services of the Senators and Representatives shall take effect, until an election of Representatives shall have intervened.

Source: National Archives. https://www.archives.gov/founding-docs/constitution

The Louisiana Purchase (1803)

In 1803, President Thomas Jefferson, through his secretary of state, James Monroe, negotiated a treaty with France that was ratified by the U.S. Senate. It nearly doubled the territory of the United States. It also set the precedent of granting U.S. citizenship on the basis of a treaty, used again in 1848 in the Treaty of Guadalupe Hidalgo, and by the Treaty of Paris in 1898 after the Spanish-American War, by which Spain ceded Puerto Rico and Guam to the United States, and the residents thereof became U.S. citizens.

Treaty between the United States of America and the French Republic

The President of the United States and the First Consul of the French Republic in the name of the French People desiring to remove all Source of misunderstanding relative to objects of discussion mentioned in the Second and fifth articles of the Convention of the 8th Vendémiaire an 9 (30 September 1800) relative to the rights claimed by the United States in virtue of the Treaty concluded in Madrid the 27 of October 1795, between His Catholic Majesty & the Said United States, & willing to Strengthen the union and friendship which at the time of the Said Convention was happily reestablished between the two nations have respectively named their Plenipotentiaries to wit The President of the United States, by and with the advice and consent of the Senate of the Said States: Robert R. Livingston Minister Plenipotentiary of the United States and James Monroe Minister Plenipotentiary and Envoy extraordinary of the Said States near the Government of the French Republic; And the First Consul in the name of the French People, Citizen Francis Barbe Marbois Minister of the public treasury who after having respectively exchanged their full powers have agreed to the following Articles.

Article I: Whereas by the Article the third of the Treaty concluded at St. Ildefonso the 9th Vendemiaire an 9 (1st October 1800) between the First Consul of the French Republic and his Catholic Majesty it was agreed as follows. "His Catholic Majesty promises and engages on his part to cede to the French Republic six months after the full and entire execution of the conditions and Stipulations herein relative to his Royal Highness the Duke of Parma, the Colony or Province of Louisiana with the Same extent that is now has in the hand of Spain, & that it had when France possessed it; and Such as it Should be after the Treaties subsequently entered into between Spain and other States. . . .

Article II: In the cession made by the preceding article are included the adjacent Islands belonging to Louisiana all public lots and Squares, vacant lands and all public buildings, fortifications, barracks and other edifices which are not private property. . . . The Archives, papers & documents relative to the domain and Sovereignty of Louisiana and its dependences will be left in the possession of the Commissaries of the United States, and copies will be afterwards given in due form to the Magistrates and Municipal officers of such of the said papers and documents as may be necessary to them.

Article III. The inhabitants of the ceded territory shall be incorporated into the Union of the United States and admitted as soon as possible according to the principles of the federal Constitution to the enjoyment of all these rights, advantages and immunities of citizens of the United States, and in the mean time they shall be maintained and protected in the free enjoyment of their liberty, property and the Religion which they profess . . .

Article V. Immediately after the ratification of the present Treaty by the President of the United States and in case that of the first Consul's shall have been previously obtained, the commissary of the French Republic shall remit all military posts of New Orleans and other parts of the ceded territory to the Commissary or Commissaries named by the President to take possession—the troops whether of France or Spain who may be there shall cease to occupy any military post from the time of taking possession and shall be embarked as soon as possible in the course of three months after the ratification of this treaty.

Article VI. The United States promise to execute Such treaties and articles as may have been agreed between Spain and the tribes and nations of Indians until by mutual consent of the United States and the said tribes or nations other Suitable articles Shall have been agreed upon. . . .

Article VIII. In future and for ever after the expiration of the twelve years, the Ships of France shall be treated upon the footing of the most favoured nations in the ports above mentioned. . . .

Article X. The present treaty Shall be ratified in good and due form and the ratifications Shall be exchanged in the Space of Six months after the date of the Signature by the Ministers Plenipotentiary or Sooner if possible.

In faith whereof the respective Plenipotentiaries have Signed these articles in the French and English languages; declaring nevertheless that the present Treaty was originally agreed to in the French language; and have thereunto affixed their Seals.

Done at Paris the tenth day of Floreal in the eleventh year of the French Republic, and the 30th of April 1803. Robt. R. Livingston [seal] Jas. Monroe [seal] Barbe Marbois [seal]

Source: Louisiana Purchase Treaty, April 30, 1803; General Records of the U.S. Government; Record Group 11; National Archives.

The Missouri Compromise (1820)

On March 6, 1820, Congress passed a law allowing the territory of Missouri to join the Union as a slave state and territories north, when formed, to enter the Union as free states, with a provision that slaves fleeing to the territory from other slave states be returned to their owner. The law had an impact on naturalization law and further legalized the institution of slavery. The compromise postponed conflict over the issue until the Civil War. This document excerpts some key provisions of the act.

Be it enacted by the Senate and the House of Representatives of the United States of America, in Congress assembled, That the inhabitants of that portion of the Missouri territory included within the boundaries herein after designated, be, and they are hereby authorized to form for themselves a constitution and state government, and to assume such name as they shall deem proper; and the said state, when formed, shall be admitted into the Union, upon an equal footing with the original states, in all respects whatsoever.

SEC. 2. And be it further enacted, That the said state shall consist of the territory included within the following boundaries, to wit: Beginning in the middle of the Mississippi River, on the parallel of thirty-six degrees of north latitude; thence west, along that parallel of latitude, to the St. Francois river; thence up, and following the course of that river, in the middle of the main channel thereof, to the parallel of latitude thirty-six degrees and thirty minutes; thence west, along the same, to a point where the said parallel is intersected by a meridian line passing through the middle of the mouth of the Kansas river, where the same empties into the Missouri river, thence, from the point aforesaid north, along the said meridian line, to the intersection of the parallel latitude which passes through the rapids of the river Des Moines, make the said line to correspond with the Indian boundary line, thence east, from the point of the intersection last aforesaid, along the said parallel of latitude, to the middle of the channel of the main fork of the said river Des Moines, thence down and along the middle of the channel of the main fork of the said river Des Moines, to the mouth of the same, where it empties into the Mississippi river; thence, due east, to the middle of the main channel of the Mississippi river; thence down, and following the course of the Mississippi river, in the middle of the main channel thereof, to the place of beginning; Provided, The said state shall ratify the boundaries aforesaid. And provided also, That the said state shall have concurrent jurisdiction on the river Mississippi, and every other river bordering on the said state so far as the said rivers shall form a common boundary to the said state; and any other state or states, now or herewith to be formed and bounded by the same, such rivers to be common to both; and that the river Mississippi, and the navigable rivers and waters leading into the same, shall be common highways, and forever free, as well to the inhabitants of the said state as to other citizens of the United States, without any tax, duty impost, or toll, therefor, imposed by the said state.

SEC. 3. And be it further enacted, That all free white male citizens of the United States, who shall have arrived at the age of twenty-one years, and have resided in said territory: three months previous to the day of election, and all other persons qualified to vote for representatives to the general assembly of the said territory, shall be qualified to be elected and they are hereby qualified and authorized to vote, and choose representatives to form a convention, who shall be appointed amongst the several counties . . .

SEC. 4. And be it further enacted, That the members of the convention thus duly elected, shall be, and they are hereby authorized to meet at the seat of government of said territory on the second Monday of the month of June next . . . to form a constitution and state government for the people within the said territory, as included within the boundaries above designated; and if it be deemed expedient, the convention shall be, and hereby is authorized to form a constitution and state government . . .

SEC. 5. And be it further enacted, That until the next general census shall be taken, the said state shall be entitled to one representative in the House of Representatives of the United States . . .

SEC. 7. And be it further enacted, That in case a constitution and state government shall be formed for the people of the said territory of Missouri, the said convention or representatives, as soon thereafter as may be, shall cause a true and attested copy of such constitution or frame of state government as shall be formed and provided, to be transmitted to Congress.

SEC.8. And be it further enacted, That in all that territory ceded by France to the United States, under the name of Louisiana, which lies north of the thirty-six degrees and thirty minutes north latitude, not included within the limits of the state, contemplated by this act, slavery and involuntary servitude, otherwise than in the punishment of crimes, whereof the parties shall have been duly convicted, shall be, and is hereby, forever prohibited: Provided always, That any person escaping into the same, from whom labour or service is lawfully claimed, in any state or territory of the United States, such fugitive may be lawfully reclaimed and conveyed to the person claiming his or her labour or service as aforesaid.

Approved, March 6, 1820

Source: Conference committee report on the Missouri Compromise, March 1, 1820; Joint Committee of Conference on the Missouri Bill, March 1, 1820, to March 6, 1820; Record Group 128l; Records of Joint Committees of Congress, 1789–1989; National Archives.

Permanent Apportionment Act (1929)

This act permanently set the number of House seats at 435. It also created a procedure to automatically reapportion House seats after every census. This number and process are still used today.

(a) On the first day, or within one week thereafter, of the first regular session of the Eighty-second Congress and of each fifth Congress thereafter, the President shall transmit to the Congress a statement showing the whole number of persons in each State, excluding Indians not taxed, as ascertained under the seventeenth and each subsequent decennial census of the population, and the number of Representatives to which each State would be entitled under an apportionment of the then existing number of Representatives by the method known as the method of equal proportions, no State to receive less than one Member.

(b) Each State shall be entitled, in the Eighty-third Congress and in each Congress thereafter until the taking effect of a reapportionment under this section or subsequent statute, to the number of Representatives shown in the statement required by subsection (a) of this section, no State to receive less than one Member. It shall be the duty of the Clerk of the House of Representatives, within fifteen calendar days after the receipt of such statement, to send to the executive of each State a certificate of the number of Representatives to which such State is entitled under this section. In case of a vacancy in the office of Clerk, or of his absence or inability to discharge this duty, then such duty shall devolve upon the Sergeant at Arms of the House of Representatives.

(c) Until a State is redistricted in the manner provided by the law thereof after any apportionment, the Representatives to which such State is entitled under such apportionment shall be elected in the following manner: (1) If there is no change in the number of Representatives, they shall be elected from the districts then prescribed by the law of such State, and if any of them are elected from the State at large they shall continue to be so elected; (2) if there is an increase in the number of Representatives, such additional Representative or Representatives shall be elected from the State at large and the other Representatives from the districts then prescribed by the law of such State; (3) if there is a decrease in the number of Representatives but the number of districts in such State is equal to such decreased number of Representatives, they shall be elected from the districts then prescribed by the law of such State; (4) if there is a decrease in the number of Representatives but the number of districts in such State is less than such number of Representatives, the number of Representatives by which such number of districts is exceeded shall be elected from the State at large and the other Representatives from the districts then prescribed by the law of such State; or (5) if there is a decrease in the number of Representatives and the number of districts in such State exceeds such decreased number of Representatives, they shall be elected from the State at large.

Source: 2 U.S. Code §2a. Reapportionment of Representatives.

U.S. Declaration of War against Japan (December 8, 1941)

Immediately following President Franklin D. Roosevelt's stirring "Day of Infamy" speech before a joint session of Congress asking for a declaration of war against the Empire of Japan, the American Congress acted on that request. The following is the full text of the formal declaration of war.

JOINT RESOLUTION Declaring that a state of war exists between the Imperial Government of Japan and the Government and the people of the United States and making provisions to prosecute the same.

Whereas the Imperial Government of Japan has committed unprovoked acts of war against the Government and people of the United States of America: Therefore be it Resolved by the Senate and House of Representatives of the United States of

America in Congress assembled, That the state of war between the United States and the Imperial Government of Japan which has thus been thrust upon the United States is hereby formally declared; and the President is hereby authorized and directed to employ the entire naval and military forces of the United States and the resources of the Government to carry on war against the Imperial Government of Japan; and, to bring the conflict to a successful termination, all of the resources of the country are hereby pledged by the Congress of the United States.

Approved, December 8, 1941, 4:10 p.m. E.S.T.

Source: Enrolled Acts and Resolutions of Congress, 1789–2011. Record Group 11: General Records of the U.S. Government, 1778–2006. Identifier 299850. National Archives.

The War Powers Resolution (November 7, 1973)

On occasion, the American Congress conflicts with the president over war policy. Congress asserted its "checks and balances" power vis-à-vis the president spurred by the Vietnam War and a Democratic-controlled Congress with a Republican president, Richard Nixon. Congress passed a war powers resolution meant to check or limit the president's use of the commander in chief powers. The documents excerpts some key provisions of the joint War Powers Resolution, Public Law 93–148, concerning the war powers of Congress and the president.

Resolved by the Senate and House of Representatives of America in Congress assembled.

Short Title

Section 1. This joint resolution may be cited as the "War Powers Resolution."

Purpose and Policy

Sec. 2. (a) It is the purpose of this joint resolution to fulfill the intent of the framers of the Constitution of the United

States and insure that the collective judgment of both the Congress and the President will apply to the introduction of United States Armed Forces into hostilities, or into situations where imminent involvement in hostilities is clearly indicated by the circumstances, and to the continued use of such forces in hostilities or in such situations.

(b) Under Article 1, section 8, of the Constitution, it is specifically provided that the Congress shall have the power to make all laws necessary and proper for carrying it into execution, not only its own powers but also all other powers vested by the Constitution in the Government of the United States, or in any department or officer thereof.

(c) The constitutional powers of the President as Commander-in-Chief to introduce United States Armed Forces into hostilities, or into situations where imminent involvement in hostilities is clearly indicated by the circumstances, are exercised only pursuant to (1) a declaration of war, (2) specific statutory authorization, or (3) a national emergency created by attack upon the United States, its territories or possessions, or its armed forces.

Consultation

Sec. 3. The President in every possible instance shall consult with Congress before introducing United States Armed Forces into hostilities or into situations were imminent involvement in hostilities is clearly indicated by the circumstances, and after every such introduction shall consult regularly with the Congress until United States Armed Forces are no longer engaged in hostilities or have been removed from such situations.

Reporting

Sec. 4. (a) In the absence of a declaration of war, or in any case in which United States Armed Forces are introduced—

(1) Into hostilities or into situations where imminent involvement in hostilities is clearly indicated by the circumstances;

(2) Into the territory, airspace or waters of a foreign nation while equipped for combat, except for deployments which relate solely to supply, replacement, repair, or training such forces, or

(3) In numbers which substantially enlarge United States Armed Forces equipped for combat already located in a foreign nation; the President shall submit within 18 hours to the Speaker of the House of Representatives and to the President pro tempore of the Senate, a report, in writing, setting forth—

(A) The circumstances necessitating the introduction of United States Armed Forces;

(B) The constitutional and legislative authority under which such introduction took place; and

(C) The estimated scope and duration of the hostilities or involvement.

(b) The President shall provide such other information as the Congress may request in the fulfillment of its constitutional responsibilities with respect to committing the nation to war and to the use of United States Armed Forces abroad.

(c) Whenever United States Armed Forces are introduced in to hostilities or into any situation as described in subsection (a) of this section, the President shall, so long as such armed forces continue to be engaged in such hostilities or situation, report to the Congress periodically on the status of such hostilities or situation as well as on the scope and duration of such hostilities or situation, but in no event shall he report to the Congress less often than once every six months.

Congressional Action

Sec. 5 (a) Each report submitted . . . shall be transmitted to the Speaker of the House and to the President pro tempore of the

Senate on the same calendar day. Each report so transmitted shall be referred to the Committee on Foreign Affairs of the House of Representatives and to the Committee on Foreign Relations for appropriate action . . .

(b) Within 60 calendar days after a report is submitted or is required to be submitted . . . whichever is earlier, the President shall terminate any use of United States Armed Forces with respect to which such report was submitted (or required to be submitted), unless the Congress has declared war or has enacted a specific authorization for such use of United States Armed Forces, (2) has extended by law such sixty-day period, or (3) is physically unable to meet as a result of an armed attack upon the United States. Such sixty-day period shall not be extended for more than an additional thirty days . . .

(c) Notwithstanding subsection (b), at any time that United States Armed Forces are engaged in hostilities outside the territory of the United States, its possessions and territories without a declaration of war or specific statutory authorization, such forces shall be removed by the President if Congress so directs by concurrent resolution.

Source: Pub. L. No. 93–148; Statutes at Large 87 Stat. 555.

Establishment of the Congressional Budget Office (1974)

The Congressional Budget and Impoundment Control Act changed the federal government's fiscal year from July 1 to October 1, required the president to submit a budget proposal to Congress, created the House and Senate Budget Committees and the Congressional Budget Office, and established more concrete guidelines for completing the budget and appropriations bills.

Congressional Budget and Impoundment Control Act— Declares the purposes of this Act. Sets forth the definitions of terms used in the Act.

Title I: Establishment of House and Senate Budget Committees

- Establishes a Standing Committee of the Senate to be known as the Committee of the Budget. Establishes such a Committee of the House. Outlines the composition and duties of the committees.

- Provides that each such committee shall make a continuing study of the effects of budget outlays and devise methods of coordinating tax policies with budget outlays.

Title II: Congressional Budget Office

- Creates a Congressional Budget Office and outlines the duties of such Office.

- States that the function of the Office is to provide information to the Budget Committees of the two Houses and to other Committees of the two Houses with respect to the budget, appropriation bills, and other bills providing budget authority or tax expenditures.

- Abolishes the Joint Committee on Reduction of Federal Expenditures. Provides for public access to budget data.

- Directs the Director of the Office to submit to the Committees on the Budget of the House of Representatives and the Senate a report, for the fiscal year commencing on October 1 of that year, with respect to fiscal policy, including new budget authority, total outlays, levels of tax expenditures under existing law, projected economic factors, and any changes in such levels based on proposals in the budget submitted by the President for such fiscal year.

- Authorizes the Director of the Office to: (1) equip the Office with up-to-date computer capability; (2) obtain the services of experts and consultants in computer technology; and (3) develop techniques for the evaluation of budgetary requirements.

Title III: Congressional Budget Process

- Sets forth a timetable with respect to the congressional budget process for any fiscal year.
- Prescribes, under such timetable, the rules for consideration of concurrent resolutions on the budget.
- Requires that concurrent resolutions on the budget must be adopted before appropriations and changes in revenues and the public debt limit are made.
- Sets forth exceptions to this provision.

Title IV: Additional Provisions to Improve Fiscal Procedures

- Provides that it shall not be in order for either House to consider any bill which provides new advance spending authority unless that bill provides that such authority is to be effective only to the extent as is provided in appropriation Acts.
- Requires the Director of the Congressional Budget Office, to the extent practical, to prepare an estimate of costs expected to be incurred in carrying out each bill or resolution.
- Defines "new spending authority" for purposes of this Act. Provides that it shall not be in order for either the Senate or House to consider any bill authorizing a new budget authority for any fiscal year unless such bill or resolution is reported on or before May 15 preceding the beginning of such fiscal year.

Title V: Change of Fiscal Year

- Changes the fiscal year of the Treasury, beginning on October 1, 1976, to commence on October 1 of each year and to end on September 30 of the following year.
- Provides for the conversion of authorizations of appropriations to comply with the new fiscal year.

Title VI: Amendments to Budget and Accounting Act, 1921

- Provides that the Presidential budget shall include the same elements as the Congressional Budget.
- Provides for five-year budget projections.

Title VII: Program Review and Evaluation

- Requires the Comptroller General, upon request, to assist any Congressional committee in developing a statement of legislative objectives and goals, methods of assessment, and the feasibility of pilot testing.
- Requires the Comptroller General, when requested, to assist Congressional committees in analyzing program reviews or evaluation studies prepared by and for any Federal agency.
- Authorizes the Comptroller General to establish an Office of Program Review and Evaluation within the General Accounting Office.
- Authorizes the employment of up to ten experts.
- Provides for a continuing study of additional budget reform proposals designed to improve and facilitate methods of congressional budget-making.
- Requires that such proposals shall include the following: (1) improving the information base required for determining the effectiveness of new programs by such means as pilot testing, survey research, and other experimental and analytical techniques; (2) improving analytical and systematic evaluation of the effectiveness of existing programs; (3) establishing maximum and minimum time limitations for program authorization; and (4) developing techniques of human resource accounting and other means of providing noneconomic as well as economic evaluation measures.

Title VIII: Fiscal and Budgetary Information and Controls

- Provides that the Secretary of the Treasury, and the Director of the Office of Management and Budget, in cooperation with the Comptroller General of the United States, shall develop, establish and maintain information systems for fiscal, budgetary, and related information.

- Provides that such information shall be furnished to Congressional committees upon request.

Title IX: Miscellaneous Provisions: Effective Dates

- Makes technical and conforming amendments to the provisions of the Legislative Reorganization Act of 1946.

- Provides for the application of the Congressional budget process to the fiscal year 1976.

Title X: Impoundment Control

- Impoundment Control Act provides that nothing contained in this Act, or in any amendments made by this Act, shall be construed as: (1) asserting or conceding the constitutional powers or limitations of either the Congress or the President; (2) ratifying or approving any impoundment heretofore or hereafter executed or approved by the President or any other Federal officer or employee, except insofar as pursuant to statutory authorization then in effect; (3) affecting in any way the claims or defenses of any party to litigation concerning any impoundment; or (4) superseding any provision of law which requires the obligation of budget authority or the making of outlays thereunder.

- Makes technical amendments to the Antideficiency Act.

- Repeals the existing impoundment reporting provision of the Budget and Accounting Procedure Act of 1950.

Source: Summary of Congressional Budget and Impoundment Control Act of 1974 (Pub. L. No. 93–344, 88 Stat. 297, 2 U.S.C. §§ 601–688).

INS v. Chadha et al. (1983)

In 1983, the U.S. Supreme Court rendered a decision that had importance beyond the immediate issue of immigration. In INS v. Chadha et al., *a class action suit was filed against the INS over its deportation proceedings. The court ruled that a House of Representatives' use of the "legislative veto" of the executive branch's rules and regulations (i.e., those of the INS) was unconstitutional. It is an example of the checks and balances power of one branch (the judiciary) over another branch (the Congress).*

Section 244(c)(2) of the Immigration and Nationality Act (Act) authorizes either House of Congress, by resolution, to invalidate the decision of the Executive Branch, pursuant to authority delegated by Congress to the Attorney General, to allow a particular deportable alien to remain in the United States. Appellee-respondent Chadha, an alien who had been lawfully admitted to the United States on a nonimmigrant student visa, remained in the United States after his visa had expired and was ordered by the Immigration and Naturalization Service (INS) to show cause why he should not be deported. He then applied for suspension of the deportation, and, after a hearing, an Immigration Judge, acting pursuant to § 244(a)(1) of the Act, which authorizes the Attorney General, in his discretion, to suspend deportation, ordered the suspension, and reported the suspension to Congress as required by § 244(c)(1). Thereafter, the House of Representatives passed a resolution pursuant to § 244(c)(2) vetoing the suspension, and the Immigration Judge reopened the deportation proceedings. Chadha moved to terminate the proceedings on the ground that § 244(c)(2) is unconstitutional, but the judge held that he had no authority to rule on its constitutionality, and ordered

Chadha deported pursuant to the House Resolution. Chadha's appeal to the Board of Immigration Appeals was dismissed, the Board also holding that it had no power to declare § 244(c)(2) unconstitutional. Chadha then filed a petition for review of the deportation order in the Court of Appeals, and the INS joined him in arguing that § 244(c)(2) is unconstitutional. The Court of Appeals held that § 244(c)(2) violates the constitutional doctrine of separation of powers, and accordingly directed the Attorney General to cease taking any steps to deport Chadha based upon the House Resolution.

Held:

1. This Court has jurisdiction to entertain the INS's appeal in No. 80–1832 under 28 U.S.C. § 1252, which provides that "[a]ny party" may appeal to the Supreme Court from a judgment of "any court of the United States" holding an Act of Congress unconstitutional in "any civil action, suit, or proceeding" to which the United States or any of its agencies is a party. A court of appeals is "a court of the United States" for purposes of § 1252, the proceeding below was a "civil action, suit, or proceeding," the INS is an agency of the United States and was a party to the proceeding below, and the judgment below held an Act of Congress unconstitutional. Moreover, for purposes of deciding whether the INS was "any party" within the grant of appellate jurisdiction in § 1252, the INS was sufficiently aggrieved by the Court of Appeals' decision prohibiting it from taking action it would otherwise take. An agency's status as an aggrieved party under § 1252 is not altered by the fact that the Executive may agree with the holding that the statute in question is unconstitutional.

2. Section 244(c)(2) is severable from the remainder of § 244. Section 406 of the Act provides that, if any particular provision of the Act is held invalid, the remainder of the Act shall not be affected. This gives rise to a presumption that

Congress did not intend the validity of the Act as a whole, or any part thereof, to depend upon whether the veto clause of § 244(c)(2) was invalid. This presumption is supported by § 244's legislative history. Moreover, a provision is further presumed severable if what remains after severance is fully operative as a law. Here, § 244 can survive as a "fully operative" and workable administrative mechanism without the one-House veto.

3. Chadha has standing to challenge the constitutionality of § 244(c)(2), since he has demonstrated "injury in fact and a substantial likelihood that the judicial relief requested will prevent or redress the claimed injury."

4. The fact that Chadha may have other statutory relief available to him does not preclude him from challenging the constitutionality of § 244(c)(2), especially where the other avenues of relief are at most speculative.

5. The Court of Appeals had jurisdiction under § 106(a) of the Act, which provides that a petition for review in a court of appeals "shall be the sole and exclusive procedure for the judicial review of all final orders of deportation . . . made against aliens within the United States pursuant to administrative proceedings" under § 242(b) of the Act. Section 106(a) includes all matters on which the final deportation order is contingent, rather than only those determinations made at the deportation hearing. Here, Chadha's deportation stands or falls on the validity of the challenged veto, the final deportation order having been entered only to implement that veto.

6. A case or controversy is presented by these cases. From the time of the House's formal intervention, there was concrete adverseness, and prior to such intervention, there was adequate Art. III adverseness even though the only parties were the INS and Chadha. The INS's agreement with Chadha's position does not alter the fact that the INS would have deported him absent the Court of Appeals' judgment.

Moreover, Congress is the proper party to defend the validity of a statute when a Government agency, as a defendant charged with enforcing the statute, agrees with plaintiffs that the statute is unconstitutional.

7. These cases do not present a nonjusticiable political question on the asserted ground that Chadha is merely challenging Congress' authority under the Naturalization and Necessary and Proper Clauses of the Constitution. The presence of constitutional issues with significant political overtones does not automatically invoke the political question doctrine. Resolution of litigation challenging the constitutional authority of one of the three branches cannot be evaded by the courts simply because the issues have political implications.

8. The congressional veto provision in § 244(c)(2) is unconstitutional.

    (a) The prescription for legislative action in Art. I, § 1—requiring all legislative powers to be vested in a Congress consisting of a Senate and a House of Representatives—and § 7—requiring every bill passed by the House and Senate, before becoming law, to be presented to the President, and, if he disapproves, to be repassed by two-thirds of the Senate and House—represents the Framers' decision that the legislative power of the Federal Government be exercised in accord with a single, finely wrought and exhaustively considered procedure. This procedure is an integral part of the constitutional design for the separation of powers.

    (b) Here, the action taken by the House pursuant to § 244(c)(2) was essentially legislative in purpose and effect, and thus was subject to the procedural requirements of Art. I, § 7, for legislative action: passage by a majority of both Houses and presentation to the President. The one-House veto operated to overrule the Attorney General and mandate Chadha's deportation.

The veto's legislative character is confirmed by the character of the congressional action it supplants; *i.e.*, absent the veto provision of § 244(c)(2), neither the House nor the Senate, or both acting together, could effectively require the Attorney General to deport an alien once the Attorney General, in the exercise of legislatively delegated authority, had determined that the alien should remain in the United States. Without the veto provision, this could have been achieved only by legislation requiring deportation. A veto by one House under § 244(c)(2) cannot be justified as an attempt at amending the standards set out in § 244(a)(1), or as a repeal of § 244 as applied to Chadha. The nature of the decision implemented by the one-House veto further manifests its legislative character. Congress must abide by its delegation of authority to the Attorney General until that delegation is legislatively altered or revoked. Finally, the veto's legislative character is confirmed by the fact that, when the Framers intended to authorize either House of Congress to act alone and outside of its prescribed bicameral legislative role, they narrowly and precisely defined the procedure for such action in the Constitution.

634 F.2d 408, affirmed.

Source: *Immigration and Naturalization Service v. Jagdish Rai Chadha et al.* (462 U.S. 919, 1983).

Clinton v. City of New York (1998)

The Supreme Court decided in Clinton v. City of New York *that the line-item veto, which was passed by a Republican Congress in the Line Item Veto Act of 1996, was unconstitutional.*

Last Term, this Court determined on expedited review that Members of Congress did not have standing to maintain a constitutional challenge to the Line Item Veto Act (Act), because they had not alleged a sufficiently concrete injury. Within two months, the President exercised his authority under the Act by canceling §4722(c) of the Balanced Budget Act of 1997, which waived the Federal Government's statutory right to recoupment of as much as $2.6 billion in taxes that the State of New York had levied against Medicaid providers, and § 968 of the Taxpayer Relief Act of 1997, which permitted the owners of certain food refiners and processors to defer recognition of capital gains if they sold their stock to eligible farmers' cooperatives. Appellees, claiming they had been injured, filed separate actions against the President and other officials challenging the cancellations. The plaintiffs in the first case are the City of New York, two hospital associations, one hospital, and two unions representing health care employees. The plaintiffs in the second are the Snake River farmers' cooperative and one of its individual members. The District Court consolidated the cases, determined that at least one of the plaintiffs in each had standing under Article III, and ruled, *inter alia,* that the Act's cancellation procedures violate the Presentment Clause. This Court again expedited its review.

Held:

1. The appellees have standing to challenge the Act's constitutionality. They invoked the District Court's jurisdiction under a section entitled "Expedited review," which, among other things, expressly authorizes "any individual adversely affected" to bring a constitutional challenge. § 692(a)(I). The Government's argument that none of them except the individual Snake River member is an "individual" within § 692(a)(I)'s meaning is rejected because, in the context of the entire section, it is clear that Congress meant that word to be construed broadly to include corporations and other entities. The Court is also unpersuaded by the Government's argument that appellees' challenge is nonjusticiable. These cases differ from *Raines,* not only because the President's exercise of his cancellation authority has removed any

concern about the dispute's ripeness, but more importantly because the parties have alleged a "personal stake" in having an actual injury redressed, rather than an "institutional injury" that is "abstract and widely dispersed." There is no merit to the Government's contention that, in both cases, the appellees have not suffered actual injury because their claims are too speculative and, in any event, are advanced by the wrong parties. Because New York State now has a multibillion dollar contingent liability that had been eliminated by § 4722(c), the State, and the appellees, suffered an immediate, concrete injury the moment the President canceled the section and deprived them of its benefits. The argument that New York's claim belongs to the State, not appellees, fails in light of New York statutes demonstrating that both New York City and the appellee providers will be assessed for substantial portions of any recoupment payments the State has to make. Similarly, the President's cancellation of § 968 inflicted a sufficient likelihood of economic injury on the Snake River appellees to establish standing under this Court's precedents. The assertion that, because processing facility sellers would have received the tax benefits, only they have standing to challenge the § 968 cancellation not only ignores the fact that the cooperatives were the intended beneficiaries of § 968, but also overlooks the fact that more than one party may be harmed by a defendant and therefore have standing.

2. The Act's cancellation procedures violate the Presentment Clause.

    (a) The Act empowers the President to cancel an "item of new direct spending" such as § 4722(c) of the Balanced Budget Act and a "limited tax benefit" such as § 968 of the Taxpayer Relief Act, § 691(a), specifying that such cancellation prevents a provision "from having legal force or effect," §§ 691e(4)(B)-(C). Thus, in both legal and practical effect, the Presidential actions at issue have amended two Acts of Congress by repealing a portion of each. Statutory repeals must conform with Art. I, but there is no constitutional authorization for the President to amend or repeal. Under the Presentment Clause, after a bill has passed both Houses, but "before it become[s] a Law," it must be presented to the President, who "shall sign it" if he approves it, but "return it," i.e., "veto" it, if he does not. There are important differences between such a "return" and cancellation under the Act: The constitutional return is of the entire bill and takes place *before* it becomes law, whereas the statutory cancellation occurs *after* the bill becomes law and affects it only in part. There are powerful reasons for construing the constitutional silence on the profoundly important subject of Presidential repeals as equivalent to an express prohibition. The Article I procedures governing statutory enactment were the product of the great debates and compromises that produced the Constitution itself. Familiar historical materials provide abundant support for the conclusion that the power to enact statutes may only "be exercised in accord with a single, finely wrought and exhaustively considered, procedure." What has emerged in the present cases, however, are not the product of the "finely wrought" procedure that the Framers designed, but truncated versions of two bills that passed both Houses.

(b) The Court rejects two related Government arguments. First, the contention that the cancellations were merely exercises of the President's discretionary authority under the Balanced Budget Act and the Taxpayer Relief Act, read in light of the previously enacted Line Item Veto Act, is unpersuasive. *Field* v. *Clark,* on which the Government relies, suggests critical differences between this cancellation power and the President's statutory power to suspend import duty exemptions that was there upheld: such suspension was contingent on a condition that did not predate its statute, the duty to suspend was absolute once the President determined the contingency had arisen, and the suspension executed congressional policy. In contrast, the Act at issue authorizes the President himself to effect the repeal of laws, for his own policy reasons, without observing Article I, §7, procedures. Second, the contention that the cancellation authority is no greater than the President's traditional statutory authority to decline to spend appropriated funds or to implement specified tax measures fails because this Act, unlike the earlier laws, gives the President the unilateral power to change the text of duly enacted statutes.

(c) The profound importance of these cases makes it appropriate to emphasize three points. First, the Court expresses no opinion about the wisdom of the Act's procedures and does not lightly conclude that the actions of the Congress that passed it, and the President who signed it into law, were unconstitutional. The Court has, however, twice had full argument and briefing on the question and has concluded that its duty is clear. Second, having concluded that the Act's cancellation provisions violate Article I, §7, the Court finds it unnecessary to consider the District Court's alternative holding that the Act impermissibly disrupts the balance of powers among the three branches of Government. Third, this decision rests on the narrow ground that the Act's procedures are not authorized by the Constitution. If this Act were valid, it would authorize the President to create a law whose text was not voted on by either House or presented to the President for signature. That may or may not be desirable, but it is surely not a document that may "become a law" pursuant to Article I, §7. If there is to be a new procedure in which the President will play a different role, such change must come through the Article V amendment procedures.

985 F. Supp. 168, affirmed.

Source: *Clinton v. City of New York* (524 U.S. 417, 1998).

Articles of Impeachment against William Jefferson Clinton (1998)

On December 19, 1998, the House of Representatives, then under majority control by the Republican Party, issued a resolution of articles of impeachment against President Clinton.
  They are presented herein in full.

Resolution

Resolved, That William Jefferson Clinton, President of the United States, is impeached for high crimes and misdemeanors, and that the following articles of impeachment be exhibited to the United States Senate:

Articles of impeachment exhibited by the House of Representatives of the United States of America in the name of itself and of the people of the United States of America, against William Jefferson Clinton, President of the United States of America, in maintenance and support of its impeachment against him for high crimes and misdemeanors.

Article I

In his conduct while President of the United States, William Jefferson Clinton, in violation of his constitutional oath faithfully to execute the office of President of the United States and, to the best of his ability, preserve, protect, and defend the Constitution of the United States, and in violation of his constitutional duty to take care that the laws be faithfully executed, has willfully corrupted and manipulated the judicial process of the United States for his personal gain and exoneration, impeding the administration of justice, in that:

On August 17, 1998, William Jefferson Clinton swore to tell the truth, the whole truth, and nothing but the truth before a Federal grand jury of the United States. Contrary to that oath, William Jefferson Clinton willfully provided perjurious, false, and misleading testimony to the grand jury concerning one or more of the following: (1) the nature and details of his relationship with a subordinate Government employee; (2) prior perjurious, false and misleading testimony he gave in a Federal civil rights action brought against him; (3) prior false and misleading statements he allowed his attorney to make to a Federal judge in that civil rights action; and (4) his corrupt efforts to influence the testimony of witnesses and to impede the discovery of evidence in that civil rights action.

In doing so, William Jefferson Clinton has undermined the integrity of his office, has brought disrepute on the Presidency, has betrayed his trust as President, and has acted in a manner subversive of the rule of law and justice, to the manifest injury of the people of the United States.

Wherefore, William Jefferson Clinton, by such conduct, warrants impeachment and trial, and removal from office and disqualification to hold and enjoy any office of honor, trust, or profit under the United States.

Article II

In his conduct while President of the United States, William Jefferson Clinton, in violation of his constitutional oath faithfully to execute the office of President of the United States and, to the best of his ability to preserve, protect, and defend the Constitution of the United States, and in violation of his constitutional duty to take care that the laws be faithfully executed, has prevented, obstructed, and impeded the administration of justice, and has to that end engaged personally, and through his subordinates and agents, in a course of conduct or scheme designed to delay, impede, cover up, and conceal the existence of evidence and testimony related to a Federal civil rights action brought against him in a duly instituted judicial proceeding.

The means used to implement this course of conduct or scheme included one or more of the following acts:

(1) On or about December 17, 1997, William Jefferson Clinton corruptly encouraged a witness in a Federal civil rights action brought against him to execute a sworn affidavit in that proceeding that he knew to be perjurious, false and misleading.

(2) On or about December 17, 1997, William Jefferson Clinton corruptly encouraged a witness in a Federal civil rights action brought against him to give perjurious, false and misleading testimony if and when called to testify personally in that proceeding.

(3) On or about December 17, 1997, William Jefferson Clinton corruptly engaged in, encouraged, or supported a scheme to conceal evidence that had been subpoenaed in a Federal civil rights action brought against him.

(4) Beginning on or about December 7, 1997, and continuing through and including January 14, 1998, William Jefferson Clinton intensified and succeeded in an effort to secure job assistance to a witness in a Federal civil rights action brought about against him in order to corruptly prevent the truthful testimony of that witness in that proceeding at a time when the truthful testimony of that witness would have been harmful to him.

(5) On January 17, 1998, at his deposition in a Federal civil rights action brought against him, William Jefferson Clinton corruptly allowed his attorney to make false and misleading statements

to a Federal judge characterizing an affidavit, in order to prevent questioning deemed relevant by the judge. Such false and misleading statements were subsequently acknowledged by his attorney in a communication to that judge.

(6) On or about January 18, and January 20, 21, 1998, William Jefferson Clinton related a false and misleading account of events relevant to a Federal civil rights action brought against him to a potential witness in that proceeding, in order to corruptly influence the testimony of that witness.

(7) On or about January 21, 23, and 25, 1998, William Jefferson Clinton made false and misleading statements to potential witnesses in a Federal grand jury proceeding in order to corruptly influence the testimony of those witnesses. The false and misleading statements made by William Jefferson Clinton were repeated by the witnesses to the grand jury, causing the grand jury to receive false and misleading information.

In all of this, William Jefferson Clinton has undermined the integrity of his office, has brought disrepute on the Presidency, has betrayed his trust as President, and has acted in a manner subversive of the rule of law and justice, to the manifest injury of the people of the United States.

Wherefore, William Jefferson Clinton, by such conduct, warrants impeachment and trial, and removal from office and disqualification to hold and enjoy any office of honor, trust, or profit under the United States.

Attest: Speaker of the House of Representatives

Source: House Resolution 611, 105th Congress, Second Session.

Authorization for the Use of Force (September 18, 2001)

After the international terrorist attacks on the United States on September 11, 2001, the Congress passed a joint resolution authorizing the use of military force against the perpetrators of the attacks and a country (Afghanistan) that supported and harbored them. It illustrates the authorization to use force option of Congress rather than a formal declaration of war. Based on the War Powers Resolution of 1973, it should have required reauthorization and in any case was to have lasted only two years. In fact, the war in Afghanistan, legally justified by this resolution, has lasted more than sixteen years, the longest-running war in American history. It has been used by presidents George W. Bush, Barack Obama, and Donald Trump as the legal basis for armed forces engagement in several countries since 2001 and clearly against terrorist groups and countries having nothing to do with the attacks of September 11, 2001. It illustrates well the "elastic" nature of the authorization to use force resolution as opposed to a formal declaration of a state of war. It is excerpted herein.

Joint Resolution

To authorize the use of United States Armed Forces against those responsible for the recent attacks launched against the United States.

Whereas, on September 11, 2001, acts of treacherous violence were committed against the United States and its citizens; and

Whereas, such acts render it both necessary and appropriate that the United States exercise its rights to self-defense and to protect United States citizens both at home and abroad; and

Whereas, in light of the threat to the national security and foreign policy of the United States posed by these grave acts of violence; and

Whereas, such acts continue to pose an unusual and extraordinary threat to the national security and foreign policy of the United States; and

Whereas, the President has authority under the Constitution to take action to deter and prevent acts of international terrorism against the United States: Now, therefore, be it

Resolved by the Senate and House of Representatives of the United States of America in Congress assembled,

Section 1. Short Title

This joint resolution may be cited as the "Authorization for Use of Military Force."

Sec. 2. Authorization for Use of United States Armed Forces

(a) IN GENERAL.—That the President is authorized to use all necessary and appropriate force against those nations, organizations, or persons he determines planned, authorized, committed, or aided the terrorist attacks that occurred on September 11, 2001, or harbored such organizations or persons, in order to prevent any future acts of international terrorism against the United States by such nations, organizations or persons.

(b) WAR POWERS RESOLUTION REQUIREMENTS—

    (1) SPECIFIC STATUTORY AUTHORIZATION.— Consistent with section 8(a) (1) of the War Powers Resolution, the Congress declares that this section is intended to constitute specific statutory authorization within the meaning of section 5(b) of the War Powers Resolution.

    (2) APPLICABILITY OF OTHER REQUIREMENTS— Nothing in this resolution supercedes any requirement of the War Powers Resolution.

    Approved September 18, 2001.

Source: Pub. L. No. 107–40, 107th Congress.

Honest Leadership and Open Government Act (2007)

Following the lobbying scandals that plagued both chambers of Congress and the Bush administration in 2005 and 2006, Congress responded with passage of the Honest Leadership and Open Government Act of 2007. This bill was signed into law by President George W. Bush on September 14, 2007. Its goals included increasing transparency in the legislative process through additional disclosure requirements and clarified ethics requirements. Many on both sides of the equation believe it achieved these goals. It succeeded in curtailing interaction between lobbyists, interest groups, and grassroots organizations and members of Congress and their staff on government time. Instead, these interactions have moved primarily to political fundraisers. An additional unintended consequence has been less social interaction between staff of different parties and chambers. Following is the Congressional Research Service's summary of the bill.

Title I: Closing the Revolving Door

(Sec. 101) Amends the federal criminal code to extend from one to two years the ban on lobbying contacts by former: (1) very senior executive personnel with any Member, officer, or employee of the entity in which such person served before his or her tenure terminated; and (2) Senators with any Member, officer or employee of either chamber, or employee of any other legislative office.

Continues the one-year ban on lobbying contacts by former: (1) Members of the House of Representatives with any Member, officer, or employee of either chamber, or employee of any other legislative office; (2) elected officers of the House with any House Member, officer, or employee; and (3) Senate officers, or a Senate employee (who, for at least 60 days during the one-year period before such employee's service terminated, was paid a salary equal to or greater than 75% of a Senator's salary) with any Senator or Senate officer or employee.

Provides that the one-year ban on lobbying contacts by former legislative office employees shall apply to employees who, for at least 60 days during the one-year before such employee's service terminated, was employed in a position for which his or her salary, exclusive of any locality-based pay adjustment (currently, or any comparable adjustment pursuant to interim authority of the President), is equal to or greater than the salary for level IV of the Executive Schedule (currently, level 5 of the Senior Executive Schedule). . . .

(Sec. 102) Subjects to a fine or imprisonment of up to 15 years, or both, a Member of Congress or a congressional employee who with the intent to influence, solely on the basis of partisan political affiliation, an employment decision or employment practice of any private entity: (1) takes or withholds, or offers or threatens to take or withhold, an official act; or (2) influences, or offers or threatens to influence, the official act of another. . . .

Title II: Full Public Disclosure of Lobbying

(Sec. 204) Amends the Federal Election Campaign Act of 1971 to require an authorized committee of a candidate, a leadership PAC, or a political party committee to include in its disclosure report after each covered period a separate schedule setting forth the name, address, and employer of each person reasonably known by the committee to be a current registered lobbyist, an individual who is listed on a LDA registration or report, or a political committee established or controlled by such a registrant or individual who provided two or more bundled contributions to the committee in an aggregate amount greater than $15,000 (applicable threshold) during the covered period, and the aggregate amount of the bundled contributions provided by each such person during such period.

. . .

Defines "leadership PAC," with respect to a candidate for election to federal office or an individual holding federal office, as a political committee that is directly or indirectly established, financed, maintained or controlled by the candidate or the officeholder, but which is not an authorized committee of the candidate or officeholder, and is not affiliated with such an authorized committee. Excludes a political committee of a political party from the meaning of "leadership PAC."

. . .

(Sec. 206) Amends the LDA to prohibit a registered lobbyist, any registered organization that employs one or more lobbyists, and any employee listed as a registered lobbyist from making a gift or providing travel to a covered legislative branch official, if such individual or organization has knowledge that the gift or travel may not be accepted under the rules of the House or the Senate.

(Sec. 207) Revises requirements for the contents of lobbyist registrations, particularly disclosure of the identity of any organization, other than the client, that: (1) contributes over $5,000 to the registrant or the client in a quarterly period to fund the registrant's lobbying activities (currently, over $10,000 toward the registrant's lobbying activities in a semiannual period); and (2) participates actively in the planning, supervision, or control of such lobbying activities (currently, in whole or in major part plans, supervises, or controls such lobbying activities) . . .

(Sec. 208) Amends the requirements for the registration of a lobbyist to extend from two to 20 years the look-back period during which an employee of the lobbyist may have served as a covered executive branch official or a covered legislative branch official. . . .

(Sec. 211) Increases from $50,000 to $200,000 the civil penalty for failure to comply with LDA requirements.

Subjects anyone who knowingly and corruptly fails to comply with LDA to imprisonment for up to five years or a specified fine, or both. . . .

(Sec. 214) Expresses the sense of Congress that: (1) the use of a family relationship by a lobbyist who is an immediate family member of a Member of Congress to gain special advantages over other lobbyists is inappropriate; and (2) the lobbying community should develop proposals for multiple self-regulatory organizations which could provide for creation of standards, legal and ethical training, development of educational materials for the public on how to responsibly hire a lobbyist or lobby firm, standards for reasonable client fees, creation of a third-party certification program including ethics training, and disclosure to clients of fee schedule requirements and conflict of interest rules.

Title III: Matters Relating to the House of Representatives

. . . Prohibits a Member, Delegate, or Resident Commissioner (Member) from directly negotiating or having any agreement of future employment or compensation until after the election for his or her successor, unless such Member files a statement about such negotiations or agreement with the Committee on Standards of Official Conduct within three business days after their commencement. Requires inclusion in such a statement of: (1) the name of the private entity or entities involved in the negotiations or agreement; and (2) the commencement date.

. . . Requires such Member, officer, or employee to recuse himself or herself from any matter in which there is or appears to be a conflict of interest under the Rule, and to notify the Committee of such recusal. Requires such individual also to submit to the Clerk of the House, for public disclosure, the statement of disclosure for which such recusal was made. . . .

(Sec. 305) Prohibits a Member, during the dates on which the Member's national political party holds its convention to nominate a candidate for President or Vice President, from participating in an event honoring him or her, other than in his or her capacity as a candidate for such office, if such event is directly paid for by a registered lobbyist or a private entity that retains or employs such lobbyist.

Title IV: Congressional Pension Accountability

(Sec. 401) Amends federal civil service law regarding the Civil Service Retirement System (CSRS) and the Federal Employees' Retirement System (FERS) to exclude from retirement accounting any service as a Member of Congress of an individual finally convicted of a felony involving: (1) bribery of public officials and witnesses; (2) acting as an agent of a foreign principal while a federal public official; (3) fraud by wire, radio, or television, including as part of a scheme to deprive citizens of honest services; (4) prohibited foreign trade practices by domestic concerns; (5) engaging in monetary transactions in property derived from specified unlawful activity; (6) tampering with a witness, victim, or an informant; (7) racketeer influenced and corrupt organizations; (8) conspiracy to commit an offense or to defraud the United States; (9) perjury; or (10) subornation of perjury. Entitles such individual, all the same, to so much of his or her lump-sum credit as is attributable to such service. . . .

Title V: Senate Legislative Transparency and Accountability

Subtitle C: Revolving Door Reform—(Sec. 531) Amends Rule XXXVII (Conflict of Interest) to prohibit a former: (1) Member, who is employed by an entity that employs or retains a registered lobbyist, from lobbying Members, officers, or employees of the Senate for two years after leaving office; or (2) employee on the staff of a Member, who is employed by an entity that employs or retains a registered lobbyist, from lobbying the Member for whom he or she worked or that Member's staff for one year after leaving that position.

Prohibits a former employee on the staff of a committee, who becomes a registered lobbyist or is employed or retained by a registered lobbyist or an entity that employs or retains a registered lobbyist, from lobbying the members of the committee for which he or she worked, or the staff of that committee, for one year after leaving his or her position.

Imposes a one-year lobbying moratorium, upon leaving such position, on an officer of the Senate or an employee on the staff of a Member or on the staff of a committee whose salary is equal to or greater than 75% of a Member's salary, and is employed at such salary for more than 60 days in a calendar year.

(Sec. 532) Prohibits a Member from negotiating or having any arrangement concerning prospective private employment until after the election for his or her successor has been held, unless such Member files a signed statement with the Secretary of the Senate, for public disclosure, regarding such negotiations and arrangements within three business days after their commencement. Requires inclusion in such a statement of: (1) the name of the private entity or entities involved; and (2) the commencement date.

Prohibits a Member from negotiating, or having any arrangement concerning, prospective employment for a job involving lobbying activities until after a successor has been elected. . . .

Source: Congressional Research Service. Summary of S. 1 (110th): Honest Leadership and Open Government Act of 2007. https://www.govtrack.us/congress/bills/110/s1/summary#libraryof congress

Introduction

This chapter lists and discusses briefly some major sources of information the reader is encouraged to consult. It begins with print sources: scholarly books on the American Congress are cited and annotated. It then lists and discusses scholarly refereed journals that publish articles pertinent to Congress. Finally, it lists and discusses nonprint sources: several feature-length films and videos that give "life" and faces to the subject, illustrating the discourse about the politics and processes of the American Congress.

Books

Alden, E. Scott. *Why Congressional Reforms Fail.* Chicago: University of Chicago Press, 2002.

> Alden addresses the resistance to change so apparent in the House of Representatives. He contends that House members resist rearranging committee powers and structures because the current structure works to their

Speaker of the House Nancy Pelosi (D-CA) smiles after receiving the gavel from Rep. Kevin McCarthy (R-CA) following her election as the next Speaker of the House during the first session of the 116th Congress at the U.S. Capitol on January 3, 2019, in Washington, D.C. Under the cloud of a partial federal government shutdown, Pelosi reclaimed her former title as Speaker and her fellow Democrats took control of the House of Representatives for the second time in eight years. (Win McNamee/Getty Images)

advantage for reelection by helping them attain funds and favors for their districts. He uses extensive evidence from three reform periods—the 1940s, 1970s, and 1990s—to show that reelection is still the most determining factor of the outcome of committee reforms and why committee reforms have not, and probably never will, succeed.

Alden, E. Scott, and John D. Wilkerson. *Congress and the Politics of Problem Solving*. New York: Cambridge University Press, 2013.
The authors show that when voters are willing to hold their member accountable for their problem-solving abilities, it can produce novel insights into the legislative organization, behavior, and output. They discuss program oversight and policy development, what drives legislative policy change, lawmakers' support for structures that enhance their capacity to address societal problems, and what encourages members to contribute to nonparticularistic policy making. They show how Congress's collective performance affects reelection prospects of incumbents of both political parties and how the electoral imperative to address societal problems offers a compelling explanation for their provocative findings.

Baker, Ross K. *Is Bipartisanship Dead? A Report from the Senate*. Boulder, CO: Paradigm Press, 2014.
Congressional scholar Ross Baker's book is a counterintuitive look at bipartisanship in the U.S. Senate. He acknowledges the trend of increasing partisanship and polarization but argues that the practice of working across the aisle is not dead, and examples are there if one knows where to look. While he was on sabbaticals in 2008 and 2012, Baker worked out of the office of Senate Majority Leader Harry Reid and talked with senators from both parties as they made bipartisan deals. He assesses the decline in bipartisanship over a forty-year period, but he addresses what he calls "boutique bipartisanship" in committees, where cooperation is more common than

on the floor. He notes how interest groups such as the National Rifle Association and the Sierra Club use items in their annual legislative scorecards to ward off bipartisan compromise.

Barone, Michael, Chuck McCutcheon, Sean Trende, and John Kraushaar. *The Almanac of American Politics*. Washington, D.C.: University of Chicago Press, 2014.
    The American Congress and all the House districts and the states selecting the U.S. senators are analyzed and described in narrative history and current statistical data.

Binder, Sarah. *Stalemate: Causes and Consequences of Legislative Gridlock*. Washington, D.C.: Brookings Institution Press, 2002.
    Gridlock has been since the earliest Congresses and stalemate seems endemic to American politics, as so well noted in this book. Binder examines the causes and consequences of gridlock. She focuses on the ability to secure policy compromise on major national issues. She examines fifty years of legislative history measuring the frequency of gridlock and revisits the structural basis for gridlock as an unintentional consequence of constitutional design. She explores ways in which elections and institutions shape the capacity of Congress and the president to make public law. She analyzes two facets of institutional evolution in the U.S. Senate: the emergence of the Senate as a coequal partner of the U.S. House of Representatives and the insertion of political parties into the legislative arena. She offers a new empirical approach for testing the accounts of policy stalemate during the decades since World War II.

Bishin, Benjamin. *Tyranny of the Minority: The Subconstituency Politics Theory of Representation*. Philadelphia: Temple University Press, 2009.
    Author Bushin explains how the desires of small groups— what he terms "subconstituencies"—so often trump the

preferences of much larger groups. He provides a unified theory of representation, based on social psychology and identity theory, to explain how citizen intensity fosters knowledge and participation and drives candidates' behavior in campaigns and legislators' behavior in connection with a wide range of issues. He posits a unique explanation of when, why, and how special interests dominate American national politics.

Boller, Paul. *Congressional Anecdotes*. New York: Oxford University Press, 1991.

Boller captures the comedy and brilliance as well as the buffoonery, the integrity as well as corruption, and the leadership as well as demagoguery of the Congress. He captures the institution with a sweeping, informative, and delightful look at the national legislature. He shows his gift for lively and revealing stories, providing a fascinating view of congressional history. Organizing the anecdotes by subject into ten chapters, each contains essays and stories that are amusing, dramatic, and poignant and that collectively reveal a rich and vital past of the great national institution, showing its indispensable part in the nation's development.

Brady, David W., and Craig Volden. *Revolving Gridlock: Politics and Policy from Jimmy Carter to George W. Bush*, 2nd ed. Boulder, CO: Westview Press, 2005.

The political scientist authors of this provocative book show that gridlock is not a product of divided government, party politics, or any of the usual suspects. They argue that instead it is an instrumental part of American government, built into our institutions and sustained by leaders acting rationally to achieve a set of goals and to thwart inadvertencies. They look at key legislative issues from divided government under Carter, Reagan, Clinton, and Bush. They analyze key points in the lawmaking of swing votes, the veto, the filibuster, and the rise of tough budget politics. They demonstrate that when it comes to divided government, it doesn't matter who occupies the White House or which party is in control of Congress. Gridlock is as American as an apple pie, and can result in stability and democracy.

Brill, Stephen. *America's Bitter Bill*. New York: Random House, 2015.

Journalist Steven Brill's near-death experience from a heart issue helped him to analyze health care from a patient's viewpoint. He realized that in addition to a tough political issue because of the great amount of money involved, the issue is politically toxic because of all the fear and emotion involved. His book discusses the political fights and lobbying of medical and pharmaceutical industries that led to the compromises of the Affordable Care Act (ACA) but added many confusing new regulations and new layers of bureaucracy. He exemplifies the confusing effects on the bills from thirty-six different pieces of paper from the same insurance company that he received on the same day. He argues that the ACA does not curb the marketplace of exorbitant bills and profiteering on the part of hospitals, medical device makers, and the drug companies and argues that, in the long run, the ACA is "unsustainable."

Brunell, Thomas L. *Redistricting and Representation: Why Competitive Elections Are Bad for America*. London: Routledge, 2008.

In this provocative book, the author argues that competition in general elections is not the sine qua non of healthy democracy. Rather, he argues, it contributes to low levels of approval of Congress and its members. He posits an argument for a radical departure from traditional approaches to redistricting—namely, that we need to "pack" districts with as many like-minded partisans as possible to maximize the number of winning voters, not losers.

Cooper, Joseph, ed. *Congress and the Decline of Public Trust: Why Can't the Government Do What's Right?* Boulder, CO: Westview Press, 1999.

> Cooper discusses the marked trend in the decline in the trust in government, clearly revealed in a host of poll data. This volume presents nine essays that detail the present character of that distrust. It analyzes the causes and dangers it poses for the future of representative government. The essays suggest remedies and focus on the pivotal role Congress plays in representative government. The authors examine patterns in trust in societal institutions and the presidency; the Clinton impeachment controversy; the emergence of far more ideological, candidate-centered members; Congress as interest-group controlled; the importance of the media; the mounting costs of campaigns; contradictions in public attitudes toward political leaders and processes; the causes and consequences of public misconceptions of democratic politics; and the need to reform campaign finance, media practices, and civic education.

Cormack, Lindsey. *Congress and U.S. Veterans: From the G.I. Bill to the VA Crisis.* Santa Barbara, CA: Praeger, 2018.

> A compelling look at veterans' policy, this book describes why the Republican Party is considered to be *the* party for veterans despite the fact that congressional Democrats are responsible for a greater number of policy initiatives. It provides detailed descriptions of the key legislative players, proposals, and communication strategies surrounding veterans' policies and politics.

Cox, Gary, and Jonathan Katz. *Eldridge Gerry's Salamander: The Electoral Consequences of the Reapportionment Revolution.* New York: Cambridge University Press, 2002.

> Since *Baker v. Carr* (1962), the case has sparked a wave of extraordinary redistricting. Both state legislative and congressional districts have been redrawn more

comprehensively than at any time in America's history. The book provides a detailed analysis of how judicial partisanship affected redistricting outcomes, arguing that the reapportionment led to three fundamental changes in the nature of congressional elections: the abrupt eradication of a 6 percent pro-Republican bias in the transition of congressional votes into seats outside the south; the abrupt increase in the advantage of incumbents; and the abrupt alterations of the two parties' success in congressional recruitment and elections.

Cox, Gary W., and Matthew D. McCubbins. *Legislative Leviathan: Party Government in the House*, 2nd ed. Cambridge; New York: Cambridge University Press, 2007.

Cox and McCubbins examine the inner workings of the House of Representatives in the years since 1945. They reevaluate the role of parties and committees. They view parties as types of "legislative cartels" that usurp power to make rules governing the structure and process of legislating. They argue that rulemaking power leads to two main consequences. First, the legislative process and the committee system are stacked in favor of majority party interests. Second, because the majority party has all the structural advantages, the key players are members of that party and its central agreements are facilitated by cartel rules and policies by carter leadership. They debunk arguments about the weakening of congressional parties and illuminate ways in which parties exercise discretion in organizing the House of Representatives to carry out its work.

Currinder, Marian. *Money in the House: Campaign Funds and Congressional Party Politics*. Boulder, CO: Westview Press, 2008.

Currinder provides a compelling look at how the drive to raise campaign money has come to dominate congressional party politics. The book examines the rise in member-to-member and member-to-party giving as part of a broader process that encourages ambitious House members to compete for power by raising money for the party and its candidates. As the margin between the parties in the House has narrowed, the political environment has become increasingly competitive. Electoral success is largely equated with fundraising success. The party that raises the most money is at a distinct advantage. Fundraising expectations are even higher for those seeking to advance in the chamber. The book argues that the new "rule of money" is fundamentally altering the way House members pursue power and the way congressional parties define and reward loyalty.

Dabros, Matthew S. *Careers after Congress: Do Jobseeking Legislators Shortchange Constituents?* Santa Barbara, CA: Praeger, 2017.
Dabros's book notes that the vast majority of legislators transition to other careers after leaving elective office. He examines the question of how many of these noncareer legislators acted in office to serve their postcongressional career motivations rather than the people they represent. Citizens, journalists, and watchdog organizations claim members of congress serve special interests in return for lucrative jobs after leaving office. Dabros examines the veracity of that claim. He focuses on 346 senators and representatives who left office between 2001 and 2011, making a counterintuitive argument that job-seeking legislators provide stalwart service to their constituents during their term in office for fear that damaging their reputations imperils their postcongressional career options. He investigates the major factors that prompt legislators to remain in public service, leave to take up lobbying or otherwise work in the private sector, or retire from work altogether.

Davidson, Roger H., Walter Oleszek, Frances E. Lee, and Eric Scheckler. *Congress and Its Members*, 16th ed. Washington, D.C.: Congressional Quarterly Press, 2017.
This comprehensive textbook on Congress and the legislative process explores the tension between Congress as

an institution and as a collection of politicians constantly seeking reelection. This new edition examines the 2016 election and the agenda of the new Congress. It covers a wide range of topics such as White House-Capitol Hill relations, party and committee leadership, judicial appointments, partisan polarization, budgeting, campaign finance, lobbying, public attitudes about Congress, reapportionment, and congressional rules and procedures. The topics are covered in a balanced fashion, with current case material and relevant data, charts, exhibits, maps, and photographs.

Devins, Neal, and Keith E. Whittington, eds. *Congress and the Constitution*. Durham, NC: Duke University Press, 2005.

This edited volume is an important collection of essays by leading scholars in law and political science that examines the role of Congress in constitutional interpretation. It demonstrates how better to integrate the legislative branch into understanding of constitutional practice. Essays look at lawmakers' attitudes toward the role of Congress as a constitutional interpreter, the offices within Congress that help lawmakers learn about constitutional issues, the willingness of Congress to use its confirmation power to shape constitutional decisions by the executive and judicial branches, and the frequency with which committees take constitutional questions into account. Other essays examine how Congress and the courts respond to each other's decisions, suggesting how the courts should evaluate Congress's work and considering how lawmakers respond to court decisions that strike down federal laws. The essays underscore the pervasive and pivotal role Congress plays in shaping the meaning of the Constitution.

Dodson, Debra L. *The Impact of Women in Congress*. Oxford; New York: Oxford University Press, 2006.

Dodson provides a study that is a major assessment of the impact women members of the American Congress have on public policy. She focuses on three related public policy case studies: reproductive health, women's health, and health policy overall. She examines the role of women in the 103rd and 104th Congresses. The book highlights the complex forces that shape what women members do and their influence on the institution of Congress.

Draper, Robert. *When the Tea Party Came to Town*. New York: Simon and Schuster, 2013.

Author Draper provides what is perhaps the definitive account of what may well turn out to be the worst congressional term in U.S. history. He burrows deep inside his subject, gaining cooperation from the major players and thereby providing an "insiders" look. The book is a colorful account, unsparingly detailed. It is an evenhanded narrative of how and why the U.S. House of Representatives evolved into the "house of ill-repute." Given the bitterly divided, highly partisan political atmosphere of current U.S. politics, Draper's look at the behind-the-scenes machinations of the House of Representatives is captivating and certainly timely. He reveals a complete "picture" of the House of Representatives, from the process of how laws are made—or not made—to an eye-popping cast of lawmakers, perhaps more contentious than ever before in U.S. history.

Evans, Jocelyn Jones. *One Nation under Siege: Congress, Terrorism, and the Fate of American Democracy*. Lexington: University Press of Kentucky, 2010.

Since the attacks of September 11, 2001, American political institutions have all undergone change, at times radical change, as they adapted to new security problems. Media attention has focused more on the executive branch. As a congressional fellow living in Washington, D.C., Evans was an eyewitness to the institutional culture of Capitol Hill before and after the attacks and the subsequent anthrax scare aimed directly at Congress. She uses her personal experiences as a base on which to build this richly researched analysis of how Congress changed as an institution and as a national symbol in the aftermath of the international terrorist attacks. She looks at the physical transformations and at the internal policy shifts that threaten democracy by limiting citizens' access to their elected representatives.

Farrier, Jasmine. *Passing the Buck: Congress, the Budget, and Deficits*. Lexington: University Press of Kentucky, 2004.

The author probes the numerous policy debates of the past few decades that have caused the institution to question whether or not its powers are vital to advancing national interest or, rather, to serve to thwart it. Farrier examines several cases in which Congress delegated powers: such as fast-track presidential trade authority, commissions to oversee military base-closing, and the line-item veto. The author notes that Congress has not declared war since World War II but instead has opted to support undeclared presidential-led military actions, from Korea to the Persian Gulf. He covers the delegation of powers and representation, then reforming the reforms—a brief history of congressional budgeting and congressional attacks on the deficits and the new tools of self-restraint such as the line-item veto act of 1996.

Fenno, Richard F., Jr. *Learning to Govern: An Institutional View of the 104th Congress*. Washington, D.C.: Brookings Institution Press, 1997.

The election of 1994 resulted in the first Republican-led Congress in forty years. Fenno argues that after four decades out of power, the Republicans were without the experience they needed to properly govern. He focuses on the confrontational style of Newt Gingrich, the deterioration of cross-party civility, the general support for term limits, and the growing loss of public confidence. The book examines the attitudes and agendas of the inexperienced freshman class of legislators and the problem-plagued attempt to use the *Contract with America* as a blueprint for governing.

Fenno, Richard F., Jr. *The Power of the Purse*. Boston: Little, Brown, 1966.

In his now classic and then groundbreaking book, Richard Fenno describes his use of semistructured, open-ended questions that he conducted in interviews with all respondents that ranged from less than one hour to three hours. His book has been widely assessed as the most comprehensive treatment of the appropriations process, covering every aspect of the process. He interviewed respondents over a six-year period and analyzed public records and appropriation debates and hearings.

Fisher, Louis. *On Appreciating Congress: The People's Branch*. Boulder, CO: Paradigm Publishers, 2010.

Louis Fisher was employed at the Congressional Research Office from 1970 to 2006. He has written nineteen books on Congress and is a highly respected specialist on constitutional law at the Law Library of the Library of Congress. This volume presents a brief investigation of an aspect of government aimed at the general reader. Fisher argues the need for a restoration of congressional authority, which he shows has been eroded since World War II to the executive and judicial branches. He notes how the system of checks and balances has been weakened. He covers presidents from Truman to Bush. He includes a good discussion of judicial rulings that were eventually overturned by congressional legislation. He mentions how excessive partisanship amounts to self-inflicted wounds that have alienated the public and led to an increase in independents. His book is a compelling call for returning Congress to its place of eminence.

Fisher, Louis. *The Supreme Court and Congress: Rival Interpretations*. Washington, D.C.: Congressional Quarterly Press, 2008.

The author, a senior scholar in the Law Library of the Library of Congress, wrote more than a dozen books on Congress. In this award-winning book, Fisher explores how the U.S. Supreme Court operates in relation to legislative action and has defined the extent and limits of congressional power. He traces conflicts between the court and Congress over the power of judicial review and other key separation of power issues: civil rights for African Americans and women, individual liberties, and the regulation of the national economy. Essays and documents examine the different interpretations of the Constitution by the judicial and legislative branches and how the dialog between the institutions helps to reconcile constitutional interpretation with democratic government.

Frank, Barney. *Frank: A Life in Politics from the Great Society to Same-Sex Marriage*. New York: Farrar, Straus, and Giroux, 2015.
Former member of Congress Frank's book is a funny yet sophisticated and expansive analysis of his life in American politics and particularly in the American Congress. The book covers issue advocacy and uses his personal experiences to argue cogently and cleverly those issues. He is noted as one of the most idiosyncratic and influential persons to serve in the U.S. House of Representatives. Frank represented the Fourth Congressional District of Massachusetts for nearly fifty years. He is the first openly gay member of Congress to enter a same-sex marriage while serving in office.

Frantzich, Steven, and John Sullivan. *The C-SPAN Revolution*. Norman: University of Oklahoma Press, 1999.
Frantzich's and Sullivan's book is the first history of the C-SPAN network. It offers a behind-the-scenes look at C-SPAN's evolution, operation, and impact on the Congress and on public affairs more broadly.

Frisch, Scott A., and Sean Q. Kelly. *Committee Assignments in the U.S. House of Representatives*. Norman: University of Oklahoma Press, 2006.
The authors draw on new data from congressional archives to reveal the complex process through which members of

Congress get assigned to powerful committees and subcommittees in the U.S. House of Representatives. They conclude that the parties differ in their committee assignment methods and show how the party's approaches have changed over time depending on the party's leadership. They focus on the increasing role of gender and race in the assignment process. Using extensive primary and secondary research sources, their book advances our grasp of the internal dynamics of the Congress as gleaned through the committee assignment process.

Garrett, R. Sam. *Campaign Crises: Detours on the Road to Congress.* Boulder, CO: Lynne Rienner Publishers, 2009.

Garrett uses extensive interviews with political professionals to highlight aspects of the campaign process often missed by detached scholars. The book is enlightening as well as entertaining. He helps to unpack the dynamics behind the scenes of campaigning and electioneering. The book provides an insightful look at the tense moments that often make or break a campaign. Garrett is well qualified to write the book as a research fellow at American University's Center for Congressional and Presidential Studies as well as an analyst for the Congressional Research Service at the Library of Congress.

Gertzog, Irwin N. *Women and Power on Capitol Hill: Reconstructing the Congressional Women's Caucus.* Boulder, CO: Lynne Reinner Publishers, 2004.

Irwin Gertzog is professor emeritus of political science at Allegheny College. In this book he analyzes the origin, development, and influence of the Congressional Caucus for Women's Issues, an effective bipartisan caucus in the U.S. House of Representatives. He explores how women associated with the caucus have cast off their veils and reasserted their roles in the legislative process of the so-long considered "boys' club."

Geyh, Charles G. *When Courts and Congress Collide: The Struggle for Control of America's Judicial System*. Ann Arbor: University of Michigan Press, 2006.

Charles Geyh is a law professor and served as director of the American Judicature Society's Center for Judicial Independence as well as counsel to the Judiciary Committee of the U.S. House of Representatives. Geyh's book is a balanced and important contribution to the literature on the give-and-take between the congressional effort to control the judiciary and historical norms of judicial independence. Though written more than a decade ago, it remains a timely and gripping historical insight into the world of contentious confirmation hearings. He makes a strong argument that the independent judiciary depends more on the inter-branch norms than on the text of the Constitution. The book raises concerns over the withering of those norms.

Green, Matthew N. *The Speaker of the House: A Study of Leadership*. New Haven, CT: Yale University Press, 2010.

Green's award-winning book provides a comprehensive analysis of the Speaker of the House and how various Speakers have exercised legislative leadership from 1940 to 2010. Green finds that the Speaker's party loyalty is tempered by a host of competing objectives, including reelection, passage of desired public policy laws, handling the interests of the party's president, and meeting demands of the House as a whole. The book deftly combines theory and empirical data, providing insight into the behavior of House Speakers. It offers historical context of the office with a rich discussion of specific instances of legislative leadership and depicts the real-world complexities of the decision-making of the Speaker's office.

Hallett, Brien, ed. *The Powers of the U.S. Congress: Where Constitutional Authority Begins and Ends*. Santa Barbara, CA: ABC-CLIO, 2016.

Hallett's book offers a useful resource for students, scholars, and citizens. It explains all twenty-one of the enumerated powers of the American Congress, from the power of the purse to the power to declare war. It provides essays by recognized experts that collectively enable readers to connect the perspectives and goals of the founders to current issues and controversies. It provides an accessible gateway to further research of each of the individual congressional powers. The book explores the extent and limitations of congressional power in domestic and foreign policy.

Hibbing, John R., and Elizabeth Theiss-Morse. *Congress as Public Enemy*. Cambridge: Cambridge University Press, 1995.
The book describes and explains the American people's alleged hatred of the Congress despite reelecting such a high percentage of incumbents. It is based on focus group sessions held across the country and a specially designed national survey. The authors conclude that much of the negativity is generated by popular perceptions of the processes of governing visible in Congress and that the public's unwitting desire to reform democracy out of the legislative body is a cure more dangerous than the disease.

Howell, William G., and Jon C. Pevehouse. *While Dangers Gather: Congressional Checks on Presidential War Powers*. Princeton, NJ: Princeton University Press, 2007.
The authors provide a comprehensive and compelling analysis of Congress's influence on presidential war powers that have profound implications for the current debates about war, presidential power, and Congress's constitutional obligation to provide a check on presidential power. The book focuses on the 2003 invasion of Iraq but analyzes the last half-century of U.S. military policy. They conclude that presidents are less likely to exercise military force when the other party controls Congress.

The partisan competition of Congress matters most for proposed deployments that are large in size and directed at less strategically important locales. Congressional influence is most often achieved through public posturing that engages the media and public concerns, stirring domestic and international doubt about U.S. resolve to see a fight through to its end.

Jacobson, Gary C. *The Politics of Congressional Elections*, 6th ed. New York: Longman, 2004.

Jacobson presents a comprehensive review and synthesis of the current literature on congressional elections. He uses three levels of analysis: the individual (voter), district, and aggregate—the balance of parties. He examines the effect of gerrymandering, the rise of primaries, and the increasing importance of candidates over parties in the past few decades. He surveys and explains how districts and states vary in geographic size, population demographics, economic base, the number of media markets, ethnicity, age, and political habits. He examines such topics as incumbency advantage, including fundraising, the growing role of political action committees (PACs), presidential versus midterm election years, and the effects of electoral politics on congressional performances.

Janis, Irving. *Groupthink*, 2nd ed. Boston: Houghton Mifflin, 1982.

This is the second edition of Janis's groundbreaking 1972 book. Janis explains the conditions that cause the problem of group decision-making that he labels "groupthink." He delineates its symptoms and a variety of indicators. He emphasizes eight symptoms: (1) an illusion of invulnerability, (2) a collective effort to rationalize away warnings that might lead members of the group to reconsider their assumptions, (3) an unquestioned belief in the group's inherent morality, (4) stereotyped views of enemy leaders,

(5) direct pressure on any dissenting members to conform, (6) self-censorship of deviations from the apparent group consensus, (7) a shared illusion of unanimity, and (8) the emergence of self-appointed mindguards. It is characterized as excessive consensus seeking and is especially apparent in "crisis decision-making" situations. It provides a useful perspective on why and how Congress makes laws in response to a "crisis" situation and why such laws typically have many unanticipated consequences.

Jones, David R., and Monika L. McDermott. *Americans, Congress, and Democratic Responsiveness*. Ann Arbor: University of Michigan Press, 2009.

The authors use new empirical analysis to demonstrate that both politicians and voters take a hand in reconfiguring the House and Senate when the majority party is unpopular, as was the case in the 2008 election. Candidates run under the party banner but distance themselves from party ideology. Voters throw hard-line party members out of office. Public approval and democratic responsibility affect policy shifts and turnover at election times. They argue that Congress is responsive to the public—that voters enforce collective responsibility. They frame substantive and normative questions and combine disparate data sets and analytical techniques to develop new and important findings about the relationships between citizen preferences, legislative actions, and government policies.

Kanstroom, Daniel. *Deportation Nation: Outsiders in American History*. Cambridge, MA: Harvard University Press, 2007.

Kanstroom examines the chilling history of how America treated outsiders as a result of communal self-idealization and self-protection. From the Alien and Sedition Acts to the Fugitive Slave laws to Indian removal to the Chinese Exclusion Act to the Palmer Raids to the incarceration of Japanese Americans, he traces how congressional policy making sought to remove those whom Congress deemed unworthy or unable to become "true" Americans. He illuminates a dark side of American history, showing that deportation has long been a legal tool to control immigrants' lives and is used with increasing crudeness in a globalized but xenophobic world all the more heightened by the fear of terrorism.

Keith, Robert, and Allen Schick. *The Federal Budget Process.* New York: Nova Science Publishers, 2003.

Authors Keith and Schick detail an overview of the federal budget process. They discuss a framework for budget enforcement, the impact of the presidential budget versus congressional budget resolution and reconciliation processes. They examine revenues and borrowing, authorizations and direct spending, annual appropriations, and congressional oversight of the implementation of spending laws.

Kowert, Paul. *Groupthink or Deadlock: When Do Leaders Learn from Their Advisors?* Albany: State University of New York Press, 2002.

Groupthink is now a widely accepted explanation for policy-making fiascoes. Efforts to avoid it, however, can lead to another problem—deadlock. Kowert explores these dual decision-making problems, using the Eisenhower and Reagan administrations to demonstrate how both leaders were capable of learning and changing their policies. He points to the need for leaders—in both executive branch and the Congress—to organize their staff in a way that fits their learning and leadership styles and allows them to negotiate a path between groupthink and deadlock.

Kroger, Gregory. *Filibustering: A Political History of Obstruction in the House and Senate.* Chicago: University of Chicago Press, 2010.

In this comprehensive book, Kroger shows how filibustering is a game with slippery rules in which legislators who think fast and try hard can overcome superior numbers. The book explains how and why obstruction has been institutionalized in the Senate over the past fifty years and how it has transformed politics and policy making. He traces the history of filibustering in the U.S. House of Representatives in the nineteenth century and measures the effects of filibustering in several ways: in bills killed, compromises struck, and new issues raised by obstruction. Notable for its breadth of theory and its combination of historical and political analyses, it is a definitive study of the subject.

Krutz, Glen S., and Jeffrey S. Peake. *Treaty Politics and the Rise of Executive Agreements: International Commitments in a System of Shared Powers*. Ann Arbor: University of Michigan Press, 2009.

Krutz's and Peake's book offers a provocative analysis of treaties and executive agreements. They use theoretical and empirical data to challenge the more usual explanations to account for the growth in the use of executive agreements. They carefully analyze the treaty process in the Senate and when the Senate can be decisive in the diplomatic process. They conclude that executive agreements represent a mutual adaptation of the executive and legislature in the system of shared power.

LaLoup, Lance T. *Parties, Rules, and the Evolution of Congressional Budgeting*. Pullman: Washington State University Press, 2005.

LaLoup traces how congressional macrobudgeting has fundamentally changed the way in which Congress frames and enacts budget choices. The book analyzes the 1974 Budget Act, the Reagan tax cuts in 1981, the Graham-Rudman-Hollings mandatory budget-deficit reduction plan of 1985, the Bush and Clinton deficit reduction packages in 1990 and 1993, the balanced budget agreement in 1997, and the Bush tax cuts in 2001 and 2003.

He shows how the process moved from a fragmented to a more centralized process, restructuring congressional rules and institutions and changing the way Congress legislates, and altered how Congress negotiates with the president.

Lee, Francis E. *Beyond Ideology: Politics, Principles, and Partisanship in the U.S.* Chicago: University of Chicago Press, 2009.
Lee seeks to explain partisan discord by showing that many partisan battles are rooted in competition for power rather than disagreement over the proper role of government. The book systematically distinguishes Senate disputes centering on ideology from the large proportion of disputes that do not center on ideology. It shows the role of power struggle in partisan conflict. Lee shows how presidential leadership polarizes legislators who can influence public opinion by how they handle the president's agenda. He details how legislators exploit good government measures and floor debate to embarrass opponents and burnish their own party's image. He argues how the congressional agenda amplifies conflict by focusing on issues that differentiate the parties.

LeMay, Michael C. *The American Political Party System: A Reference Handbook.* Santa Barbara, CA: ABC-CLIO, 2017.
This volume presents a comprehensive discussion of how political parties, both major and minor, developed in American politics from 1790 to 2016. It details their successes and failures in achieving election of their members to the American Congress and the presidency. It discusses the legislative influence of political parties within the American Congress.

LeMay, Michael C. *Illegal Immigration*, 2nd ed. Santa Barbara, CA: ABC-CLIO, 2015.
This volume defines the concept and analyzes the flow of unauthorized immigration to the United States since

1970. It focuses on why immigration reform is such a vexing problem. It demonstrates the problems and issues resulting from bad policy, the gaps, failures, and unanticipated consequences of provisions in legal immigration lawmaking that contribute so significantly to the illegal immigration flow. It discusses the groups that advocate for or oppose immigration reform. It emphasizes that both legal and illegal immigration policies are intermestic—involving both domestic and international concerns. It details how immigration flows wax and wane in response to push and pull factors that make the problem increasingly difficult in complexity and scope, thereby making policy responses by the American Congress all the more difficult. It shows how, since 9/11, a sense of "fortress America" has permeated the political debate regarding both legal and illegal immigration and how the unauthorized immigration flow has become an important element in congressional stalemate and policy making.

LeMay, Michael C. *Religious Freedom in America: A Reference Handbook*. Santa Barbara, CA: ABC-CLIO, 2018.
A comprehensive discussion of how the First Amendment's religious freedom guarantee through the free exercise and the no establishment clauses have been elaborated upon and expanded by court cases and by laws enacted by the American Congress.

LeMay, Michael C., and Elliott R. Barkan, eds. *U.S. Immigration and Naturalization Laws and Issues: A Documentary History*. Westport, CT; London: Greenwood Press, 1999.
This edited volume excerpts summaries of all the laws and court cases that interpret immigration and naturalization law from colonial times to 1996.

Loomis, Burdett A., and Wendy J. Schiller. *The Contemporary Congress*, 6th ed. Lanham, MD: Rowman and Littlefield, 2016.
Their book is a concise yet comprehensive and analytical text that covers all the foundations of a course on

Congress: from the underlying theory of representative democracy and the process of elections to committee dynamics and the legislative process on the House and Senate floors to the relationship between Congress and the presidency under unified and divided government. It presents a succinct and comprehensive view into the rules, politics, and party strategy that determine the policy decisions in the American Congress.

Magleby, David B., J. Quinonson, and Kelly D. Patterson. *Electing Congress: New Rules for an Old Game: Real Politics in America*. Upper Saddle River, NJ: Prentice-Hall, 2007.
    This book communicates how the Bipartisan Campaign Reform Act has changed the playing field for congressional elections in some ways and, in other ways, how it has not. It covers how it will affect future congressional elections. It is a collection of thoughtful essays on the subject that is a part of the publisher's series entitled Real Politics in America.

Mann, Thomas E., and Norman J. Ornstein. *The Broken Branch: How Congress Is Failing America and How to Get It Back on Track*. Oxford: Oxford University Press, 2006.
    Mann and Ornstein are two of the most renowned and knowledgeable congressional scholars. Their provocative book shows how partisanship has increased tribal warfare. They argue persuasively how voter turnout fosters partisan extremism in Congress and enhances the power of ideological activists.

Mann, Thomas, and Norman Ornstein. *It's Even Worse Than It Looks*. New York: Basic Books, 2012.
    The authors detail how acrimony and hyperpartisanship have seeped into part of the political process. They show how it influences Congress toward deadlock and contributes to the record-low approval ratings of government, in general, and of Congress, in particular. They identify two sources of congressional dysfunction: (1) the parties are

now so polarized and vehemently adversarial as to resemble parliamentary parties and (2) that the Republican party is an insurgent outlier—ideologically extreme; contemptuous of the inherited social and economic policy regime; scornful of compromise; unpersuaded by conventional understanding of facts, evidence, and science; and dismissive of the legitimacy of its political opposition and asymmetrical polarization—Republicans are more partisan than Democrats.

Masket, Seth E. *No Middle Ground: How Informal Party Organizations Control Nominations and Polarize Legislatures.* Ann Arbor: University of Michigan Press, 2009.

Masket's book is an insightful account of the polarization of American politics over the past few decades. He shows how policy-motivated activists have organized to influence political parties in nominations and in policy making. Masket shows that legislators can be content without parties that control agendas. He explains the transition from freewheeling legislators to rigidly partisan voting blocs. It is a thoughtful book that uses qualitative and quantitative research to argue his points.

Mayhew, David R. *America's Congress: Actions in the Public Sphere—James Madison through Newt Gingrich.* New Haven, CT: Yale University Press, 2000.

One of the most distinguished political scientists and scholars of Congress, Mayhew examines the actions of members of Congress throughout American history. He assesses their patterns and the importance of their role in the system of separation of powers. He offers insights into a wide range of matters, from the nature of congressional opposition to presidents and the frequency of foreign policy actions to the timing of notable activity within congressional careers. He sheds new light on the contributions to U.S. history made by members of Congress.

Mayhew, David. *Congress: The Electoral Connection*, 2nd ed. New Haven, CT: Yale University Press, 2004.

In this new edition of his now classic book, Mayhew argues persuasively that the principal motivation of legislators in reelection and the pursuit of that affect the way they behave and make public policy. Its first edition revolutionized the study of Congress.

Mayhew, David. *Divided We Govern: Party, Control, Lawmaking, and Investigating: 1946–2002*, 2nd ed. New Haven, CT: Yale University Press, 2005.

This prize-winning book debunks the myth that the American national government functions effectively only when one party controls the presidency and Congress. It updates the historical narrative to include the years from 1990 through 2002. Mayhew finds that divided government is no less production of important legislative than does unified government. The book's use of tabulations and analysis is unimpeachable.

Migration Policy Institute. *America's Challenge: Domestic Security, Civil Liberties, and National Unity after September 11*. Washington, D.C.: Migration Policy Institute, 2003.

This report is based on eighteen months of extensive research and interviews with detainees, lawyers, senior government officials engaged in domestic security and immigration issues, and leaders of Arab American and Muslim American communities across the country. It is a comprehensive compilation and analysis of persons detained post–9/11. It concludes that the harsh measures enacted by the American Congress against immigrants since the attacks have had dire consequences for antiterrorism efforts, fundamental civil liberties, and national unity. The authors conclude that authorities have placed too much emphasis on immigration in its counterterrorism efforts and that immigration enforcement is of limited effectiveness. It discusses the widespread discrimination experienced by Arab Americans and Muslim Americans since the 9/11 attacks and explains how rampant discrimination undermines national unity.

Monroe, Nathan M., Jason M. Roberts, and David W. Rohle. *Why Not Parties? Party Effects in the U.S. Senate*. Chicago: University of Chicago Press, 2008.

This book studies senatorial partisanship. It offers a collection of original essays that focus inclusively on the effects of parties in the workings of the upper chamber. Its essays explore the electoral foundations of parties, partisan procedural advantage, and partisan implications for policy. It is a timely book that shows that political parties do matter and that, in the U.S. Senate, their impact is far more similar to the House of Representatives than suggested by conventional wisdom.

Ngai, Mae M. 2004. *Impossible Subjects: Illegal Aliens and the Making of Modern America*. Princeton, NJ: Princeton University Press.

This multiaward-winning book traces the origin of the illegal alien in American law and society, explaining how and why it became a central issue in American immigration policy. She offers a close reading of the legal regime of restriction since 1920 and shows how restriction laws passed by the American Congress changed and reshaped America, creating new categories of racial difference. A deeply stimulating book or impressive scholarship, it delves beneath the tip of the iceberg of formal policy and lawmaking.

Oleszek, Walter J., Mark Oleszek, and Elizabeth Rybicki. *Congressional Procedures and the Policy Process*, 10th ed. Washington, D.C.: Congressional Quarterly Press, 2015.

This tenth edition is one of the most respected books on Congress. It is fair and evenhanded in addressing controversies in which Capitol Hill is engrossed. It is well researched and accessible to students and general readers, and it covers important topics and questions about Congress. It emphasizes congressional procedures, amendments, and the budget and appropriations processes. It incorporates history, current events, and theory in a nonpartisan posture and is openly "pro-Congress" as an institution.

Parker, David C. *The Power of Money in Congressional Campaigns, 1880–2006*. Norman: University of Oklahoma Press, 2008.
Author David Parker challenges the notion that over the past century, the pivot of American political campaigns shifted from parties to candidates. He examines the historical development of party, interest groups, and candidate power in congressional elections, covering both primaries and general elections since 1880. He posits a theoretical model: that the need for candidates to accumulate enough resources to be successful drives the competition. Campaigns, he states, simply are resource dependent. He analyzes case studies spanning more than a century, arguing that campaign behavior is determined by the resources needed to win. He shows how changes in electoral rules impact strategies used by candidates and parties to accumulate campaign resources, showing how the Bipartisan Campaign Reform Act of 2002 may influence the relationships among political actors and affect the quality of democratic discourse.

Polsby, Nelson W. *How Congress Evolves: Social Bases of Institutional Change*. Oxford; New York: Oxford University Press, 2004.
A distinguished political scientist, Polsby argues persuasively that from the 1950s to the 1990s, Congress evolved. This evolutionary process led to the U.S. House of Representative's liberalization and later to its transformation

into an arena of sharp partisanship. His book sheds light into the dusty corners of institutional history. He offers an explanation for important transformations in the congressional environment.

Paludi, Michele A., ed. *Why Congress Needs Women: Bringing Sanity to the House and Senate.* Santa Barbara, CA: Praeger, 2016.
In her intriguing book, Poludi addresses women's civil strategies for negotiation and leadership through careful analysis of social science research and management theory, as well as in-depth interviews with women legislators. She documents how women in Washington, D.C., are affecting the development of the world at all levels. The book is especially timely as women candidates enter the political arena in record levels.

Reingold, Beth, ed. *Legislative Women: Getting Elected, Getting Ahead.* Boulder, CO: Lynne Rienner Publishers, 2008.
Reingold's book provides a wide-ranging study of the increasingly complex array of opportunities and challenges that more and more women face as legislative candidates and as elected officials. She and her contributors use original research to expand our knowledge on several critically important topics: campaign finance, race and ethnicity, media relations, and how women advance within the ranks of the nation's elites. They examine how and under what circumstances gender matters most. The book offers new depth to the study of women and politics.

Remini, Robert V., and the Library of Congress. *The House: The History of the House of Representatives.* New York: Harper Collins, 2006.
A distinguished historian and the official historian of the U.S. House of Representatives, author Robert Remini shows how throughout U.S. history, the House of Representatives played a central role in shaping the nation. He traces the institution from a struggling, nascent body

to a venerable powerhouse as America rose to a preeminent role on the world stage. His narrative portrays the drama of democracy as the struggle between principle and pragmatism. He is an award-winning author whose narrative documents America's successful experiment with democracy.

Ritchie, Donald A. *The U.S. Congress: A Very Short Introduction*, 2nd ed. New York: Oxford University Press, 2016.

An eminent congressional historian, Ritchie takes readers behind the scenes of Capitol Hill, profiling key players, explaining their behavior, and translating parliamentary language to plain English. His eye-opening book provides an insider's view of Congress matched with a professional historian's analytical insight. He covers such topics as campaigning for Congress, how to attract large donors, committee assignments, the role of lobbyists and staffers, floor proceedings, parliamentary rules, coalition building, constituent services, media relations, and news coverage. He covers such key concepts as checks and balances, advise and consent, and congressional oversight. He provides a portrait of how Congress really works.

Rosenblum, Marc R. *U.S. Immigration Policy since 9/11: Understanding the Stalemate over Comprehensive Immigration Reform.* Washington, D.C.: Migration Policy Institute, 2011.

Rosenblum was deputy director of the Migration Policy Institute (MPI). This book is a report of MPI's Regional Migration Study Group. It reviews the history of immigration legislation since 9/11, focusing on the new enforcement mandates and the unsuccessful attempts to pass comprehensive immigration reform. It finds that the history and asymmetries of the political process favor the enforcement responses and that the economic downturn stack the deck against comprehensive reform.

Rubin, Irene S. *Balancing the Federal Budget.* New York: Chatham House, 2003.

Rubin explains how the government successfully balanced the budget in 1998. In her lively narrative, she describes the efforts of Congress and the administration over seventeen years to shape the process to encourage balance as well as the reactions of federal agencies to the pressures for workforce reduction. It covers contractors and clientele groups as well as the bureaucracy and the Congress struggling over complex budget issues.

Schick, Allen. *The Federal Budget.* Washington, D.C.: Brookings Institution Press, 2000.

Schick's book analyzes political and economic aspects of the budget process. Politics means change, and process means stability and incrementalism. Schick shows how the budget process has those two features together. He covers how the government takes in and spends more than $2 trillion annually. He details how the budget process entails the active participation of the president, key advisers, members of Congress, the efforts of thousands of staff in both the executive and legislative branches, and the attention of numerous interest groups. It entails literally thousands of decisions, big and small, in a difficult, conflict-laden process. The book features case studies that dramatize budgetary politics.

Schrug, Peter. *Not Fit for Our Society: Nativism and Immigration.* Berkeley: University of California Press, 2010.

Schrug presents a view on how the immigration debate and policies have shaped America since the founding. That helps us to better understand how the immigration debates have gotten us to where we are today. He provides a sweeping review of the current congressional immigration debates in a historical context, uncovering the dark impulses that have long undergirded nativist thought. The book is a lively and thoughtful interpretation of America's ambivalence toward immigration and its place in history.

Shaw, Greg M. *The Dysfunctional Politics of the Affordable Care Act*. Santa Barbara, CA: Praeger. 2017.

This comprehensive review of the politics of Obamacare analyzes the contentious debates over health-care reform and challenges the argument that treating medical patients like shoppers can significantly reduce health expenditures.

Sinclair, Barbara. *Party Wars: Polarization and the Politics of National Policy Making*. Norman: University of Oklahoma Press, 2006.

Sinclair's book describes the ideological gulf separating the two major parties and how the gulf developed and how today's fierce partisan competition affects the political process and national-level policy making. She traces it to changes in the Republican Party in the 1970s and 1980s, focusing on neoconservatism and the rise of the religious right. The parties, their voters and the politicians they elect, differ substantially on what they consider good public policy. She describes the institutional consequences for the House and the Senate of this polarization. She identifies weaknesses of the highly polarized system and offers suggested remedies.

Sinclair, Barbara. *Unorthodox Lawmaking: New Legislative Processes in the U.S. Congress*, 2nd ed. Washington, D.C.: Congressional Quarterly Press, 2000.

Sinclair argues that budget bills and the budget process are part of what she calls unorthodox lawmaking. Changes in the internal structure of Congress stemming from changes in the political environment have created problems for and opportunities to members of Congress to modify the legislative process. Individual members participate more fully in the legislative process. Those problems created issues for both chambers and for the majority parties making legislating more difficult. Divided government, big deficits, and increasing party polarization exacerbated problems of legislating, especially for the majority congressional Democrats in the House throughout the 1980s and 1990s.

Skinner, Richard M. *More Than Money: Interest Groups and Congressional Elections*. Lanham, MD: Rowman and Littlefield, 2007.
Skinner's book examines issue advocacy, independent expenditures, and voter mobilization that go beyond the limits set by federal law. It is an attempt to understand this world of interest group action in a theoretical fashion. The book links data gathered through case studies to broader ideas about interest groups, political parties, and congressional elections. Skinner examines what resource groups possess for political action, how they are linked to incentive groups, and how groups can apply those resources effectively. It looks at how interest groups adapt to changing political and legal contexts. It does so in a clear, accessible style.

Smith, Steven S. *The Senate Syndrome: The Evolution of Procedural Warfare in the Modern U.S. Senate*. Norman: University of Oklahoma Press, 2014.
Smith's book examines tensions that have been building for years. He examines the Senate and how and why senators became so obsessed with parliamentary procedure. He notes lessons from the story about the role of the Senate and that blame can be attributed to senators and the parties and the prospects for reform.

Smith, Steven S., Jason M. Roberts, and Ryan J. Vander Wielen. *The American Congress*, 8th ed. Cambridge; New York: Cambridge University Press, 2013.

This congressional textbook is updated with new learning features and, like its early editions, is a crisp introduction to congressional politics. It covers the 2012 elections and health-care reform and provides an early take on the 113th Congress. It shows the importance of a strong legislature in American democracy. The authors all have Capitol Hill experience and scholarship. The book examines the two congressional sessions of the Obama presidency. The text engages students by emphasizing the importance of Congress and has new end-of-chapter discussion questions and suggestions for further study.

Sollenberger, Michael A. *The President Shall Nominate: How Congress Trumps Executive Powers.* Lawrence: University Press of Kansas, 2008.

Sollenberger takes readers behind the scenes to explain what happens before presidents publicly announce their nominees. It presents a comprehensive history of the appointment process. He shows how political practice has shaped the use of a power that the Constitution declares must be shared by the executive and legislative branches. Skinner sheds new light on issues related to express and implied powers, the validity of the unitary executive model, the tensions between politics and professionalism, and the limits of originalism and textualism in interpreting the appointment process. It stimulates reconsideration and rethinking of fundamental principles of constitutional government.

Stewart, Charles H. *Analyzing Congress*, 2nd ed. New York: Norton, 2012.

Stewart's text introduces the fundamental concepts of rational choice theory and includes many empirical studies drawn from classic scholarship on Congress. Chapters include exercises that encourage students to apply rational choice. His book is highly readable and a convincing argument that politicians pursue their own self-interest dictated by the determination to get reelected—at all costs. Positions taken, votes cast, and gestures are made with the reelection imperative first and foremost in mind. His central point is that to understand democratic government, one must understand politics.

Strahan, Randall. *Leading Representatives: The Agency of Leadership in the U.S. House.* Baltimore: Johns Hopkins University Press, 2007.

Strahan argues that legislators as agents of their followers are an incomplete picture. He demonstrates why and explores the independent contributions that leaders make in congressional politics. He draws on historical and contemporary cases to show how leaders in the House have advanced changes in Congress and in national policy. He explores the tactics, tenure, and efficacy of the leadership of three prominent Speakers: Henry Clay, Thomas Reed, and Newt Gingrich. He employs a range of resources: papers, correspondence, and interviews with Gingrich and his staff. He offers a new framework—the conditional agency perspective—that links contextual perspectives with characteristics of individual leaders.

Sulkin, Tracy. *Issue Politics in Congress.* Cambridge; New York: Cambridge University Press, 2005.

Sulkin explores how legislators' experiences as candidates shape their subsequent behavior as policy makers. The book shows that winning legislators take up their challenger's priority issues from the last campaign and act on them. Attentiveness to their challenger's issues reflects a widespread, systematic, yet largely unrecognized mode of responsiveness in Congress. It reveals why doing so provides important benefits for these legislators as well as for the legitimacy of the representative process.

Taylor, Andrew, and Norman Ornstein. *Elephants Edge: The Republicans as a Ruling Party*. Westport, CT: Praeger, 2005.

Taylor and Ornstein's book describes the Republican Party's edge in Congress, state politics, judicial rulings, party finances, the media, public attitudes, and economic developments. They explore how these conditions facilitate the establishment of Republican rule. The book explores how they are using the courts to move policy forward and to mobilize parts of the electorate. They note, however, that Republican rule should not be confused with Republican realignment. They explain factors that prohibit them from fully exploiting their advantages in the way that Democrats did during the New Deal: internal and intractable tension within the party, their information gathering strategies, and the innate risk aversion of the campaign industry.

Theriault, Sean M. *The Gingrich Senators*. New York: Oxford University Press, 2013.

Theriault documents the Senate's demise over the past thirty years by showing how one group of senators—whom he dubs the Gingrich Senators—has been at the forefront of the transformation. He defines them as the Republican senators who previously served in the House after 1978, the year Newt Gingrich was first elected to the House. He demonstrates that these senators are more conservative and more likely to engage in tactics that obstruct the legislative process and prove more likely to oppose Democratic presidents than do their fellow Republicans. He shows how they behave as partisan warriors who have radically transformed the way the Senate operates as an institution, using cutthroat tactics, obstructionism, and legislative games. He concludes by examining their fate and the future of the U.S. Senate.

Theriault, Sean M. *Party Polarization in Congress*. New York: Cambridge University Press, 2008.

Theriault's book is a comprehensive account of the rise of party conflict in Congress since the early 1970s. He examines factors both inside and outside Congress that drive the parties further apart. His analysis reveals that external factors, such as the extremism of party activists, redistricting, demographic changes, and the decline in split-ticket voting cannot fully explain polarization. Internal institutional factors in both chambers must also be considered to fully understand the dramatic changes in party politics. He uses roll call votes and the conditional party government theory of Rohde and Aldrich and contends that the growing homogeneity of the party caucuses has led members to cede more power to their party's leadership. He finds that the rise of congressional partisanship is far more dramatic on procedural votes, which have comprised a larger share of the roll call record.

Volden, Craig, and Alan E. Wiseman. *Legislative Effectiveness in the United States Congress: The Lawmakers*. New York: Cambridge University Press, 2014.

This award-winning book explores why some members of Congress are more effective than others in navigating the legislative process and what this means for how Congress is organized and what policies it produces. They develop a new metric of individual legislator effectiveness that is useful to the study of party influence in Congress, the success or failures of women and African Americans in Congress, policy gridlock, and specific strategies lawmakers use to advance their agendas.

Wheeler, Darren A. *Congress and the War on Terror*. Santa Barbara, CA: Praeger, 2018.

Well researched, Wheeler's book examines the regular-order process in U.S. foreign policy making. He focuses on the battle against terrorism and on Congress as representative of the American people and argues that the United States must develop long-term policies that provide for national security while protecting the civil liberties of the American people.

Wucker, Michele. *Lockout: Why America Keeps Getting Immigration Wrong When Our Prosperity Depends on Getting It Right.* New York: Public Affairs Press, 2006.

Wucker's narrative history reviews how we shut the door to immigration after World War I, only to realize the error of doing so and reopening the door in 1965. The current record-high foreign-born population, global turbulence, and economic instability have once again pushed Americans past a tipping point about immigration and the global role of the United States. She documents the mistakes that led to our predicament today and clarifies why it would be a catastrophic error of judgment and a colossal lack of self-knowledge for America to again turn its back on the rest of the world, and in doing so, on the best of itself.

Zelizer, Julian E. *The Fierce Urgency of Now.* New York: Penguin, 2015.

Zelizer, professor of history and public affairs at Princeton University, takes the full measure of the sweeping changes spearheaded by Lyndon Johnson to transform the agenda of American politics since the New Deal. The Great Society, in three years, passed the Civil Rights and the Voting Rights Acts, the War on Poverty, and Medicare and Medicaid. Zelizer provides insight into the battles that raged in Congress and the administration. He details the bitterly divided forces at play in the United States—from religious groups and civil rights activists to labor unions and the media and how they influenced the ideal of a Great Society.

Zelizer, Julian E. *On Capitol Hill: The Struggle to Reform Congress and Its Consequences, 1948–2000*. Cambridge; New York: Cambridge University Press, 2006.

> Clearly written, Zelizer explains how Congress got to where it is today and how conservatives in Congress proved to be much better than liberal reformers in thriving in the new system put in place in Congress since the 1950s. He shows why scandals have become so important in modern politics and demonstrates why current Congresses seem unable to accomplish much. He shows how changes in the media changed the way the House and Senate operate.

Zolberg, Aristide. 2008. *A Nation by Design: Immigration Policy in the Fashioning of America*. Cambridge, MA: Russell Sage Foundation, Harvard University Press.

> The late Harvard professor explores American immigration policy from the colonial period to the present, discussing how it has been used as a tool of nation building. It covers policy at the local and state levels as well as federal immigration policy. It profiles the vacillating currents of opinion on immigration throughout American history. It examines legal, illegal, and asylum-seeking immigration.

Leading Scholarly Journals

American Journal of Political Science

This is a peer-reviewed academic journal published by the Midwest Political Science Association. It is published quarterly since 1973, ranks fourth among political science journals, and publishes original research articles in all areas of political science, quite often related to Congress and congressional politics.

American Political Science Review

This quarterly, peer-reviewed scholarly journal covers all areas of political science. It is the official journal of the American Political Science Association and is published by Cambridge University Press. Established in 1906, it is the premier research journal of the field of political science. It frequently publishes original research studies of the American Congress.

American Prospect

This monthly magazine covers politics, culture, and policy from a liberal perspective. It is based in Washington, D.C. It frequently has critical articles dealing with congressional issues and concerns, especially pertaining to civil rights and privacy issues.

American Sociological Review

Founded in 1936, the *American Sociological Review* is the flagship, peer-reviewed academic journal of the American Sociological Association. It is a Sage published journal of original works of interest to sociology in general and is committed to advance understanding of fundamental social processes. It is published bimonthly. It is ranked second among 143 journals of sociology. It frequently has articles on minority groups and population affected by congressional lawmaking, such as the Patriot Act, and immigration law designed to crack down on immigration enforcement and border control.

American Studies

This is a quarterly, interdisciplinary academic journal sponsored by the Mid-America American Studies Association, the University of Kansas College of Liberal Arts. It began in 1959 and has one thousand subscribers. It offers provocative perspectives on various issues and has frequent special sections and special issues devoted to in-depth treatment of a single topic.

Its book review section keeps abreast of the latest in contemporary scholarship. It has an online e-version that provides free access to all past issues.

Congressional Quarterly

This is a division of Sage Publications and publishes books, directories, periodicals, and electronic products on American government and politics and on the American Congress, notably *CQ Recall* and *CQ Weekly*. It was founded in 1945. It publishes news and analysis about the American Congress.

Georgetown Immigration Law Journal

This quarterly law review is the most specifically related law journal dealing with U.S. immigration law, its current developments, and reform-related matters concerning all three branches of government. It frequently focuses on illegal immigration and occasionally on how the American Congress treats issues and concerns that impact immigration. It contains case reviews, articles, notes, and commentaries. It publishes workshop reports devoted to immigration lawmaking.

Harvard Law Review

This law review is published eight times per year. It contains original articles, case reviews, essays, commentaries, and book reviews that occasionally focus on lawmaking and legal reforms. It began publication in 1887. It is published by an independent group of students at Harvard Law School. It is ranked number 1 of 143 law journals.

Independent Review

The *Independent Review* is a journal of political economy that is a peer-reviewed periodical published quarterly since 1997. It is an interdisciplinary journal devoted to the study of political economy and the critical analysis of government policy and lawmaking. It is provocative, lucid, and engaging in style. Its articles range across the fields of economics, political science, law, history, philosophy, and sociology. It features in-depth examination of past, present, and future policy issues by leading scholars and experts. It has frequently featured articles on civil rights and civil liberties and on immigration and race-related legal issues.

Journal of Politics

This peer-reviewed journal of political science was established in 1939, and it now publishes quarterly by the University of Chicago Press for the Southern Political Science Association. It publishes original research articles in all fields of political science, often concerning Congress, and it ranks 9th of 161 political science journals.

Legislative Studies Quarterly

Ranked 80th of 161 political science journals, it has been published since 1976 by Washington University and has articles on legislative systems, processes, behavior, parliaments, and their relations to other institutions, their functions in the political system, and activity by its members. It is a quarterly, peer-reviewed academic journal published by Wiley-Blackwell and is the official journal of the Legislative Studies section of the American Political Science Association.

National Journal

The *National Journal* is based in Washington, D.C. It is a monthly magazine about current political environment that has been published since 1969. It is now part of the National Journal Group and is described as the "premier source on nonpartisan insight on politics and public policy."

National Review

The *National Review* is a semimonthly magazine founded by William F. Buckley Jr. in 1965. It is a leading conservative magazine covering news, politics, and current events and culture with analysis and commentary and is described as the "most widely read and influential magazine for conservative news, commentary, and opinion."

Perspectives on Politics

Perspectives on Politics is a quarterly, peer-reviewed academic journal established in 2003 and is published by Cambridge University Press. It publishes articles for the political science profession as well as the broader society. It seeks to nurture political science as a field, publishing important scholarly topics, ideas, and innovations. It ranks 11th of 161 political journals.

Policy Studies Journal

This journal of the Policy Studies Organization is produced at Iowa State University, College of Education. It is published quarterly and contains articles related to all issues of public policy, including immigration reform issues and policies. It also publishes occasional symposium issues and regular book reviews.

Political Science Quarterly

Political Science Quarterly is a double-blind, peer-reviewed academic journal covering government, politics, and policy. It has been published since 1886 by the Academy of Political Science. Each issue contains six articles and up to forty book reviews. It is a journal of public and international affairs and is ranked 117th of 161 political science journals.

Polity

This is a Palgrave Macmillan journal published on behalf of the Northeastern Political Science Association since 1968. It publishes original research articles of general interest to political scientists across all fields. It has occasional studies of Congress, congressional behavior, and congressional politics. It is ranked 92nd of 161 political science journals.

Public Affairs Report

This is an annual publication of the Institute of Governmental Studies at the University of California, Berkeley. It is published as a public service to inform scholars, policy makers, and the public about activities of the institute. It does not represent the official position of the institute or of the university. The institute also publishes the *California Journal of Politics and Policy*. It supports research programs and seminars.

Public Choice

This is a peer-reviewed academic journal that studies the intersection between economics and political science. The journal plays a central role in fostering exchange between economists and political scientists, enabling both to explain and learn from each other's perspective. Its roots are in the application of economic methods to problems normally dealt with by political scientists—such as congressional policy making. While it retains strong traces of economic methodology, currently it also addresses newly developed, effective techniques that are not within the domain of economists.

Public Interest

Public Interest was a quarterly public policy journal established in 1965 by the New York intellectuals Daniel Bell and Irving Kristol. It was published until 2005. It was a leading neoconservative journal on political economy and culture aimed at journalists, scholars, and policy makers. It was based in Washington, D.C., and published 159 issues.

Publius: The Journal of Federalism

Publius is the world's leading journal devoted to federalism. It publishes original empirical and theoretical research on federalism and intergovernmental relations. It is published for the Center for the Study of State and Local Government, Lafayette College, Eastern Pennsylvania. In 2016, it was ranked 60th of

165 journals of political science and is the official journal of the Section on Federalism of the American Political Science Association. It has been published since 2006. Each year it issues an annual review of American federalism, which highlights and analyzes federalism and intergovernmental issues in the preceding year. It also publishes occasionally special issues on timely and significant trends and events.

The Review of Policy Research

The *Review of Policy Research* is a bimonthly, peer-reviewed academic journal published by Wiley-Blackwell for the Policy Studies Organization. It has been published since 1981. It is a political science discipline journal that focuses on the politics and policy of science, technology and environmental issues, science policy, environment resource management, information networks, cultural industries, biotechnology, security and surveillance, privacy, globalization, education, research and innovation, development, intellectual property, health, and demographics.

Roll Call

This news service provides Capitol Hill and Washington, D.C., with news, objective facts, and analysis along with coverage of political campaigns and elections. It rates each House and Senate race. It offers opinions and analysis on a host of topics and issues concerning Congress.

Social Science Research

Social Science Research publishes papers devoted to quantitative social science research and methodology. It features articles to illustrate the use of quantitative methods to empirically test social science theory. Its research cuts across traditional disciplinary boundaries. It publishes special feature issues. They concern current pressing issues in world society, typically with a political angle in keeping with the tradition of the New School for Social Research's politically conscious history. It organizes and publishes the proceedings of a conference series. It is published by Elsevier for the New School for Social Research and has been published since 1934.

White House Studies

White House Studies is a quarterly, peer-reviewed journal of scholarship and commentary on the politics and history of the presidency and the White House. It reviews current books and publishes original and timely scholarly articles. It has a regular feature on White House history and regularly features profiling first couples. Though scholarly, its articles are generally shorter than most academic journals to be more suitable to a wide audience that includes scholars, libraries, presidential sites and institutions, and White House enthusiasts. It is published by Nova Science Journals for the University of Southern Mississippi.

Yale Law Journal

This student-run and edited law review is affiliated with Yale Law School. It has been published since 1891 and is one of the most widely known of the eight law reviews published by students at Yale Law School. The review is one of the most often cited publications in the United States and often generates the highest number of citations per published article. Published eight times per year, each issue contains articles, essays, features, and book reviews by professional legal scholars as well as student-written notes and comments.

Nonprint Sources

This section presents an annotated list of nonprint sources useful to the study of the American Congress: feature-length films, videos, and key websites.

Films

The following annotated list describes eight feature-length films that involve depictions of how the American Congress impacts lawmaking and American politics. They are listed in order of their date of release and cover American political films from 1939 to 2017.

Mr. Smith Goes to Washington (1939). Black and white, 1:30 minutes, Sony Pictures.

> This classic comedy-drama film was directed by Frank Capra and stars James Stewart. Stewart's role is archetypal, and it is one of the quintessential films about American politics and broadly considered one of Stewart's best acting jobs. It portrays a young, idealistic senator fighting corruption in Washington, D.C., and is a powerful statement about American ideals.

The Washington Story (1952). Black and white, 1:21 minutes.

> This Metro-Goldwyn-Mayer (MGM) film was directed by Robert Pirosh and stars Van Johnson and Patricia Neal. Van Johnson portrays a member of Congress being investigated by a reporter (played by Patricia Neal) who is determined to uncover a tabloid-worthy scandal who instead falls for the member of Congress and comes to discover that he is innocent of the scandalous behavior his political enemies are charging against him.

Advise and Consent (1962). Color, 2:20 minutes.

> This neo-noir movie is based on the Pulitzer Prize–winning 1959 novel written by Allen Drury. It was directed by the famed Otto Preminger. It stars Henry Fonda as the nominee for secretary of state and focuses on the U.S. Senate battle to confirm him. A Warner Brothers picture, it examines American politics, blind hypocrisy, idealism, and self-interest. It is an excellent political drama with a top-flight cast.

The Congress (1988). Color, 1:33 minutes.

A PBS DVD video, it is a TV movie or documentary directed by the famed documentary filmmaker, Ken Burns. It stars David McCullough and Barbara Fields. It was produced by Florentine films.

Congress is one of the nation's most important and misunderstood political institutions. Ken Burns tells the story behind this branch of the U.S. government.

The American President (1995). Color, 1:54 minutes.

Rated eight stars on a ten-star rating system, this comedy/drama/romance film was directed by Rob Reiner, one of the most politically astute directors. It stars Michael Douglas, Annette Bening, Martin Sheen, and Michael J. Fox. Witty and funny, it is an engaging story about a widowed president who falls in love with a lobbyist. A rival for the presidential office, a U.S. senator played by Richard Dreyfuss, opens an attack on the president's character because of his romance with the lobbyist. It is a Warner Brothers–distributed Universal Pictures/Castle Rock Entertainment production.

Charlie Wilson's War (2007). Color, 1:42 minutes.

This biography/drama/comedy film was directed by Mike Nichols and stars Tom Hanks and Julia Roberts. It is a drama based on the Texas member of Congress, Charlie Wilson, and his covert dealings in Afghanistan to assist Afghan rebels against the Soviet Union. Wilson, a member of two congressional foreign policy and covert-ops committees, uses his canny political efforts to supply the Afghan mujahideen rebels with U.S. weapons. The rebels achieve a military victory but with unforeseen consequences and prices. It is a Paramount and Universal Studios–distributed movie produced by Relativity Media.

Lincoln (2012). Color, 2:30 minutes.

This biography/drama/history film was directed by Steven Spielberg and stars Daniel Day-Lewis as Lincoln and Sally Field as his wife. As the Civil War winds down, President Lincoln endeavors to achieve the landmark constitutional amendment to forever ban slavery from the United States. He clashes with a recalcitrant Congress. Distributed by Dreamworks and 20th Century Fox Studios, it was produced by Reliance Entertainment.

LBJ (2017). Color, 1:57 minutes.

This biography/drama is a compelling bio-picture that well captures the tumultuous career of Lyndon B. Johnson, from his career in the Congress—first the House and then the Senate—as well as his service as vice president and then president. It focuses on his role as Senate majority leader and on his commitment to get Congress to enact the landmark 1964 Civil Rights Act. It was directed by Rob Reiner and stars Woody Harrelson. It was produced by Electric Entertainment.

Videos

The following are nine short-length videos related to the American Congress and how it operates in addressing various public policy issues.

Liberty and Security in an Age of Terrorism (2003). Color, 23 minutes, Film Media Group.

This film grapples with the issues of balance between homeland security in the post–9/11 world and the basic civil liberty values central to American society. Using a hypothetical scenario, a panel of persons confronts the issues and wrestles with the high-stakes questions in discussing the implications of the USA Patriot Act, surveillance of suspects, closed deportation hearings, demands for student information, and just what constitutes an unaligned combatant.

The Patriot Act under Fire (2003). Color, 23 minutes, Film Media Group.

For many, worrying about constitutional rights seems like an archaic luxury in the age of international terrorism. The need for tighter security made civil liberties seem less critical when the nation confronted terrorism by passing urgent measures such as the USA Patriot Act, designed to defend the country. Two years after its passage, ABC News and anchor Ted Koppel took a hard look at the law with representatives from the Justice Department, the American Civil Liberties Union, and others.

What Is the House of Representatives? (YouTube), 17:31, Saylor POLSC 231, U.S. Government and Politics, Lesson 16.

A discussion on the structure of the House of Representatives.

The United States Congress (TeacherTube), 2:14.

A very brief introduction to the American Congress aimed at high school–level viewers.

How a Bill Becomes a Law (YouTube), 18:51: Mr. Raymond's Civics EOC Academy.

A basic discussion on the complex process of how a proposed law (a bill) makes a typical route through the American Congress on its way to become a law.

House Votes to Censure Representatives Charles Rangel (*PBS News-Hour*), 4:09.

Video from a December 2, 2010, *PBS NewsHour* broadcast that covers the vote in the U.S. House of Representatives to censure Representative Charlie Rangel for ethics violations.

The Enumerated Powers of the Legislative Branch of the U.S. Government (YouTube), 7:23.
> This video from October 22, 2012, looks at Article I of the U.S. Constitution to examine the wording and import of the enumerated powers of the American Congress.

Just the Facts: Historical Icons—Edward Kennedy (YouTube/Worldwide Academic Program), 2:12.
> This brief video from 2009 was produced for high school social science classes and is a brief tribute to the late U.S. senator Edward Kennedy featuring his career and important impact on several public policy issues.

A House of Representatives Session (C-SPAN), variable length, www.c-span.org/video/?/442060-2/us-house-meets.
> This video covers the March 6, 2018, session of the U.S. House of Representatives in which the House passed H.R. 4607, a bill requiring bank regulators to review and identify outdated regulations every seven years and illustrating the current "deregulation" emphasis of the Republican-controlled Congress.

Websites

Congressional Budget Office: www.cbo.gov/

Federal Courts: www.uscourts.gov

Federal Elections Commission: www.fec.gov/

Government Accountability Office: www.gao.gov/

House of Representatives: www.house.gov/

House Committees: https://www.house.gov/committees

House Lobbying/Clerk of the House: http://clerk.house.gov/index.aspxHouse Party Leaders/Organization: https://www.house.gov/leadership

House Rules/Committee on Rules: https://rules.house.gov/

Library of Congress—Congress Information: https://www.congress.gov/

Roll Call Data: www.voteview.com

Senate: www.senate.gov/

Senate Committees: https://www.senate.gov/committees/

Senate Party Leaders/Organizations: http://www.senate.gov/senators/leadership.htm

Senate Rules: https://www.senate.gov/reference/reference_index_subjects/Rules_and_Procedure_vrd.htm

Supreme Court: www.supremecourtus.gov

White House and Executive Agencies: https://www.whitehouse.gov/

This chapter provides some of the most important of historical events connected to the American Congress. The events mentioned are only a small selection of all possible items.

1776 The Continental Congress declares independence from Great Britain. They first passed a resolution introduced by Robert Lee (Virginia) on July 2 and then on July 4 passed the more formal Declaration of Independence, which was written by the Committee of Five. This committee consisted of Thomas Jefferson (Virginia), Roger Sherman (Connecticut), Benjamin Franklin (Pennsylvania), John Adams (Massachusetts), and Robert Livingston (New York).

1777 The Continental Congress establishes a national government in the Articles of Confederation. The states ratified the Articles in 1781 and remained in effect until the ratification of the Constitution in 1787. Under the Articles, there was no executive branch and the Congress had very little power. All laws required a super majority of state approval.

Senate Judiciary Committee Chairman Charles Grassley (R-IA), back to camera, swears in Judge Neil Gorsuch during the first day of his Supreme Court confirmation hearing before the Senate Judiciary Committee in the Hart Senate Office Building on March 20, 2017, in Washington, D.C. Gorsuch was nominated by President Donald Trump to fill the vacancy left on the court by the February 2016 death of Associate Justice Antonin Scalia. (Alex Wong/Getty Images)

1784 The Continental Congress passes the Treaty of Paris, which ends the Revolutionary War.

1787 The Constitution of the United States is ratified, which creates a bicameral legislative branch, consisting of a U.S. House of Representatives and a U.S. Senate. Every state has two representatives in the Senate, and the House is made up of proportional representation for all states.

1789–1791 The First Congress convenes in New York City. The House achieved a quorum on April 1 and elected their first Speaker, Representative Frederick Muhlenberg (R-PA). The Senate achieved a quorum on April 6.

1789 The First Congress submits the first twelve constitutional amendments to the states for ratification. Over the next two years, the states approved ten of them, creating the Bill of Rights.

1789 Congress passes the Judiciary Act of 1789. As outlined in Article III, Section 1 of the Constitution, the Act established the Supreme Court comprised of five associate justices and one chief justice and thirteen judicial districts.

1790 President George Washington gives the first State of the Union speech to a joint session of Congress in New York.

1790 Congress passes and President Washington signs the Permanent Seat of Government Act, which establishes Washington, D.C., as the seat of the federal government. Congress spent the next ten years in Philadelphia, while a Capitol Building was built in Washington, D.C.

1792 President Washington exercises his constitutional power to veto a bill passed by Congress for the first time. The bill was a new plan to divide seats in the House of Representatives, which would have given more seats to northern states.

1793 President Washington lays the cornerstone for the new U.S. Capitol Building.

1795 The Senate, exercising their advice and consent power, rejects their first Supreme Court justice nominee, John Rutledge.

1797   Senator William Blount (D-R-TN) becomes the first senator to be impeached by the House of Representatives. The Senate decided to expel him from the Senate in 1799. He was accused of treasonous activities.

1800   Congress passes a law, and it is signed by President John Adams, which moves the capital from Philadelphia to Washington, D.C. The House and Senate moved into the unfinished Capitol Building.

1803   Congress passes an act, and President Thomas Jefferson signs, which authorizes $11 million for the Louisiana Purchase from France.

1804   Justice Samuel Chase is the first Supreme Court justice to be impeached, for his political bias and partisan decisions. The Senate acquitted him, and he was not convicted.

1812   Congress passes its first declaration of war against Great Britain and Ireland.

1814   The British army sets the Capitol Building on fire during the War of 1812, destroying the entire congressional book collection. Burn marks are still visible in the Capitol crypt today. Thomas Jefferson offered to sell his own book collection of over six thousand books to Congress for $23,950 for the new Library of Congress. The new collection came to Washington in 1815 and today comprises over 167 million items, which includes 39 million books and 72 million manuscripts.

1816   The U.S. Senate establishes their still-in-use system of permanent standing committees.

1820   The Missouri Compromise is passed, which admitted slave state Missouri and free state Maine to the union. This act also prohibited slavery in the new Louisiana Purchase north of the 36 30 latitude line. This Compromise was fully repealed in 1854 by the Kansas-Nebraska Act and deemed unconstitutional in 1857 with the Dred Scott case.

1822   Delegate Joseph Marion Hernandez (No party-FL) becomes the first Hispanic American to serve in Congress.

Since then, 117 Hispanic Americans have served as representatives, delegates, resident commissioners, or senators.

1825 The House of Representatives exercises its constitutional duty of deciding the president when the Electoral College vote failed to decide a winner in the 1824 election. John Quincy Adams won the vote in the House.

1827 The Senate creates special seats for the press in its viewing gallery. These seats remain today.

1834 The Senate rejects its first cabinet nominee Roger Taney to Treasury secretary. He was nominated by President Andrew Jackson. Taney went on to be the chief justice of the Supreme Court, issuing the majority opinion in *Dred Scott v. Sandford* (1857).

1841 The first continuous filibuster is waged in the Senate from March 5 through March 11.

1844 The House of Representatives grants a seat on the House floor to former First Lady Dolley Madison for anytime she wants to use it. Madison enjoyed listening to the House debate. She remains one of the very few nonmembers to receive House floor privileges.

1845 A presidential veto is overridden by Congress for the first time. President John Tyler vetoed a bill regarding prohibiting the president spending money without appropriations from Congress. Congress overrode the veto. President Franklin Roosevelt had his veto overridden the most time of any president with nine. He vetoed a total of 635 bills.

1852 Henry Clay, former member of the House of Representatives, who served as Speaker three separate times, secretary of state, and U.S. senator, is the first person to lie in state in the rotunda of the U.S. Capitol Building. Since then less than forty people have received this highest of honors, the most recent being Senator John McCain in 2018.

1860 The House of Representatives receives a letter from South Carolina's representatives, announcing their secession from the union. The Confederate States of America forms in 1861 and the Civil War begins in April 1861 at Fort Sumter.

1862 Congress passes and President Lincoln signs the Homestead Act. This act granted up to 160 acres of government-surveyed land (they can purchase for $1.25 per acre after six months) to any adult citizen who agrees to occupy the land for five years and makes improvements to it. This act distributed over 500 million acres in the American West.

1865 Congress passes, and the states ratify, the Thirteenth Amendment to the Constitution, which abolishes slavery in the United States.

1867 Tenure of Office Act goes into law, over a President Johnson veto. This act would prevent the president from firing cabinet officials, which the Senate has previously confirmed. When President Johnson violated this act, he was impeached. This act was fully repealed in 1887.

1868 President Johnson becomes the first president to be impeached by the House of Representatives, for violating the Tenure of Office Act. He was not removed but acquitted by the Senate. In 1875, he became the first former president to serve as a U.S. senator.

1870 Senator Hiram Revels (R-MS) and Representative Joseph Rainey (R-SC) become the first African Americans to serve in Congress. Senate Democrats tried to block Senator Revels from being able to take his seat, but Senate Republicans came to his defense, and he was eventually seated in the Senate. One hundred fifty-three African Americans have served in Congress since then.

1872 Congress establishes the first National Park, Yellowstone, and President Ulysses S. Grant signed it into law.

1873 The first Congressional Record is published. The Record is a verbatim account of everything that happens on the House and Senate floor. It also includes all introduced legislation and votes.

1876 The first and only cabinet official to ever be impeached is acquitted by the Senate. Secretary of War William Belknap was impeached by the House for receiving payments from contracts.

1877 All senators begin sitting with their party in the Senate chamber, instead of keeping an equal number of seats on each side of the center aisle.

1883 Congress passes and President Chester Arthur signs the Pendleton Civil Service Reform Act into law. This act was a key component of the Progressive Era reforms. The act sought to end the practice of the spoils system, which gave government jobs for political reasons rather than being qualified. Government workers would thus be hired for merit and could not be fired for political reasons.

1884 The Senate acquires its first personal office staff members, when the chamber provides each member with clerical staff.

1900 Delegate Robert M. Wilcox (Home Rule Party-HI) is the first Asian Pacific American to serve in Congress. Since then, sixty Asian Pacific Americans have served in Congress.

1906 Congress passes the Pure Food and Drug Act to address the conditions in the country's food manufacturing facilities, particularly in meat processing and packing plants in Chicago. This act was a major piece of the progressive reforms passed by Congress in the early part of the century.

1906 The cornerstone is laid for the Russell Senate office building, named for Senator Richard Russell Jr. of Georgia. This building opened in 1909. It houses the personal offices of senators as well as numerous committees.

1907 Senator Charles Curtis (R-KS) becomes the first Native American to serve in the Senate. He was of Kaw, Osage, and Potawatomi ancestry. Only three Native Americans have served in the U.S. Senate.

1907 The first House office building, where members have their personal offices and committees are housed, is completed. This building would become the Cannon House Office Building, named for Joseph Cannon, Speaker of the House, from 1903 to 1911.

1909 The first congressional baseball game is played, made up of members of both parties in Congress. This game is still played every summer, with proceeds going to charities in Washington, D.C. In 2017, during a Republican practice for the annual game, a lone shooter fired upon team members, seriously injuring Majority Whip Steve Scalise (R-LA).

1910 The House remains in a marathon all-night session discussing a change to the House Rules, which would strip the Speaker (Joe Cannon) of his chairpersonship of the Rules Committee. The rule change was adopted after twenty-nine hours, and the fifty-year reign of powerful House Speakers came to an end.

1913 President Woodrow Wilson (D) gives the first in-person State of the Union speech since President Thomas Jefferson (D-R) abandoned the practice for being too monarchical. All presidents after him, until Wilson, sent written statements to Congress to comply with the constitutional requirement laid out in Article II, Section 3, Clause 1.

1913 The Senate Democrats officially designate their floor leader for the first time. Republicans would not designate a floor leader until 1925. These positions of majority and minority leader are still in use today.

1913 The Sixteenth Amendment to the Constitution is ratified, which allows for Congress to create an income tax on individuals and corporations.

1913 The Seventeenth Amendment is ratified, which requires the direct election of senators rather than being selected by state legislatures. This followed years of bribery cases brought to the Senate, where members were bribing the state legislators to seat them and many states moving to a direct election system on their own.

1916   Rural Post Roads Act is passed by Congress, which provided for the constructions of roads in rural areas and national forests. This act was the precursor to the federal highway system and the transportation bill, which is reauthorized every five years.

1917   Representative Jeannette Rankin (R-MT) becomes the first woman to be elected to serve in Congress. She represented the state of Montana and was the only member of Congress to vote against U.S. participation in both World War I and World War II. Since then, 330 women have served in Congress.

1917   The cloture rule is adopted in the Senate, which allows a filibuster to be stopped with a two-thirds super majority vote. It was first used in 1919 to stop a filibuster on the Treaty of Versailles.

1917   Congress passes a war resolution against Germany, formally entering the United States into World War I.

1920   The Nineteenth Amendment to the Constitution is ratified, which allows women to vote in federal elections.

1921   Congress passes the Budget and Accounting Act, which requires the president to submit a budget to Congress at the beginning of the year, between the first Monday in January and the first Monday in February.

1923   The Senate Committee on Public Lands and Surveys begins hearings that would become the Teapot Dome investigation. The Teapot Dome scandal involved the secretary of the Interior, Albert Fall, leasing federal oil reserves to private oil developers, without any sort of competitive bidding process.

1924   Congress passes and President Calvin Coolidge signs the Indian Citizenship Act, which gives citizenship to all Native Americans born in the United States. They were not immediately given the right to vote, however, as that was left up to the states. It took up to thirty years for all Native Americans to have the right to vote in this country.

1927 The U.S. Supreme Court in *McGrain v. Daugherty* establishes the power of congressional committees to compel witnesses to testify. Witnesses still retain their Fifth Amendment rights, however.

1928 The first attending physician of the Capitol, Dr. George Calver, is directed by the secretary of the navy to provide medical attention and health care to all members of Congress. Dr. Calver would serve Congress until his retirement in 1966.

1929 Congress passes the Permanent Apportionment Act of 1929, setting the number of House members at 435. They created a procedure to automatically reapportion House seats after every census.

1932 Senator Hattie Ophelia Wyatt Caraway (D-AR) becomes the first woman to be elected to the U.S. Senate. The first woman to serve in the Senate was Rebecca Latimer Felton (D-GA), who was appointed to fill a vacancy. She served only twenty-four hours. Since then fifty-two women have served in the Senate.

1933 The Twentieth Amendment is ratified, which stipulated that the terms of all members of Congress end at noon on January 3 and the new terms begin on the same day. It also required Congress to meet on January 3 of each year.

1935 Congress passes and President Franklin D. Roosevelt signs into law the Social Security Act of 1935. This act was a key component of the New Deal legislation. Others included creation of the Tennessee Valley Authority (1933), the Communications Act (1934), Soil Conservation (1935), rural electrification (1936), and the Pittman-Robertson Act or the Wildlife Restoration Act (1937).

1938 The Fair Labor Standards Act is passed by Congress and signed by President Roosevelt. This is considered the last major piece of the New Deal legislation. This act created a forty-hour workweek, made child labor illegal, and set a minimum wage.

1940 Sam Rayburn (D-TX) is elected Speaker of the House. He would serve ten nonconsecutive terms as Speaker and led the Democrats as both minority leader and Speaker from 1940 to 1961. In 1961, he proposed a resolution that would increase the Rules Committee membership by three members, to take some of the power from the chairperson. This resolution passed by five votes.

1941 On December 8, following a joint address to both chambers of Congress by President Roosevelt regarding the attack on Pearl Harbor, Congress voted on a war resolution declaring war on Japan. Representative Rankin (R-MT) was the lone "no" vote against the war. On December 11, Congress declared war on Germany and Italy. Representative Rankin voted "present" on these two votes. No members in either chamber voted against the declarations.

1946 President Harry S. Truman signs the Legislative Reorganization Act. This act sought to streamline the committee process, by drastically cutting the number of standing committees in both the House and Senate while also creating the subcommittee structure. The act also increased the number of staff in Congress (in 1947, each member and committee hired professional staff), provided additional oversight of the executive branch, required lobbyist registration, provided a congressional pay raise, created the Legislative Reference Service (later Congressional Research Service), and provided free education for House and Senate pages.

1947 Congress passes and President Truman signs into law the National Security Act of 1947. This act reorganized much of America's defense and intelligence agencies following the end of World War II and the beginning of the Cold War. The War and Navy Departments were put under one secretary of defense; it created the National Security Council and the Central Intelligence Agency.

1948   Congress passes the Displaced Persons Act of 1948. This act was a response to the millions of people in Eastern and Central Europe who were left homeless and destitute following World War II. It allowed for four hundred thousand people to come to the United States for resettlement over the next four years. The hearing was televised and became one of the most infamous House hearings.

1948   The House Committee on Un-American Activities begins a public hearing looking into the allegations by Whittaker Chambers, a former communist spy, that Alger Hiss, a former State Department official, was a spy for the Soviet Union.

1948   Senator Margaret Chase Smith (R-ME) becomes the first woman to be elected to both the House and Senate.

1950   The Senate creates a Special Committee to Investigate Organized Crime in Interstate Commerce, also known as the Kefauver Crime Committee, named for Senator Estes Kefauver (D-TN) who chaired the committee. The committee visited fourteen cities in fifteen months, some of which was televised.

1954   Four Puerto Rican nationalists open fire on the House floor from the visitors' gallery on March 1. The House was in the middle of a vote to reauthorize a bill allowing Mexican farm works to work in the country; thus, the floor was full of members and staff. Five members were wounded, but miraculously no one was killed.

1954   The Army-McCarthy hearings begin. These televised hearings initially were set up by Senator Joseph McCarthy (R-WI) to investigate army security, which followed years of his allegations that Communists had infiltrated American government. The army responded by accusing Senator McCarthy of using his influence to give special treatment to one of his aides who had been drafted. Senator McCarthy's popularity plummeted after these hearings, and he was censured by the Senate on December 2, 1954.

1957   Senator Strom Thurmond (R-SC) carries out the longest filibuster in Senate history, talking for twenty hours and eighteen minutes. He was trying to delay passage of the Civil Rights Act of 1957.

1957   In *Watkins v. United States*, the court determined Congress can investigate individuals but cannot in the process expose their private affairs without justification.

1961   Congress passes and President Kennedy signs into law a bill creating the Peace Corps. Even though this bill was signed by President Kennedy, it was an important precursor to the Great Society legislation.

1964   The Civil Rights Act of 1964 passes, following a fourteen-hour thirteen-minute filibuster by Senator Robert C. Byrd (D-WV). The bill was on the floor for sixty days. A cloture vote was taken, with a vote of 71–29, the first cloture invoked on a civil rights bill. Senator Clair Engle of California was very ill with brain cancer and could not speak but still was on the floor for the vote; he pointed to his eye to vote for cloture. The act provided for minority voting rights, outlawed discrimination at public facilities, and created equal employment protections. This act was a key component of the Great Society legislation.

1965   The Voting Rights Act of 1965 is passed by Congress and signed by President Lyndon Johnson. This legislation banned "Jim Crow" laws, primarily being used in the South, specifically literacy tests and poll taxes. It also required the Judiciary Department approve state and county voting practices in the South.

1966   Congress passes and President Johnson signs the Freedom of Information Act. This act gave the American people and press access to federal executive records.

1968   Senator Robert Kennedy (D-NY) is running for president and, following his win in the California primary, is assassinated in a hotel in Los Angeles, California.

1969   Representative Shirley Anita Chisholm (D-NY) becomes the first African American member of Congress. She was the only female in her freshman class of members of the House. She went on to serve seven terms in Congress.

1969   The Apollo 11 crew members are honored by a joint meeting of Congress. The three astronauts were the first men to walk on the moon.

1970   Congress passes and President Nixon signs the Legislative Reorganization Act of 1970 into law. The most significant change in the bill was the implementation of an electronic voting system in the House. The first electronic vote would occur in 1973.

1971   The Twenty-Sixth Amendment is ratified, which lowered the voting age to eighteen.

1972   House Majority Leader Hale Boggs (D-LA) and Nicholas Begich (D-AK) vanish in a small plane over Alaska. Boggs was in Alaska campaigning for Begich when their plane disappeared. The wreckage was never found. Begich's son, Mark, went on to serve as a U.S. senator from Alaska.

1973   Congress passes, President Nixon vetoes, and Congress overrides the veto on the War Powers Act. This act was an effort by Congress to reclaim some of their constitutional war powers. It requires the president to notify Congress within forty-eight hours of military action. Congress then has sixty days, with a possible thirty-day extension, to approve the action.

1973   The Endangered Species Act of 1973 is passed by Congress and signed by President Nixon. This act endeavored to save species from extinction, one of the first being the American bald eagle.

1973   The Senate Select Committee on Presidential Campaign Activities, which is more commonly known as the Watergate Committee, begins open public hearings. This committee was tasked with investigating campaign activities during the 1972 presidential campaign, including the break-in at the

Democratic National Committee headquarters in the Watergate Hotel. These hearings and the unprecedented action of the committee suing President Nixon for access to his White House tapes eventually led to the House Judiciary Committee passing three articles of impeachment. President Nixon resigned on August 9, 1974, before the full House could vote on impeachment.

1974 The Congressional Budget and Impoundment Control Act of 1974 is passed. This act changed the federal government's fiscal year from July 1 to October 1, required the president to submit a budget proposal to Congress, created the House and Senate Budget Committees and the Congressional Budget Office, and established more concrete guidelines for completing the budget and appropriations bills.

1975 The Senate cloture rule is changed from requiring two-thirds of all senators to invoke cloture to three-fifths.

1976 The Supreme Court reaches a decision in the campaign finance case, *Buckley v. Valeo*. The court decided that placing limits on individual contributions to campaigns was constitutional but Congress could not restrict the amount a campaign spent.

1978 In response to Watergate, Congress passes and President Carter signs the Ethics in Government Act of 1978. It increased public disclosure for public officials and put new restrictions on lobbying.

1983 A bomb planted by members of the Resistance Conspiracy, as a retaliation against U.S. military involvement in Lebanon and Grenada, detonates on the second floor of the U.S. Capitol's Senate wing. Since it was almost 11 p.m., no one was there and there were no casualties.

1983 The Supreme Court rules in *INS v. Chadha et al.* that the legislative veto is unconstitutional. The legislative veto is a decision by at least one chamber of Congress or committee that overturns an action by the executive branch.

1983 On September 1, Representative Larry McDonald (D-GA) is killed, along with 268 other passengers and crew, in a passenger plane crash. A Soviet fighter jet shot down Korean Airlines Flight 007, which was en route to Seoul, when it accidentally flew into Russian air space.

1985 Gramm-Rudman-Hollings Balanced Budget and Emergency Deficit Control Act is signed by President Reagan. Gramm-Rudman-Hollings (named for the three senators who sponsored the legislation) was meant to gradually decrease deficits with a goal of a balanced budget by 1991. It was deemed unconstitutional and amended in 1987.

1986 The House adjourns for two hours and then passes a resolution expressing sympathy for the loss of the astronauts killed in the *Challenger* crash.

1987 On May 5, a joint hearing between the House Select Committee to Investigate Covert Arms Transactions with Iran and the Senate Select Committee on Secret Military Assistance to Iran and the Nicaraguan Opposition begins. The hearings would last forty-one days, over the course of three months, all of which were televised. The hearings were investigating the scandal regarding the sale of weapons to Iran by the Reagan administration to fund the Nicaraguan contras.

1988 The U.S. House of Representatives adds the Pledge of Allegiance to its daily business. The pledge follows the daily prayer given by the House Chaplain or a guest clergyperson.

1990 Congress passes and President G. W. Bush signs into law the Americans with Disabilities Act. It strengthened punishments for actions against people with disabilities. It also required buildings be made accessible to those with disabilities.

1991 Congress passes the Persian Gulf Resolution on January 12, which authorized the use of military force against the Iraqi military in response to their invasion of Kuwait. The United States launched air strikes against Iraq four days later, which was the first time since the Gulf of Tonkin Resolution of 1964 where Congress reapproved military action.

1994 Member of Congress Newt Gingrich (R-GA) releases the *Contract with America*, a plan for the Republicans if they take the majority in the House during the midterm elections. In the midterm elections, the Republicans gained fifty-four House seats and Gingrich became Speaker of the House.

1995 In *U.S. Term Limits, Inc. v. Thornton*, the Supreme Court decides a state cannot impose term limits upon members of Congress.

1995 Following President Clinton's veto of a continuing resolution to fund the government, the federal government partially shuts down from November 13 to November 19. The government again shut down for twenty-one days from December 5, 1995, to January 6, 1996, over further disagreements between congressional Republicans and President Clinton.

1996 In a historic example of bipartisan compromise, Congress passes and President Clinton signs the Personal Responsibility and Work Opportunity Reconciliation Act of 1996 (Welfare Reform). This bill included work requirements in exchange for government assistance.

1998 On July 24, Russell Weston enters the U.S. Capitol Building with a gun, killing Capitol police officers, Officer Jacob Chestnut and Detective John Gibson. The two officers were given the honor of lying in state in the Capitol rotunda and are buried at Arlington National Cemetery. They are credited with saving numerous lives that day.

1998 The Supreme Court decides in *Clinton v. City of New York* that the line-item veto, which was passed by a Republican Congress in the Line Item Veto Act of 1996, was unconstitutional.

1998 President Clinton is impeached by the House of Representatives for perjury and obstruction of justice. The Senate acquits him in 1999, and he is not removed, remaining president for the next two years.

2000 Hillary Rodham Clinton (D-NY) becomes the first First Lady to be elected to the Senate. She would serve for eight years, until she was nominated to be secretary of state by President Obama.

2001 The U.S. Senate of the historic 107th Congress begins its session on January 3 evenly divided (fifty Republicans and fifty Democrats), with the tie-breaking vote going first to Vice President Al Gore and then after January 20 to Vice President Dick Cheney. The Senate remained thus until June 6, when Senator Jim Jeffords (R then I-VT) announced he was leaving the Republican Party to become Independent and caucus with the Democrats. This gave Democrats a one-vote majority until the midterm elections of 2002, where Republicans experience the rare occurrence of gaining seats in a midterm election during a Republican presidency.

2001 The events of September 11 force an evacuation of the U.S. Capitol and all House and Senate office buildings. Later in the afternoon, after the Capitol had been evacuated, 150 members of Congress gathered on the East Front of the Capitol, where House and Senate leaders addressed the group. Following the speeches, members spontaneously broke into song, singing "God Bless America." Congress returned to work on September 12. President Bush addressed a joint session of Congress on September 20, where he spoke passionately against the Taliban and al-Qaeda and announced the formation of an Office of Homeland Security within the White House. Typically a member of the minority party gives a response to all joint addresses, but the Democrats declined, instead desiring that America "speaks tonight with one voice" (House Minority Leader Richard Gephardt). In October, Congress passes the USA PATRIOT Act in response to September 11.

2001   A letter containing anthrax is opened by an intern in the Hart Office Building office of Senator Tom Daschle (D-SD) on October 15. The Hart Building remained closed for remediation until January 2002.

2002   The U.S. Senate and House meet in a joint session in their original home, New York City's Federal Hall, in a tribute to the victims and heroes of September 11. They initially met there from March 1789 to August 1790 before moving to Philadelphia for ten years.

2002   Congress passes and President George W. Bush signs the Bipartisan Campaign Reform Act (BCRA) of 2002 (McCain-Feingold) into law. BCRA sought to get soft money out of candidate campaigns and, in doing so, increased the amount individuals can give to campaigns. This act led to the *Citizens United v. FEC* decision in 2010 and eventually the creation of "super PAC's."

2002   Senator Paul Wellstone (D-MN) is killed in a plane crash in Minnesota while campaigning for reelection.

2002   Congress, in direct opposition to the wishes of President Bush, creates a new cabinet-level department, the Department of Homeland Security.

2005   Both the House and Senate return to Washington early from their August recess to pass emergency appropriations in response to Hurricane Katrina.

2007   Congress passes and President Bush signs the Honest Government and Open Government Act. This bill was passed as a response to congressional lobbying scandals and created more disclosure requirements as well as more gift restrictions.

2008   Senator Barack Obama (D-IL) is the first African American to be elected president of the United States. He is also only the third sitting senator to be elected president, after Warren Harding in 1920 and John Kennedy in 1960.

2010   Congress passes historic health-care legislation, the Patient Protection and Affordable Care Act. The legislation passed without a single Republican vote in either the House or the Senate.

2010   Congress passes and President Obama signs the Dodd-Frank Wall Street Reform and Consumer Protection Act, as a response to the financial crisis of 2008.

2013   Senate Democrats, led by Senate Majority Leader Harry Reid (D-NV), invoke the nuclear option, effectively ending the filibuster, or at least the sixty-vote requirement to invoke cloture, for non-Supreme Court and executive branch nominees. Instead, a simple majority vote of fifty-one can invoke cloture and end the filibuster on these nominees.

2013   Congress fails to pass its spending bills on time, largely due to a disagreement over funding for the Affordable Care Act, shutting down the government for sixteen days in October.

2017   Senate Republicans, led by Senate Majority Leader Mitch McConnell (R-KY), invoke the nuclear option for the last remaining nominees not already covered by the 2013 move by the Democrats, Supreme Court justices. Neil Gorsuch is therefore confirmed to replace Justice Antonin Scalia on the Court.

2017   Congress passes the Tax Cuts and Jobs Act of 2017, a historical tax cut bill. The bill passed without a single Democratic vote in either chamber.

2018   Speaker Paul Ryan (R-WI) dismisses House Chaplain, Reverend Patrick Conroy, following member complaints. The position in both the House and Senate goes back to the first days of both chambers and even the Continental Congress.

This glossary defines some of those terms that have been used in this book, along with some terms that one may encounter in additional research on the topic.

Adjourn　The end of a legislative or calendar day in Congress.

Albany Regency　The political party organization in New York that led the way to formation of the Jacksonian-Democratic Party in 1828.

Amendments　Legislative proposals presented by members of Congress to change or replace bill language. These can be offered in committee markup or on the House or Senate floor.

Appropriations bill　Bills that authorize the actual spending of money from the U.S. Treasury.

Authorizing legislation　Bills that create, continue, or alter existing programs or agencies. These authorizations can last for a specific time period and then need reauthorizations or can last for an indefinite period of time.

Bicameral legislature　A structural device of the U.S. government that constitutionally divides the Congress into two chambers: the House of Representatives and the Senate. It is also used by forty-nine of the state legislatures (Nebraska being the exception) where the lower chamber is called the House of Delegates or House of Representatives. As with the national government, the upper chamber of the state legislature is called the state senate.

Bill   A proposed law that passes the appropriate committee of jurisdiction and is brought to the floor for a vote.

Bipartisan   An effort that has the support of members of both political parties.

Bipartisan Campaign Reform Act (BCRA)   Law passed in 2002 that established new limits on federal campaign contributions and attempted to eliminate soft money from campaigns.

Blue Dog Democrats   Moderate and conservative Democrat members of Congress.

Blue slip   A Senate norm in which the senators from the state from which a judicial nominee comes give their approval for the nomination to proceed to consideration.

Budget resolution   Nonbinding legislation that outlines the budget for the upcoming five years. It is not signed by the president, but Congress must abide by the limits.

Bully pulpit   The idea that the office of the president provides a powerful platform from which to speak to the public.

Bureaucratic culture   A hierarchical and formal organization that has several layers where tasks, authority, and responsibility are delegated between departments, offices, or people. This structure is held together by a central or main administration, and it has led to the development of modern civilization.

Casework/Constituency services   Work done by members of Congress and their staff on behalf of their constituents, usually in an effort to solve problems the constituents are having with federal agencies.

Caucus   An informal structural device of the Congress in which members who share a common interest or goal meet to discuss and reach some degree of consensus on how best to pursue that interest, vote on a proposed bill, and sometimes craft provisions to be incorporated into a bill.

Centrifugal forces   Influences operating in Congress that push the institution toward greater decentralization and the influence of individual members in Senate and fragmentation in the House.

Centripetal forces Centralization influences, such as caucuses and political parties operating in Congress.

Chair (committee) The leader of the majority party on the committee. This person sets the agenda of the committee and chairs all hearings.

Chamber One of the houses of the American Congress—either the House of Representatives or the Senate.

Checks and balances The constitutional system by which each branch of the U.S. federal government is able to check the power of the other branches.

Closed rule A resolution issued by the House Rules Committee forbidding any amendments from being offered to a specific bill during House floor consideration.

Cloture The process by which a filibuster is formally ended in the Senate. Sixty senators must approve of the cloture motion for it to pass and end the filibuster. Following the cloture vote, there remains thirty hours of debate on the measure.

Committee Formalized groups in the House and Senate that write legislation and conduct investigations into the executive branch. They are made up of a select number of members and all members serve on at least one committee. The legislation they prepare is then considered by the full House or Senate.

Concurrent resolution A resolution, or piece of legislation, which is passed by both the House and Senate but not signed by the president and thus does not have the force of law. The budget resolution is an example.

Conference Committee A committee made up of both House and Senate members in order to reconcile differences when the two chambers pass similar but not identical versions of the same bill. The final product must be passed by both the House and Senate before going to the president for his signature.

Congressional Budget Act   Bill passed in 1974 that established deadlines and guidelines for formulating the congressional budget.

Congressional Record   Official record of the daily proceedings of the House and Senate. Includes verbatim discussion from the House and Senate floor as well as all introduced legislation and votes. Its existence is stipulated in the Constitution—Article I, Section 5.

Congressional session   Each Congress consists of two years, made up of one-year sessions.

Constituents   The individuals whom each member of Congress represents. They do not have to be voters or citizens or support the member to be included. Each House member represents about seven hundred thousand constituents. The number is equal to the state's population for senators.

Continuing resolution   Short-term legislation passed by Congress to keep the government open and operating at current spending levels.

Descriptive representation   The type of representation where the member of Congress shares descriptive characteristics with a majority of their constituents, like race, religion, or occupation.

Discretionary spending   Spending requiring an annual appropriation bill set by the House and Senate Appropriation Committees and for new spending, based on an authorization bill.

Due process of law   The constitutional limitation on government behavior to deal with an individual according to prescribed rules and procedures.

Enumerated powers   Those powers explicitly stated in the Constitution.

Executive agreements   Treaty-like arrangements between the executives of two or more nations that are binding during the terms of office of those respective executive officers. They developed in part as a means by which a U.S. president may bypass the "advice and consent" powers of the U.S. Senate.

Executive orders Actions issued by a president, assigned numbers and published in the federal register, akin to laws passed by Congress, that direct members of the executive branch to follow a new policy or directive as to how that officer or agency shall proceed to implement a law.

Exempt An individual or class or category of individuals to whom a certain provision of the law does not apply.

Filibuster A delaying tactic of a member of the Senate who has objections to a bill or amendment. The senator can hold the Senate floor indefinitely, preventing movement on the bill or use other parliamentary tactics to hold up debate. Ending the filibuster requires invoking cloture, which requires sixty members to vote for it.

Fire-alarm oversight Congressional oversight that is more decentralized in which citizens, interest groups, agency "whistle-blowers," and the media "pull the alarm" to indicate a problem that initiates the oversight action (hearings, investigations, requirement of a special report, etc.).

Fiscalization Refers to viewing the policy process by a fiscal focus placing a central emphasis upon controlling spending levels and funding for continuing programs.

Fiscal year A year used by the federal government for budgeting purposes. The federal government fiscal year runs from October 1 to September 30 of the following year.

Franking privilege Sending mail without paying for postage. Members of Congress can communicate with their constituents via mail at the taxpayer's expense.

General election Election to choose members of Congress, usually between two candidates from the two major parties. Occurs in November of even-numbered years.

Germane Pertaining to the underlying bill subject.

Gerrymandering The postcensus drawing of electoral district lines into unusual shapes in order to give advantage to a particular party or racial or ethnic demographic group of residents of the electoral district or to dilute their vote and effectively ensure a "safe" seat for the reelection of an incumbent. In effect, it enables the incumbent to pick his or her voters rather than the voters selecting the officeholder.

Going public When a president takes his policies to the American public for approval and support. The voters then put pressure on their members of Congress to enact these policies.

Hold A stalling tactic in the Senate, similar to a filibuster, which prohibits a bill from coming to the floor for consideration

Hotline A process by which the majority and minority leaders gauge support or opposition for legislation. Can pass noncontroversial items through unanimous consent if no senators object.

Impeach The process by which the House of Representatives charges a high-level federal government official with "treason, bribery, or other high crimes and misdemeanors" according to the Constitution. Not just presidents can be impeached; anyone the Senate confirms can be impeached, including federal judges. Impeachment does not mean removal.

Incumbency advantage The advantage the current office holder has in reelection. Members of Congress are reelected at very high levels.

Incumbent The person who currently holds the elected office.

Independent expenditures Campaign spending that is outside the individual candidate campaigns. It is an independent campaign, or communication, that advocates for the election or defeat of a specific federal candidate. It cannot be coordinated with any specific candidate.

Joint resolution Passed by both the House and Senate and signed by the president. Differs little from a bill. Usually reserved for continuing resolutions or emergency appropriations.

King Caucus   Signified a principal difference between the organization of the first political parties and that which emerged with the mass party system of the Jacksonian era, implying an undemocratic, nonrepublican system in which elite members in Congress in their party caucuses selected national party nominees.

Law   The enacted bill that is passed in identical language by both chambers of the Congress and signed by the president or repassed by a two-thirds vote by members of both chambers overriding the objections of the president.

Legislative veto   A method or strategy of legislative oversight that is disputed as to its constitutionality wherein certain provisions are written into a law delegating authority for certain actions to the president or an executive agency subject to the approval or disapproval of one or both chambers of Congress or its committee or committee leadership as a way to check executive branch action without having to pass new legislation requiring a presidential signature but thereby retaining a final say over executive decisions.

Line-item veto   A veto that allows the president to strike out specific portions of a bill and leave the rest. The Supreme Court said this violated the Constitution and the president no longer has this power.

Logrolling   An instance where two or more members agree to support each other's proposals.

Majority leader   The leader of the majority party in either the House or Senate. In the Senate, they are the leader of the body. In the House, they are second in command to the Speaker.

Mandatory spending   Spending enacted into law but not dependent on an annual appropriation bill consisting of transfer payments and welfare benefits such as Medicare, Medicaid, and Social Security.

Markup   The process by which bills are amended and altered in the committee of jurisdiction. Following markup, the bills can be considered by the full House or Senate.

Minority leader   The leader of the minority party in either the House or the Senate.

Motion to proceed   A motion, usually offered by the majority leader, in consultation with the minority leader, to bring a bill up for floor consideration.

Nuclear option   A parliamentary tool in the Senate that allows for the changing of the standing rules of the Senate, specifically the rule that requires sixty votes to invoke cloture and end a filibuster. Normally changing the standing rules requires a two-thirds vote, but this allows fifty-one senators to vote to approve the rule change.

Nullification   A theory espoused by Senator Henry Clay that asserted that the states could essentially veto any national law that impinged on states' rights.

Omnibus spending bill   An alternative to the regular fiscal budget. It is typically used when the regular budget process has broken down and cannot be enacted in time to meet the October 1 fiscal-year schedule. It is voted up or down in both chambers. It is typically crafted by leaders of both parties and used to bypass the regular-order committee review, hearings, and amendment processes and usually combines numerous appropriation bills or categories of funding.

Open rule   A resolution reported out of the House Rules Committee that allows any and all amendments to be offered on a specific piece of legislation. Usually reserved for appropriations bills.

Pocket veto   A method by which the president may "kill" a bill from becoming law without signing the bill but can do so only if the Congress sends the bill to the president within ten days or less of its adjournment.

Poison pill amendment   An amendment that is offered, usually by the minority, to make the bill unpassable or weakened.

Polarization   The process by which the two parties in Congress get further apart in terms of policy preferences.

Police-patrol oversight Routine, systematic surveillance by Congress of executive-branch agencies under congressional initiative, such as hearings, investigations, and so on.

Political action committee (PAC) An organization regulated by the Federal Election Commission, which aims to raise money to support federal election candidates.

Political incorporation A model that holds that for a minority community to witness an effective response to its needs, minority leaders must come to occupy positions of government authority.

Preside (or presiding officer) The person who presides over the floor activities of the House or Senate. In the Senate, the vice president as the president of the Senate is the constitutional presiding officer. In his absence, it is the president pro tempore.

President of Senate The vice president of the United States. Only power in the Senate is to break tie votes.

President pro tempore of Senate In the absence of the president of the Senate, the pro tempore will preside over the Senate. This is usually the longest-serving member of the majority party and as such delegates a great deal of presiding duties to junior members of the Senate.

Primary election The election that occurs before the general election. It allows voters to decide which candidates from the major parties will appear on the general election ballot.

Pro forma session From the Latin meaning "as a matter of form." The Senate convenes for a brief session every day, usually only lasting a few minutes. Normally no major legislation is taken up. This topic came up during the question of if the president could recess appoint executive branch officials during these sessions. Since the Senate is in session and not in recess, the president cannot.

Public law A bill that has been passed in identical form by both chambers of Congress and signed by the president.

Designated by "P.L" and the number of the Congress which it passed. For instance P.L. 111–148 is the Affordable Care Act, which passed during the 111th Congress in 2010 and was the 148th bill to be passed and signed by the president.

Quorum The number of members of Congress who need to be present for business to be conducted. In the Senate it is 51; in the House it is 218 (simple majorities).

Ranking member The leader of the minority party on a committee. Not only works with the chair to set the committee's agenda but also comes up with policy alternatives.

Reapportionment The process by which the 435 seats in the House of Representatives are divided among the fifty states. This occurs after the U.S. Census, which occurs every ten years. Every state will get at least one seat or district. Each district has approximately seven hundred thousand people in it.

Reauthorization Acts of Congress to reenact a law whose previous passage included a time limit or sunset provision that ends the law unless it is reauthorized.

Recess A brief break in the legislative day in Congress. Different from an adjournment that ends a legislative day. Congress usually recesses in midday for party caucus meetings or committee votes. The month-long break in August is also called a recess by members and their staffs, even though it is much longer and is actually an adjournment.

Recess appointment A means to temporarily appoint an individual to an office in the U.S. Senate while the Senate is in recess. The person can then hold that office or position until the end of the congressional session. The Senate can block this bypass action by the president by simply not officially going into recess.

Redistributive A government program or benefit that goes to one group of people and is paid for by another group of taxpayers.

Redistricting The process by which congressional districts are drawn in individual states. This occurs after the Census and reapportionment.

Resolution   A written measure adopted by a deliberative body. It refers to measures that do not become laws and are passed by only one chamber and not signed by the president. Resolutions may be nonbinding or procedural and substantive.

Revolving door   Members of Congress, or their staff, leaving Congress and seeking employment in the world of lobbying or elsewhere in the private sector and back again.

Riders   Language or amendments added to must-pass legislation. They are usually nongermane and thus are often added in the Senate.

Roll call   A vote in a chamber of the American Congress that records the yea or nay vote by each member of that chamber and recorded in the "Journal" of that chamber (the Congressional Record).

Rules Committee (House)   The standing committee in the House that governs how and when legislation will be debated on the House floor. It determines what, if any, and how many amendments will be offered. It also sets rules for debate on legislation. It is one of the most powerful committees in Congress and is often called the Speaker's Committee.

Select Committee   A temporary committee in Congress created for a specific purpose. They only last for the two-year Congress. Both the House and Senate, however, have select or special committees that operate like permanent standing committees.

Separation of powers   The idea that each branch of the federal government has their own distinct powers. The branches are all independent of each other.

Speaker of the House   The leader of the House of Representatives and the head of the majority party. The Speaker is a constitutional position and formally elected by the full House.

Stakeholder   A person or organization with an interest or concern in something, especially a business, or one who is involved or is affected by a policy or course of action.

Standing committee   A permanent committee in Congress. They exist from one Congress to the next. They have jurisdiction over a specific policy area and usually oversee a specific executive branch department.

Substantive representation   When a member of Congress carries out the policy preferences of their constituents in Congress.

Sunset provision   A provision written into a law that provides for an automatic expiration of the law after a specified time period. *See* reauthorization.

Super PAC (political action committee)   An organization that can raise and spend unlimited funds to advocate for the election or defeat of a candidate. This organization cannot give money or coordinate directly with any candidate.

Sweetener amendment   An amendment added to a piece of legislation to entice more members to support the overall bill and assure its final passage.

Unanimous consent   An agreement in the Senate that every member agrees to and allows the Senate to set limits on debate and amendments and also pass noncontroversial bills and amendments. Since all members must agree, any one member can object and delay progress on a bill or amendment.

Unfunded mandates   Requirements by the federal government upon state and local governments without offsetting funding for their implementation.

Veto   A legislative power of the office of president of the United States, as part of the checks and balances system established by the Constitution, by which the president refuses to sign a bill into law, and by which the president lists objections to the bill and sends it back to the Congress within ten days of having received the bill.

Veto override   The process in which the Congress, by a two-thirds vote of the members of both chambers, passes a bill into law without having the president sign the bill into law. It occurs after a president has vetoed a piece of legislation.

Whistle-blower   A person within an agency who without authorization to do so exposes to Congress or the media what that person considers illegal or unethical actions taken by the agency.

Yellow Dog Democrats   Democrats who would sooner vote for a dog than for a Republican.

Zero-sum decisions   Those in which gains in one policy area are directly related to the loss in other policy areas.

Index

About the Authors

Sara L. Hagedorn, PhD, is an assistant professor in the Department of Political Science at the University of Colorado, Colorado Springs. Her teaching and research interests focus on congressional policy making and productivity, minority and gender politics, U.S. elections, and energy policy. Her recent writings and presentations have focused on civility in politics and the role of interest groups in federal policy.

Born on the Crow Indian Reservation in Montana, Dr. Hagedorn is an enrolled member of the Northern Cheyenne Tribe of Montana. She grew up working on her parents' fourth-generation cattle ranch in Montana and attended a one-room country school through the sixth grade. After graduating from Carroll College in Helena, Montana, Dr. Hagedorn served as a legislative assistant in the office of Senator Conrad Burns, where she handled the policy areas of agriculture, Indian affairs, and judiciary for four years. Dr. Hagedorn then served as Director of Special Projects and Policy for the John Thune for U.S. Senate Campaign in South Dakota. Following the election, Dr. Hagedorn returned to Washington as Senator Thune's senior legislative assistant, handling agriculture, energy, and natural resources. Over the course of her seven years in Congress, she played active roles in the 2002 Farm Bill, the 2005 Energy Bill, drought disaster legislation (for which she was awarded the National Association of Wheat Growers "Friend of Wheat Award"), and Indian education programs. She was also the keynote speaker at numerous events both in Washington and around the country. Following her congressional service, Hagedorn earned a PhD in American government and public policy from the University of Colorado at Boulder.

Over the past ten years, she has advised numerous senatorial and congressional campaigns and served as a statewide executive committee member of one presidential campaign and two constitutional amendment ballot initiatives. She is regularly interviewed by the media regarding elections and Congress.

Michael C. LeMay, PhD, is professor emeritus from California State University–San Bernardino, where he served as director of the National Security Studies Program, an interdisciplinary master's degree program, and as chair of the Department of Political Science and assistant dean for student affairs for the College of Social and Behavioral Sciences. He has frequently written and presented papers at professional conferences on the topic of immigration. He has also written numerous journal articles, book chapters, published essays, and book reviews. He is published in the *International Migration Review, In Defense of the Alien, Journal of American Ethnic History, Southwestern Political Science Review, Teaching Political Science*, and the *National Civic Review*. He is the author of thirty academic books, more than a dozen of which are academic volumes dealing with immigration history and policy. His prior books on the subject are *Homeland Security* (ABC-CLIO, 2018); *Religious Freedom in America* (ABC-CLIO, 2018); *U.S. Immigration Policy, Ethnicity, and Religion in American History* (Praeger, 2018); *Illegal Immigration: A Reference Handbook*, Second Edition (ABC-CLIO, 2015); and *Doctors at the Borders: Immigration and the Rise of Public Health* (Praeger, 2015). He has served as series editor and contributing author of the three-volume series *Transforming America: Perspectives on U.S. Immigration* (ABC-CLIO, 2013); *Illegal Immigration*, First Edition (ABC-CLIO, 2007); *Guarding the Gates: Immigration and National Security* (Praeger Security International, 2006); *U.S. Immigration and Naturalization Laws and Issues: A Documentary History* (ed., with Elliott Barkan; Greenwood, 1999); *Anatomy of* *a Public Policy: The Reform of Contemporary Immigration Law* (Praeger, 1994); *The Gatekeepers: Comparative Immigration Policy* (Praeger, 1989); *From Open Door to Dutch Door: An Analysis of U.S. Immigration Policy since 1820* (Praeger, 1987); and *The Struggle for Influence* (University Press of America, 1985). Professor LeMay has written two textbooks that have considerable material related to these topics: *Public Administration: Clashing Values in the Administration of Public Policy*, Second Edition (Wadsworth, 2006) and *The Perennial Struggle*, Third Edition (Prentice-Hall, 2009). He frequently lectures on topics related to immigration history and policy. He loves to travel and has lectured around the world and has visited more than one hundred cities in forty countries. His forthcoming work includes *The Immigration and Naturalization Act of 1965* (ABC-CLIO).